THE SCULPTOR

"I saw the angel in the marble, and I
just chiseled until I set him free."
—*Michelangelo*

THE SCULPTOR

"I saw the angel in the marble, and I
just chiseled until I set him free."
—*Michelangelo*

This inspiring sculpture, created by Gary Price of Springville, Utah, is symbolic of working beneath the surface. Those who embark upon this great work become "sculptors" of their own souls, working from within to discover and shape their identities and destinies. The vision, power, and will to become who we really are is within each of us. We chip away all that is not us, using chisels and mallets to bring the truth of ourselves to light. The work is difficult and at times even painful, but the sculptor within us, what I call the soul's hidden agenda, will not rest until the work is finished. The soul will ultimately be whole, with or without our conscious participation.

Many thanks to Gary Price for allowing me to include this exceptional piece of art in this book.

WORKING
BENEATH
THE SURFACE

*Attending to the
soul's "hidden agenda"
for wholeness, fulfillment, and
deep spiritual healing*

THOMAS RISKAS

Executive
Excellence
Publishing

Executive Excellence Publishing
1344 East 1120 South
Provo, UT 84606
phone: (801) 375-4060
fax: (801) 377-5960
e-mail: execexcl@itsnet.com
web: http://www.eep.com

First edition: August 1997

Printed in the United States of America
10 9 8 7 6 5 4 3 2 1   02 01 00 99 98 97

ISBN: 1-890009-15-6

Cover sculpture and sculpture photo by Gary Price
Author photo by Bryant Livingston
Cover design by Ginger McGovern
Printed by Publishers Press

To my beloved companion, Annette:
Thank you will never be enough.

Contents

Acknowledgments

I feel deeply indebted to those who have in some way played a significant role in this work.

My wife, Annette, has been a tremendous inspiration and force for good in helping me work beneath the surface in my own life. She has encouraged me, endured me, and been my greatest support and most helpful critic.

My children—Nicole, T. J., Tyson, and Tessa—have also played a greater part than they know. They have put me to the test, revealed me to myself, and helped me learn humility and patience. Most of all, they have taught me how to love and have renewed me with their love.

My mother and my father, who is deceased, gave me not only the gifts of life and of love, but their own special gifts. From my mother I received a free spirit, from my father a disposition for risk-taking, together with a deep sense of responsibility and of the need to balance the demands of internal and external authority in following my own path.

To my brothers, Dean and Jim: You have been like a mirror to my soul and a touchstone in my quest for self-understanding. I love you both more than I can say.

I am indebted to my friends George Pace and Rodney Palmer, and also to Lynda Steele, Chris Robertson, David Hamblin, Gary Acevedo, and the works of Carl Jung, Murray Bowen, John Bradshaw, Thomas Moore, Robert Johnson, and Joseph Campbell for inspiring and assisting me in my journey to wholeness. Carl Jung in particular has been largely responsible for giving me new sight and insight. In my work I rely heavily on his thoughts and quote him extensively. This renowned Swiss psychologist is, in my view, a prophet for our time.

To Stephen R. Covey and my colleagues at the Covey Leadership Center, I also want to say thank you. Your work and example have been pivotal in the evolution of my work. We had some memorable experiences together that were both enjoyable and instructive. I wish you all the very best.

To my clients who have worked with me over the years, I offer my heartfelt gratitude and acknowledgment. I not only consider you colleagues and clients, but honor you as leaders and friends. Your courage, encouragement, vision, and humanity have been an inspiration to me in more ways than you know.

To my personal friend and lifelong physician, Ralph Spiegl, thank you for always being there, for always caring, and for being the initial catalyst for my own work beneath the surface.

To my dear friend, Richard Bentley, who defied rules and logic as a branch manager eighteen years ago and loaned me money to start my consulting practice, thank you for believing in me and for being there when I needed you.

To Glenna Crooks and John Hudnall for their invaluable editorial assistance and for challenging my thinking, thank you for being my friends.

To my editor, Trent Price, thank you for your insightful assistance and for encouraging my heart by believing so deeply in my work.

Finally, and most important, I would be remiss and untrue if I did not acknowledge Him who needs no acknowledgment, but who, in my view, deserves all and is the greatest person who ever lived, even Jesus Christ. He is the Author and Finisher of my faith. Without Him, I could do nothing.

"Any real change implies the breakup of the world as we have always known it, the loss of all that gave us identity, the end of safety. And at such a moment, unable to see and not daring to imagine what the future will bring forth, we cling to what we know, or thought we knew—to what we possessed, or dreamed we possessed.

"Yet it is only when we are able, without bitterness or self-pity, to surrender a dream we have long cherished or a privilege we have long possessed, that we are set free—that we set ourselves free—for higher dreams, for greater privilege."

—James Baldwin

"Your vision will become clear only when you can look into your own heart. Who looks outside, dreams; who looks inside, awakes."

—Carl Jung

"How can we remember our ignorance, which growth requires, when we are using our knowledge all the time?"

—Henry David Thoreau

Preface

PERSONAL REFLECTIONS

"All this have I proved by wisdom: I said, 'I will be wise,' but it was far from me. . . . Be [therefore] not righteous over much, neither make thyself over wise: Why shouldest thou destroy thyself?"

—Ecclesiastes 7:23 and 16

For years I taught thousands of people around the world *The 7 Habits of Highly Effective People®1* and related programs. I was both amazed and pleased by the hunger for self-improvement I found in others. It was not unusual to hear inspiring stories of people whose lives had been deeply and positively affected in some way. Some reported that they had achieved greater balance in their lives, others that their relationships at home and work had improved because they were listening more and were kinder and more considerate. These initial reports filled me with a sense of great personal and professional satisfaction.

In the midst of this success I began to notice an emerging need. Over time, as I followed up on my clients' progress, I found widespread instances of backsliding. People's sense of personal "mission" was becoming obscure. Many of those who initially had given glowing reports about their progress had fallen off the wagon. Others reported overall feelings of disappointment and frustration. The unspoken question kept repeating itself: "If I'm trying so hard to be effective, why am I still so ineffective?" I can remember going to my hotel room after teaching, feeling depressed, and wondering if what I was doing was really making a difference.

What made matters worse was my own experience; after all, I wasn't faring much better than the people I taught. It was frustrating and disheartening. For example, I could teach the habit of being proactive at a seminar, go back to my room, call home, and get in a fight with my wife or one of my children over some trivial matter.

On one occasion, while I was teaching a group of executives the habit of empathic listening, one of the participants requested that we spend more time discussing a previous issue. I was resistant. I hadn't finished teaching the habit on listening and felt I knew best what the group needed. Before I knew it, I found myself in the grip of some personal demon and in a power struggle with the entire group. In the space of a few short minutes I had violated the first six habits and had offended the client. How could I expect others to consistently practice these habits when I couldn't?

Unfortunately, my concerns didn't stop there. I thought I could write off my occasional reactive behavior to fatigue, stress, or some other external factor. But what about the times when I behaved well, but was motivated to control or manipulate others and only made things worse? All this vexed my spirit and made me far less productive than I wanted to be or thought I could be. Ironically, my passion to succeed often triggered the very intensity and extremism that were sabotaging my best efforts.

I was on a collision course with the truth—the truth about me. Unfortunately, nothing in what I had learned and taught could help me deal with the unconscious inner forces that were undermining my best conscious intentions and shaping my destiny in strange, unexplainable ways. I eventually realized that this was because none of the positive self-improvement programs I had been involved with could help me see the whole truth about myself. None of them directed me to work beneath the surface of my ego or self-image and cut through all the lies, fears, and insecurities that lay hidden in the darkness. And none of them taught me how to integrate my personality or defuse my reactivity at its source. In fact, the very philosophy of such programs, which is inherently affirming and one-sided, was my shield against the truth. I had thought that as long as I *sincerely* practiced effective behavior, I would be okay. Nothing could have been further from the truth, for the truth was—and often is—in the darkness, and no one was pointing to the darkness for answers, especially not me.

All this and more testified to me of the insufficiency of what I was teaching and practicing. What I have come to believe is that it's time, in effect, to peel the onion; that no "silver bullet" can magically and effortlessly enable us to rise above our lies, wounds, and imperfections to fulfill our destiny. Even religious conversion cannot save us from ourselves. Nor would God do so, in my estimation, for in saving us from ourselves He would, ironically, damn the very purpose and joy of our existence.[2]

Further, I realized that behavioral excellence and effectiveness, and the false security that comes with them, can be damaging and even dangerous to the soul, particularly when such goals are mixed with our definition of Self and our deeply scripted values of competition and perfection. This unhealthy mixture makes us all better liars—to ourselves and to others—and sets us up for a variety of problems related to pride. I also learned that although our desire for greater effectiveness and character development through principled behavior is certainly commendable, necessary, and worthwhile, it must not become a superficial, perfectionistic, and one-sided effort that ignores or discounts the deeper callings of the soul for healing, wholeness, meaning, and experience. These callings and needs constitute the "hidden agenda" of our life. And it's this hidden agenda that is, as Joseph Campbell would say, running the show.

With these new insights came liberation. I saw my struggles in a new light—as a movement of my soul toward greater wholeness and integrity. All that I had been doing to "fix" myself was not a waste of time. In fact, in addition to providing valuable skills and perspectives, these principles and habits of effectiveness, along with my commitment to excellence, had served a deeper, more profound purpose than I had ever imagined; they had brought my deeper needs to the surface. My reactivity, provoked by my misguided efforts to be "perfect," had been compensating for my one-sidedness and was now forcing me to care for and accept myself as a whole human being. My struggles, inconsistencies, and frustrations were simply moving me to the next level of self-realization.

All these insights, of course, are now merely hindsight. What I see now, I knew at an unconscious level years ago. I felt compelled to move onward, against my career plans and conscious intentions, to begin a different journey. I left the Covey Leadership Center and began to look inward and do the inner work I had avoided for so long. Instead of telling myself what to do, I began to listen. From the deepest parts of my soul I heard the cries of neglect and felt myself awakening to needs and values that either had been unknown or long denied and suppressed. I entered the "second" transformation of the spirit that Friedrich Nietzsche describes in *Thus Spake Zarathustra*[3]: I had moved from the stage of the "camel," which was the season of instruction and obedience, to the stage of the "lion," whose task it was to kill the dragon named "Thou Shalt" and come to my Self.

And so the conflict began: Should versus Want, Right versus Wrong, Good versus Bad, "Thou shalt" and "Thou shalt not" versus Ethical Choice. I began to see the roots of my reactivity and how my own insistence on living a "highly effective" life was hurting me. In order to be effective, I felt I had to condemn everything about me that, by definition, was not effective. This led to suppression, denial, and self-alienation. I was, in short, getting in my own way.

For the next four years I focused my attention on psychological healing and wholeness. I began to learn the art of shedding—peeling off the scales of untruth like so many layers of an onion. I attended to many of the fears and misconceptions that had kept me from the whole truth about who I am and the work

I am here to do. I began to get "in relationship" with myself. From my own depths came a wealth of information. I dreamed, and from my dreams came the keys to my wholeness.

Gradually, the notion of care replaced the notion of cure, and the experience of wholeness replaced the goal of flawless perfection. I came to see the light in the darkness and learned to let go of control, befriend my demons, hold my own authority, and put more trust in myself. I gained more respect for my powers to create and destroy, and I learned how to work with those inner forces consciously and ethically. I dismantled all my beliefs, values, and commitments and opened them up to critical evaluation.

No longer would my life be dominated by "shoulds" and "oughts." I started making choices: What do *I* believe? What do *I* stand for? What do *I* want? How do *I* want to live my life? What am *I* here to do? What do *I* need to do? Why? How? When? With whom? To answer these questions I made room for the "inconceivable," considered alternatives, and consulted only three sources: my heart, my conscience, and God. Through this process I needed to let go of my self-image and face myself as I was—the light *and* the darkness.

All this reminds me of the insightful words of Jungian analyst Robert Johnson, who wrote:

> We don't do this [inner work of individuation] by sitting rooted in our patriarchal attitudes. . . . We have to go to the parts of ourselves that we have barely touched, that we barely know. We must sail forth and steer for deep waters, risking all, yet strangely safe upon those seas of God.[4]

Taking this thought forward, Johnson continues:

> There comes a time in life when a man's ego doesn't have the answers. He doesn't know enough; he doesn't have the resources needed to resolve an impossible situation. He needs to give himself over to the unconscious and drift with its tides until he finds an island of new consciousness for that era of his life.

> One of the great strengths of the inner feminine is the ability to let go, to give up ego control, to stop trying to control the people and the situation, to turn the situation over to fate and wait on the natural flow of the universe, to . . . give oneself over to the will of God, to stop trying to understand by intellect or logic, to stop trying to force things, to . . . wait patiently, listening to a soft voice within, for the wisdom that comes not from logic or action, but from feeling, intuition, the irrational, and the lyrical.[5]

My journey is far from over. Wholeness is a daily, lifelong pursuit, and my soul's hidden agenda for wholeness and fulfillment continues to move me forward through dreams, promptings, impressions, insights, warnings, relationships, and even personal commandments. I listen, watch, pray, feel, reflect, discern, and act. I attend to my needs, my moods, my dreams, my reactivity, my feelings, and all the little coincidences in my life that I once ignored. I relentlessly pursue the truth and strive to cut mercilessly through all the self-programmed lies and self-deceptions that rob me of the freedom to be fully alive. I talk to parts of myself that need attention or that have long been neglected. I grieve my losses, nurse my wounds, and try to appreciate the sacredness of the mundane and routine. I've put away my weekly planner and abandoned my thoughtful goals and plans. Instead, I try to stay conscious, attentive, and present and respond with integrity to the call from within. I'm convinced that the soul knows what it needs, and when.

I wrote this book for others, like myself, who are deeply committed to their spiritual and psychological growth and who are, perhaps without knowing it, getting in the way of their own effectiveness and self-realization. I have personally applied, and continue to apply, everything I recommend in these pages. As you read this book, please keep in mind that nothing of enduring value can be realized without paying a dear price, particularly in matters of the soul.

Working beneath the surface is hard work that can—and probably will—involve what some psychologists refer to as "legitimate suffering": the kind of suffering that comes from letting go of who we *think* we are and why we *think* we're here. Legitimate suffering is the kind of suffering that comes as we honestly face our lies, wounds, limitations, and wrongdoings.

Even as we faithfully do this work and pass through such suffering, which continues throughout our lives in some form or another, we are likely to experience what Thomas Moore calls the "great mystery of the soul." In *Care of the Soul*, Moore writes: "This is the great mystery of the soul: Whenever something is being accomplished, it is also in some way being undone."[6] My experience confirms that this is true. Just when we think we are being more effective, spiritual, centered, or "successful" in life (whatever that means to us), something happens that shows us we have a long way to go. But why should this surprise or discourage us? Do we really expect anything else? If our eyes were truly open, would we *truly* want it any other way?

Introduction

ATTENDING TO THE SOUL'S HIDDEN AGENDA:
Essential Perspectives and Overview

"What is running the show is what is coming up from
way down below."

—*Joseph Campbell*

"Passage to India"
Sail forth—steer for the deep waters only,
Reckless O Soul, exploring, I with thee, and thou with me,
For we are bound where mariner has not yet dared to go,
And we will risk the ship, ourselves, and all.

O my brave soul!
O farther, farther sail!
O daring joy, but safe! Are they not all the seas of God?
O farther, farther, farther sail!

—*Walt Whitman*

T his book is based in part on the premise that each of us is
directed from within by a *hidden agenda* that calls us from
the center of our soul and moves us toward wholeness and self-
realization through our relationships and experiences in life. In
order to fulfill our hidden agenda for wholeness, and thereby
realize our unique purpose and calling in life, we need to work
beneath the surface of our lies, fears, insecurities, and limited
self-knowledge to get "in relationship" with ourselves and others.
This requires us to peel off the layers of untruth and face the
truth about ourselves, clear the past, integrate our personality,
and attend to the needs of the soul.

The hidden agenda I speak of has been referred to in other
terms. Abraham Maslow referred to it as the need for "self-actu-

alization" and "transcendence." Carl Jung referred to it as the "principle of individuation." In actuality, this hidden agenda, or law of progression, is nothing less than the soul's quest for reconciliation and completion that strives to put us in conscious relation with the Self, the divine center or spirit within us, and the work we are called to do. It is the ultimate goal of our existence and the desired end of our unique path or journey in life. As such it is at the heart of life's greatest triumphs, as well as at the center of our most tragic and bitter disappointments.

The hidden agenda accounts for happiness and misery, health and sickness, unity and alienation, commitment and apathy, harmony and conflict, tranquility and violence, prosperity and collapse, creation and destruction—the whole range of human experience. It drives us into the wilderness and brings us home again. It has many faces, and its truth is often elusive and irrational. It is the nemesis of the logical mind and is experienced by most as both a blessing and a curse. For most of us it is the best-kept secret of our lives, hidden even from our conscious selves. It includes fateful events and the calls of necessity, and is comprised of forces we are generally not even aware of—inner forces that can make and break us, that put us on the right path and move us in the wrong direction.

The hidden agenda does not interpret success or failure as we do. It often works to undermine our best intentions to act effectively or behave appropriately, and it seems to sabotage our sincere efforts at self-improvement and our best-laid plans for work and life. It is sometimes a paradox wherein the "right" direction, as defined by our self-made goals, our social, moral, and religious standards, or others' expectations, might be the wrong direction at a certain time in our life. Conversely, we may find ourselves pursuing "wrong," "forbidden," or "illogical" courses that are, in reality, the right way for us to go at the time.

We've often heard the saying that the heart has reasons the mind cannot understand; such is the mystery of the hidden agenda. To hearken to it is to act in faith; to fail to hearken to it is to forfeit your highest destiny. And a frightening encounter it can be—asking in some cases that everything be sacrificed to feed its desires, or in other instances nothing at all, except perhaps that we relinquish our pride and fears.

In our relationships, the hidden agenda can bring us together and tear us apart. In troubled relationships it can take the form of a "death wish" where individuals, families, groups, communities, and even nations react and counterreact to each other in an unconscious effort to resolve some deeper dysfunction that is blocking mutual growth.

Our failure or refusal to understand and accept the hidden agenda at the personal level can blind us to the deeper needs and values of the soul and to the inner work needed to live a vibrant, meaningful, and productive life. It also results in the reactivity, backsliding, strife, immorality, distrust, and the lacks of unity, commitment, and accountability that plague our lives at every turn.

I believe that each person's conscious quest for personal wholeness or individuation takes our entire world to a higher level of consciousness, morality, and interdependence. This makes "working beneath the surface" the transcendent work of humanity at its most fundamental level, and a top priority in our planned agendas for prosperity and personal growth.

Working Beneath the Surface is about peeling the onion— about facilitating individuation, or maturity to wholeness. It results in personal transformation and empowerment through the development and integration of all parts of our personality to a condition of wholeness and unity. It involves working toward complete self-knowledge, self-acceptance, and the ascent of wisdom, consciousness, relatedness, and spirituality. Such work, which enables us to get in relationship with ourselves, is fundamental to our success in living and relating effectively with others. And living and relating effectively with others is fundamental to fulfilling our hidden agenda for wholeness.

In any living system, disorder can be the source of new order, and this concept is a great paradox of progression. In this regard,

Working Beneath the Surface is a process of disintegration that paradoxically results in a re-integration to wholeness, whereby we let go of our present form in order to reemerge to a higher state that is better suited to the demands of the present environment. As human beings, we need to use disequilibrium to avoid deterioration. This can be a difficult and painful lesson to learn.

This book is dedicated to the premise that all of us, regardless of our domain, role, or specialty, need to be wise, mature, conscious, and dedicated to truth with a strong voice of internal authority and sense of Self in relation to God and all mankind. Performing the inner work prescribed in this book is very humbling because the inner work deals with the whole person. It is a call to honesty and greater integrity. And it is absolutely foundational and essential, in my view, to all serious efforts at personal development. Although such a process is difficult, it is also immensely rewarding, as it provides the basis for enduring peace, joy, and fulfillment and empowers us to deal effectively with the perplexing paradoxes and contradictions that will continue to characterize the times of opportunity, confusion, and commotion that lie ahead.

Although the work I am advocating in this book requires a degree of ego strength typically found only in the second half of life, still, regardless of what half of life you are in, the best time to begin this journey is now. For those who have already embarked, this book will help you along even further and confirm the work you've done or are doing. It's never too late to begin. And those who have begun need to continue. My only caution is to take it slow, pace yourself, and stick with it. In some cases, the help of a qualified therapist or counselor will be needed. You will know if you need help. You will feel stuck, resistant, and anxious. If you have these feelings, don't push yourself, and don't be afraid or embarrassed to reach out and get the professional help you need. I personally believe that some amount of psychoanalysis and psychotherapy can be beneficial to anyone, regardless of how "normal" we think we are.

Inner work is a radical departure from today's popular self-improvement approaches. Nothing about it is easy. And it doesn't happen merely by applying formulas, laws, behaviors, or principles of morality, effectiveness, or success. Instead, it requires the rigors of inner work—the work of honest and thorough self-analysis, reflection, integration, reconciliation, and healing. This work is done in many ways, but it is not optional if we want the kind of world we say we want. It would seem we are called to do it by virtue of our very existence on this planet, and we must do it if we want to be fully alive, effective, and empowered human beings. In my estimation, those who are engaged in this work are the true heroes and leaders in the world today.

In nearly twenty years of field experience I have found that people are generally endowed with many wonderful personality strengths. These strengths, together with faith and hope, will be needed in working beneath the surface to face yourself and integrate your personality. You will need all your strengths to make allies of your personal demons and to transform the negative forces of human interaction. You will need them to hold the tension of contradiction, paradox, and opposing values in making truly ethical decisions that go beyond common notions of right and wrong. And you will need all these strengths, together with humility, to endure the darkness of confusion, self-doubt, and powerlessness that envelop every person from time to time.

I have great faith in the strength and resilience of human beings. I have had the privilege of working with thousands of people across the world. These people, most of whom are leaders in their professions, businesses, and communities, are wonderful individuals of noble character and great competence in their work. I acknowledge their accomplishments and am inspired by their victories of spirit, ingenuity, and passion in the face of tremendous adversity. Even so, the greatest powers of the human soul—the powers of light and darkness brought together in conscious unity—remain only a potentiality to most people today, even to those who see themselves (or who are seen by others) as highly successful or effective.

One last point: Some people, after reading this book, might wonder how they can get others to work beneath the surface. Such a task will seem formidable. My response is that such a concern is part of the problem. This is a very personal journey. Your life, as manifested or expressed by your decisions, actions, and conversations will, if authentic, inspire and edify others and will encourage them to work beneath the surface. The heightened spiritual hunger and consciousness of the masses will greatly leverage the positive impact of every enlightened person who is growing toward the conscious realization of his or her true potential. It has been said that when the student is ready, the teacher enters. The reverse is also true: When the teacher is ready, the student enters.

This book will help you start the process. It will help you work beneath the surface to create and sustain productive relationships with yourself and others, thereby satisfying your inner quest for completeness and tapping the powers within you of being whole, integrated, and fully human. These are the powers that reside deep beneath our ego, or the surface we call self. To harness them, even in small measure, is to rise to a new and sustained level of effectiveness, personhood, and leadership that few have imagined possible.

Overview

Chapter One explains why popular approaches to self-improvement can't result in sustained effectiveness or personal wholeness. In my estimation, our purpose in this world is to experience the richness of life and fill the measure of our creation—to become whole, not to become perfect in our behavior. Ironically, today's emphasis on self-improvement and success often undermines the true nature of effectiveness and the soul's hidden agenda for wholeness.

In this chapter I discuss four limitations of performance-focused or formula-based approaches, and I introduce the concepts of the "personal shadow" and the "paradox of effectiveness," wherein the more we strive to be effective, the more ineffective we become, as we delude ourselves into believing that who we *think* we are is who we *really* are. This chapter draws on some of my experiences in the field of human development to show that working beneath the surface must involve the deep inner work that leads to individuation.

Chapter Two shows how our hidden agenda for wholeness becomes frustrated and how we lose vital energy and power in our lives. By understanding how we become disempowered in our life, we learn the key to our eventual full empowerment through healing and wholeness. This chapter establishes an essential theoretical foundation for the rest of the book.

Chapter Three shows the effect our frustrated hidden agenda can have on others and what can happen when we are "out of relationship" with ourselves—namely, that we live certain lies, refuse to see the truth about ourselves, become alienated from others, and lose our vital connection to wholeness—even while we are practicing principles of effective behavior. We can be nice, kind, and well-behaved, and still find ourselves out of relationship.

Relationships are social systems affected by psychic forces working beneath the surface of our awareness. These forces are more powerful than we realize and represent unconscious motives and deeply scripted beliefs, values, instincts, and patterns of behavior that constitute our reality.

In this chapter I present four levels of untruth that constitute the lies we live, and discuss how these lies cause chain reactions that lead to reactive cycles. You will see how our best efforts to work with others provoke the very behaviors we want them to change, and how such downward spirals, driven by unrealistic expectations, seek to fulfill the relationship "death wish" that is part of the soul's destructive, secret pursuit for wholeness and vitality. Finally, in this context I also discuss reactive cycles between groups and offer some thoughts on how to resolve inter-group conflict and alienation.

To fulfill our hidden agenda for wholeness we need to get in relationship with others. In *Chapter Four* you will learn what is required to cut through many of the lies we live, break free from reactive cycles, and get in relationship with others. This chapter continues the discussion started in Chapter Three and provides a practical framework for creating and sustaining productive, fulfilling relationships and for healing damaged relationships.

Chapter Five begins the discussion about the inner forces in our life that shape our destiny and move us toward wholeness, and introduces the essential inner work that we must do to achieve that end. I center the discussion on Joseph Campbell's interpretive model of the mythical hero, which leads toward individuation and personal empowerment. I present the initial phases of personal integration and describe a process of inner work that will help you get in relationship with yourself.

This chapter includes various exercises to help you learn about yourself and reclaim the power within you that will enable you to enjoy greater wholeness, fulfillment, and sustained personal effectiveness. I advise you to take this chapter slowly, participate fully in the exercises, and carefully read the corresponding notes at the back of the book.

The discussion of inner work continues in *Chapter Six*, which is about working beneath the surface of our own rationalizations to clear the past of abuse and wrongdoing. An essential part of individuation involves healing the wounds of the past and starting over. Reconciliation and deep spiritual and emotional healing help remove the obstructions that weaken our character and disempower our spirit. Clearing the past involves psychological and spiritual renewal that purifies the heart, satisfies our hidden agenda for reconciliation, and strengthens our relationships with the Self, God, and others.

Chapter Seven explores some of the unique, essential human capacities and perspectives that distinguish those who emerge from the darkness and become more individuated, or whole, through inner work. These capacities are essential to our quest for personal fulfillment and global unity, peace, and prosperity. They are characteristic of genuine, whole leaders and individuals in every walk of life and are sorely needed in today's world.

The *Notes* at the end of the book reflect additional thoughts, concepts, and quotations for more in-depth study, and include the sources for much of my thinking. I consider the information in this section to be of great value for continued learning. Although I rely heavily on quotations from other authors and texts to support and amplify certain key concepts, I suggest you take the time to read every quotation carefully, as well as the complete texts from which the quotes are taken. Researching and writing this book has been a journey of discovery for me that has invigorated my spirit. I hope these notes and sources help you in your own journey.

In writing these chapters I have drawn on both personal and professional experiences to illustrate certain points. I have also approached various concepts from the perspectives of personal, work, and family life for a broad application that includes all aspects of life experience. But, in the final analysis, social context is irrelevant in our quest for individuation.

Finally, I want to share a few words on my use of *psychological terminology*. My objective is to synthesize and build upon the concepts we already have at our disposal, not to create another lexicon. I am not a clinical psychologist, but I use some established psychological terms to convey certain concepts.

I have personally connected with the tenets of analytical psychology and the work of Carl Jung. This, I believe, is no accident. His work is fundamental to the fulfillment of my own unique calling in life. I feel no need to create new terms to take the place of words like *ego, complex, persona, shadow, wholeness, Self, individuation,* and the like. I use these and other seemingly jargony terms freely. If they seem to get in your way, I'm sorry. However, some readers may benefit more from this book by becoming familiar with these terms before beginning.

To conclude this introduction, I think it's time to get beneath the surface and start doing the real inner soul work that so desperately needs to be done. It's time to face, honestly and courageously, the one reality most of us have avoided for so long: our Self. I share the sentiments of Carl Jung, who wrote, "I am neither spurred on by excessive optimism nor in love with high ideals, but am merely concerned with the fate of the individual human being—that infinitesimal unit on whom a world depends, and in whom . . . even God seeks his goal."[1]

I believe we need to move beyond surface behavioral solutions, mindless mechanistic processes, and one-sided, reductionistic, or over-idealistic formulas for success and self-improvement that frustrate and corrupt our hidden agenda for wholeness. Life is never simple, particularly in the complex psychic and spiritual life of the individual. And so we begin, first by undoing and unknowing, and then by knowing, doing, and ultimately *being*. But first, a word of wisdom from Zorba in the motion picture "Zorba the Greek": "Damn it . . . I like you too much not to say it: You have everything except one thing—madness. A man needs a little madness, or else he dare not cut the rope and be free." With this in mind, let us all move forward with whatever madness we need, to let go of the fears, knowledge, and lies that bind and blind us—and be free.

Chapter One

ALL THE KING'S HORSES . . .

Why Popular Approaches to Human Development Don't Result in Sustained Effectiveness or Personal Wholeness

"Our very psychology has been shaken to its foundation . . . to grasp the meaning of the world today we
use a language created to express the world of yester-
day. The life of the past seems to us nearer our true
nature, but only for the reason that it is nearer our
language."

—Antoine de Saint Exupery

"Far too many people are misled into snatching at . . .
'magical' ideas and applying them externally like an
ointment. People will do anything, no matter how
absurd, in order to avoid facing their own souls."

—Carl Jung

"We wait for light, but behold obscurity; for brightness, but we walk in darkness."

—Isaiah 59:9

Our sincere efforts for self-improvement and personal effectiveness are terribly misplaced and often incur the wrath of
a human soul that was never intended to be perfect, at least not
in the Platonic sense we tend to use the term. This seems evidenced by the results of our labors. After investing vast amounts
of time, money, and energy in the pursuit of self-improvement,
we are still left wanting.

It seems we're like batteries that can't hold a charge—up today, down tomorrow. Still, we keep trying to recharge by adopting new philosophies, learning new skills, or embracing new behaviors, laws, or principles. We hype each other up, preach to each other, and remind each other that success is within our grasp. All this feels and sounds good, but it typically doesn't last, leaving us empty and frustrated. Something's missing, even if we are not ready or willing to admit it. So what is it?

What's Missing?

I believe four elements are missing in our search for wholeness and sustained effectiveness:

First, today's conventional wisdom lacks real appreciation for human limitations and the unconscious values and wisdom of the soul. The unconscious will that works toward wholeness, our hidden agenda, often works against our conscious will to improve.

Conventional wisdom would have us consider our weaknesses irrelevant, and focus on our strengths while we avoid dealing with our past wounds and wrongdoings. Our hidden agenda, however, requires us to turn our weaknesses into strengths by facing, reexperiencing, and clearing the past through essential inner work, reconciliation, and suffering. For example, it might be "wise" for you to stay in your present job, but your hidden agenda might move you to pursue another profession that responds to the call of the soul. Also, while traditional principles of life and time management require that we put "first things first," the soul often requires greater spontaneity, even occasionally putting *last* things first or first things last. Further, although conventional morality requires that we always are honest, fair, loyal, and true to our word, the unconscious wisdom of the soul may sometimes require ethical dishonesty, favoritism, disloyalty, and broken promises as a call to higher truth and a higher good.

To do the things we are told we must do to be effective, influential, or successful requires that we have *access* to the power within us. Many popular writers today assume this access, which, as I will discuss in the next chapter, is a faulty assumption. The truth is, most of us do *not* have access to enough of our natural power to function at "peak performance" on a consistent basis, and "willpower" is simply not enough. It is one thing to have the power to change and to be consistently "proactive," but it is quite another to have access to that power.

Before we can be consistently effective or influential, we must face the realities of our own limitations. These limitations include the deeply ingrained lies we live, as well as our inability to respond proactively in response to certain triggering events. Operating within the human psyche are autonomous reactive complexes that have a will of their own. These complexes, which I discuss in more depth in Chapter Two, often undermine our noblest intentions and best-developed habits of effectiveness. They cause us to react "out of character" and defy even the most self-disciplined practitioner. They are part of the human shadow, and we rarely account for their presence and operation in our lives. We simply cannot "will" or wish them away, and we cannot defuse them by merely changing our beliefs, our thinking, or our mental models.

Cognitive approaches and other methods of "paradigm shifting," including religious or spiritual conversion, are insufficient in helping us work with these autonomous complexes. Unfortunately, we too often respond to our reactive episodes by creating mental models that explain our behaviors in the best possible light to support our self-concept, rather than acknowledge these reactive complexes for what they are. Our cognitive ability, void of deep reflection, becomes a servant of the ego. This results in self-deception. Our first choice, then, is not one of changing behavior, but of choosing to be whole. This choice leads us to work beneath the surface to *reclaim* the power to which we have lost access.

Many popular thinkers in the field of self-improvement would have us believe that we already have the power within us to take complete control of our lives and to be successful and effective, or at least "proactive." However, this is only a partial truth. The fact is, we are far less in control of ourselves than we would like to think.

All this speaks to the limitation of personal insight. Related to this deficiency are the popular concepts of "paradigm" and "paradigm shifting," which are worn out and misunderstood terms, at least in their fulness. These concepts entered our vernacular as fads and have exited as jokes. All concepts that are severed from their roots in the soul will suffer such a fate.

Plato's *paradeigma*, or "pattern," takes on a deeper, more profound meaning in context of our soul's hidden agenda for wholeness and the Voice of Necessity that calls us to our highest destiny, or lot in life. James Hillman, in his thought-provoking book *The Soul's Code*, elaborates:

> So the "lot" is the image that is your inheritance, your soul's portion in the world order, and your place on earth, all compacted into a pattern that has been selected by your soul before you ever got here. . . . Since ancient psychology usually located the soul around or with the heart, your heart holds the image of your destiny and calls you to it.
>
> Unpacking the image takes a lifetime. It may be perceived all at once, but understood only slowly. Thus, the soul has an image of its fate, which time can show only as "future." Is "future" another name for fate, and are our concerns about "the future" more likely fantasies or fate?
>
> Before the souls enter human life, however, they pass through the plain of Lethe (oblivion, forgetting) so that on arrival here all of the previous activities of choosing lots and the descent from the lap of Necessity is wiped out. It is in this condition of a *tabula rasa*, or empty tablet, that we are born. We have forgotten all of the story, though the inescapable and necessary pattern of my lot remains and my companion daimon remembers.[1]

The soul indeed remembers, and the "daimon"—the hidden agenda that shapes our destiny—calls to us as a revelation from beyond, yet within, to honor the unconscious values and wisdom of the soul, and to fill the measure of our creation.

We have power to reason, discern, and choose our response; to act and not merely be acted upon. But how we use such power is largely determined by inner forces we are not even aware of. These inner forces include unconscious needs, values, goals, beliefs, and genetic predispositions, all directed through the soul by our hidden agenda for wholeness. Therefore, our freedom and ability to access the inner powers is realized only by consciously knowing about these unconscious inner forces. This means that our awareness of our motives, as well as our ability to choose between one course of action and another, is much more limited than we realize. The power to choose our response seems more a function of our degree of consciousness than sheer willpower or determination.

Second, *we lack sufficient consciousness, maturity, and wisdom to ensure balance, consistency, and true integrity.* To date, efforts in human development have focused primarily on the premise that training, imitation, and practice can make the person "perfect." Successful people are studied, and, from their lives, psychological profiles emerge in the form of prominent habits, attitudes, paradigms, and attributes. Then, we are told that to be effective we need to imitate these great people, or follow the same formulas and principles that have made them successful. The better we imitate, the more successful we are, says the theory.

This is all fine as far as it goes. Unfortunately, it doesn't go far. Ironically, the *form* is often imitated without the imitator coming anywhere near the *substance* of the virtues the model represents. Further, all the great people we seek to emulate have a very dark, human side which merits equal consideration, but is selectively ignored, creating a partial and unbalanced understanding of their true power and greatness.[2]

Although I am sure we can reap some benefit in applying such principles and behavior, I find that such efforts often amount to nothing more than a form of cosmetic surgery or character "face-lift." Such changes, which mostly entail behavioral modification, do not necessarily make us more effective.

I can know, for example, that having a "bias for action" is a trait possessed by effective people, and yet not have sufficient wisdom to know when such a quality might be detrimental or beneficial to others. In my effort to take action, I may not have sufficient maturity to act effectively, use an appropriate style, encourage dissent, value diversity, or follow and serve. And I might not be sufficiently conscious of when my passion for taking action might be transforming into the dark practices of manipulation, overbearance, impulsion, and excessive control. So it is with all the traits that characterize effective people. Even "paradigm shifts" that result in conversion to a new behavior are, for the same reasons, insufficient.

For years I taught and tried to conform to principles and behaviors of effectiveness, but I struggled personally with recurring bouts of reactive or selfish behavior, scarcity thinking, and inconsistent and erratic performance. In fact, at times I felt like Paul of the New Testament, who, even after his miraculous conversion, acknowledged: "I can see that my body follows a different law that battles against the law which my [spirit] dictates."[3]

I sometimes wondered if it was just me, but I knew I wasn't alone. The same struggles and frustrations were reported by many others. Although we acknowledged our human frailties, we viewed our adherence to principles and prescribed formulas of ideal behavior as the "silver bullet" that would enable us to rise above our humanity and become perfect. We were sadly mistaken in both our desires and expectations.

The unfortunate reality for most of us is that these new skills, habits, principles, and formulas for effectiveness and success are often employed as strategies to keep us from the truth about ourselves. We don't do this deliberately, or even consciously. But, for many, this quest for transcendence of self is, in reality, a misguided response to deeply held beliefs of powerlessness, inadequacy, and unworthiness—beliefs that lie at the core of the wounded personality. Sadly, we become so caught up in the dogma of how we ought to behave that we fail to hear the soul's call toward authenticity and wisdom, or the heart's cry for true intimacy, passion, and spontaneity. We try in vain to re-create or "reengineer" ourselves in the image of "principled" behavior and traditional notions of integrity, virtue, and honor. But these efforts are just other forms of idolatry, disguised in noble clothing.

As we worship the graven image of "highly effective" or successful people, we forget we are already created in God's image—and, if any adjustment is needed, it has nothing to do with creating a "better" person, but in shedding all the lies, false ideals, and inhuman expectations that alienate us from ourselves and others. Michelangelo put it so well: "I saw the angel in the marble, and I just chiseled until I set him free."

Third, we have become so enamored with the false notion of perfection, and neurotic in our pursuit of it, that we have lost touch with our own darkness. We have failed to acknowledge and integrate our "shadow," or alter-ego, and have set ourselves up for great disappointment, alienation, and even self-destruction.

Although the proverbial "wolf in sheep's clothing" might not represent the noble desires and intents of the heart, it certainly represents the dark extremes of our character strengths, as well as the inferior forces of our personality that demand integration to satisfy our need for completion. According to Jung, "In the unconscious is everything that has been rejected by consciousness, and the more [principled] one's consciousness is, the more heathenishly does the unconscious behave, if in the rejected heathenism there are values which are important for life."[4]

It is perfectly natural to deny this at first, particularly if we identify *only* with the ideal image of ourselves that observes the principles of moral, effective living. Again from Jung:

> Observance of customs and laws [principles] can very easily be a cloak for a lie so subtle that our fellow human beings are unable to detect it. It may help us to escape all criticism; we may even be able to deceive

ourselves in the belief of our obvious righteousness.
But deep down, below the surface of the average
man's conscience, he hears a voice whispering, "There
is something not right," no matter how much his
rightness is supported by public opinion or by the
moral code.[5]

Sometimes this "whispering voice" is revealed by the defensiveness or uneasiness we feel when we are confronted with honest
feedback, or even with the assertion that we have a dark side.
Often, our defensiveness escalates from denial to delusion, or
sincere denial, and an unwillingness to see ourselves as we really
are. Of this, Jung warns: "Our unwillingness to see our own faults,
and the projection of them onto others, is the source of most
quarrels, and the strongest guarantee that injustice, animosity, and
persecution will not easily die out."[6]

Those of us who engage in one-sided pursuits of effectiveness
or moral righteousness soon find ourselves in the grip of a
frustrating and potentially dangerous paradox, wherein the more
we strive to live effective lives, the less effective and more deluded
we become in the sincere belief that our actions and decisions are
morally and ethically right. Of this paradox, Jung writes:

People who strive to be excessively ethical, who
always think, feel, and act altruistically and idealisti-
cally, avenge themselves for their intolerable ideals by
a subtly planned maliciousness, of which they are
naturally not conscious as such, but which leads to
misunderstandings and unhappy situations. All these
difficulties appear to them as "especially unfortunate
circumstances," or the fault and the malice of other
people, or as tragic complications. Consciously they
imagine they are rid of the conflict, but it is still there,
unseen, to be stumbled over at every step.[7]

Therefore, whenever we identify ourselves with being "virtuous" or "righteous," those parts of ourselves in the shadow
that don't fit the ideal are split off and denied. We seek to build

our strengths and eliminate our weaknesses, not realizing that they are inseparably connected.

The goal of the hidden agenda is wholeness, experience, and authenticity—not idealistic perfection. So we shame our weaknesses and thereby disempower or contaminate the hidden strengths associated with them. We become one-sided, exchanging balanced self-knowledge for the unbalanced zeal of perfection, setting ourselves up for extremism and derailment.

Fourth, we lack the desire, or even the willingness, to face the truth and clear the past of our wounds, losses, and wrongdoings. The work of grieving, mourning, and repenting, or of feeling guilt, regret, or remorse, seems like such hard work, and it can be so negative and depressing to count our losses, or to suffer for our mistakes, sins, and past ignorance. No one likes to talk about such things, let alone experience them. And yet it is precisely our wounds, losses, and unresolved acts of wrongdoing that obstruct our progress and joy in life and keep us alienated from ourselves, others, and God. Such breaches cannot be repaired by simply converting to new, more effective, or more virtuous behaviors. If we do not clear the past, we remain vulnerable to reliving it again and again. The only way out of the fire is through it.

As legendary heavyweight boxing champion Joe Lewis once said about his opponent, "He can run, but he can't hide." So it is with our past—eventually it catches up with us. The mandate of the hidden agenda is learn and grow, or suffer. The inverse is also true. We must suffer to learn and grow. Any approach to personal effectiveness and spirituality that does not require legitimate suffering is at best incomplete and at worst irresponsible, and perhaps even dangerous and damaging to the soul.

The Need for Inner Work

Does all of this mean we should not teach, practice, and cultivate a virtuous and principled way of behaving or living? Not at all. The pursuit of virtue and the development of character through principled behavior are necessary and worthwhile, as long as they do not become unconscious, one-sided, or reductionistic efforts that ignore or discount the needs and realities of the human soul and the need to work beneath the surface toward greater self-realization.

This lesson is perhaps best taught in Jesus's "Parable of the Sower," found in the thirteenth chapter of Matthew in the Bible:

> Behold, a sower went forth to sow; and when he sowed, some seeds fell by the way side, and the fowls came and devoured them up. Some fell upon stony places, where they had not much earth; and forthwith they sprung up, because they had no deepness of earth; and when the sun was up, they were scorched; and because they had no root, they withered away. And some fell among thorns; and the thorns sprung up, and choked them. But other fell into good ground, and brought forth fruit, some an hundredfold, some sixtyfold, some thirtyfold. Who hath ears to hear, let him hear.[8]

In this parable we learn that from stony ground, or unprepared soil, the seed dies or weeds ultimately choke it. The soil of the soul must be adequately prepared for the seed of truth to take root and bear enduring fruit. Such preparation requires not only adequate knowledge and nourishment, but the hard work of the plow which mixes, or integrates, the nourished soil into a rich and receptive seedbed. The work of the plow is "inner work," a work most people will go to almost any length to avoid. Although sowing the seeds of virtue and effectiveness is important, it is no substitute for the work of the plow. Such plow-work entails toil and suffering, as it is met with great resistance.[9]

Without sufficient individuation—which involves differentiating and integrating all aspects of the personality to a condition of greater wholeness—there can be no real integrity or sustained effectiveness. Advocates of personal effectiveness either gloss over this point or miss it altogether. In my view, it is psychologically unsound to *sustain* a life of true effectiveness and integrity without the rigors of inner work that make us whole human beings. It is also unrealistic to assume that without sufficient consciousness, maturity, and wisdom we can be as fruitful or as productive in life as we hope.

The "Parable of the Sower" confirms the notion that the seed, which I believe pertains not only to principles of truth, but to *personal* truth concerning our particular callings and work in life, brings forth fruit—in some cases "thirtyfold," in others "sixtyfold," and in still other cases, "an hundredfold." In other words, our callings in life—our personal truths—are realized in proportion to our degree of integration or wholeness. This makes self-realization dependent on the work of individuation.

To ignore or deny the whole person is to mobilize extremism, strengthen the walls of denial, fortify pride, and essentially disempower the individual, thus setting him or her up for failure—which is exactly what will be needed to get the person back on the right track. Again, we are reminded by Jung, "Only unconscious and wholly uncritical people can imagine it possible to abide in a permanent state of moral goodness. But, because most people are devoid of self-criticism, permanent self-deception is the rule."[10]

Integration means unifying and getting in proper relationship with all aspects of our personality. The result is wholeness, or the "synergy of the soul," where the whole of who we are far exceeds the sum of all our parts. Integration to wholeness, which is the meaning of individuation, is a process that begins with challenging how we see and interpret who we are. This enables us to differentiate the various parts of our personality with our essential identity and nature.

Our ego, the part of ourselves we are aware of, is not necessarily who we really are, and is certainly not *all* we are. It is pitifully inadequate, with all its good habits and sanitized motives and intentions, to move us toward wholeness, self-realization, and true effectiveness.

Formulas and principles cannot save us from ourselves or nourish our soul, for the simple reason that they have no life of their own. The human agency that gives them life is, by nature, wounded, imperfect, and fallible to some degree, and also, then, is human performance. If we interpret our life's experiences and realities incorrectly or incompletely on the inside, then our outward behavior, regardless of how effective it is by qualitative or empirical measurements, becomes nothing more than "window dressing."

Although this point is commonly understood and accepted, what I find missing is an adequate understanding and appreciation for how internal psychic processes are changed. I believe we are faced with a far greater task than simply realizing that we need to change how we have been behaving or doing things. This might be an important start, as it is to see with understanding that certain principles, processes, and behaviors are required to obtain desired results or even simply to live a more abundant life. All these realizations are certainly necessary to initiate the change process.

A Change of Heart

But there's more—much more: There must be a change of heart that reaches into the depths of the soul and does something more than confirm the rightness of the way. That is why we need to experience a deeper, more profound level of personal change that not only reframes our core beliefs and values, but also awakens our needs, capacities, and emotions—as well as the unconscious psychic processes that determine how we interpret and respond to reality. Such a transformation begins with desire and progresses to the death of the ego-ideal and one-sided consciousness. With such a death we experience a psychological rebirth, meaning we ultimately return to ourselves and become our own person: a whole, integrated individual.

According to Eugene Pascal, "This is not an unrealistic idea; it can be achieved by understanding that we can indeed rebirth ourselves by bringing together . . . the conscious and unconscious elements in ourselves, which will produce a new state of consciousness."[11] Each of us will likely experience many psychic rebirth experiences throughout our lives. Each rebirth will essentially involve the realization, or consciousness, of some fundamental aspect of our personality or condition that was previously outside our knowledge or awareness. Through progressive self-realization, we approach substantive transformations of our psychic processes. We see and respond to reality differently, being more integrated and aligned to truth than before. Psychological rebirth, conceived by depth insight, is a forerunner to spiritual transformation and personal wholeness.

In truth, the wise, mature character of a well-rounded person is forged in the furnace of life's experiences and the refining fire of legitimate suffering, which requires facing the whole truth about ourselves, holding the tension of internal opposing forces, and reconciling ourselves to the Truth. Such is the work that needs to be done, and it involves the arduous task of honest introspection, reflection, analysis, reconciliation, and caring for the needs of the soul. It is nothing less than a descent into the darkness of our own soul, which places us "in relationship" with ourselves and others, providing the necessary insight that fosters true humility and integrity.

Without doing this work, we focus on and identify ourselves with our performance, our accomplishments, and either our strengths or our weaknesses. We remain in a condition of recurring self-deception, reactivity, and alienation that frustrates our desire for sustained effectiveness and our quest for wholeness and fulfillment. We continue to run from ourselves and unwittingly perform for all the demanding external voices and expectations that distract us from the true relatedness that makes us fully human and alive.

Chapter Two

DAMNING THE FLOW:
How We Get Stuck in Life and Stop Growing

"The person . . . in the grip of an old distress says things that are not pertinent, does things that don't work, fails to cope with the situation, and endures terrible feelings that have nothing to do with the present."

—Harvey Jackins

"We are here to ruin ourselves and to break our hearts and love the wrong people and die." This philosophy comes from the character Ronny Cammareri in the movie "Moonstruck." It describes, in veiled language, exactly what is required to become whole. It also describes the destiny of those who neglect their hidden agenda for wholeness and who live out their lives unconsciously, in quiet desperation or blissful self-deception. One way or another we'll wake up. Life has a way of getting our attention, and the hidden agenda within each of us is relentless in its quest.

In the meantime, we need to answer two questions: First, what stops our growth and keeps us stuck in old patterns of self-defeating thinking and behavior? And second, what stimulates our growth and releases us from the grip of these self-defeating patterns? Ironically, the answer to both questions is the same: wounding, and the suffering that comes with it.

Wounds and Suffering

The wounding I am referring to is psychological and spiritual in nature. To live is to be wounded, and we are all wounded in various ways. I have identified five interrelated wounds, which are diagramed in Figure 1.

Five Existential Wounds of the Soul

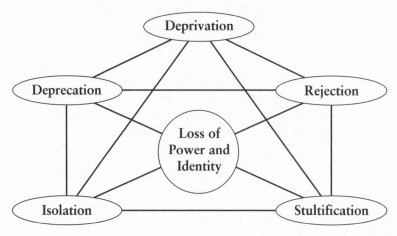

Figure 1

Deprivation is the wound of being insufficiently loved, esteemed, accepted, respected, or nurtured. *Deprecation* us the wound of being falsely accused, shamed, belittled, or disapproved. *Isolation* is the wound of being misunderstood, wrongly judged, persecuted, cast out, or overlooked. *Stultification* is the wound of being controlled, smothered, or stifled. *Rejection* is the wound of being abandoned, neglected, or unappreciated.

When we are born we incur the wounds of our progenitors through our genetic inheritance. The sins and weaknesses of the parents are passed on to the children. As we are raised, we are wounded by parents, siblings, and relatives. We are also wounded in our social interactions with friends, acquaintances, and even complete strangers. The incidents of abuse that wound the soul may be stark or subtle, malignant or benevolent in intent, or even unintentional. They take many different forms and can vary greatly in intensity. They might be emotional, physical, or sexual in nature. But, in all cases, the wounds they inflict damage the spiritual core of the person and his or her sense of identity and self-worth. This existential wounding, or shaming, continues throughout our lives among peers, at school, at work, in marriage, and in virtually every close or intimate relationship.

We also wound ourselves by the choices we make, particularly by choices that violate our internal sense of right and wrong. These constitute acts of wrongdoing wherein we commit acts of offense and moral transgression or refuse to do what we know in our hearts is right. Such self-inflicted wounds ultimately bring the legitimate suffering of guilt and genuine remorse.

All these wounds can be, and often are, destructive—blocking our development to wholeness or full personhood. They create what Jung referred to as "sore spots" in our personalities that leave us stuck in our dependency on validation, approval, and acceptance. These sore spots, also called reactive complexes, are common to all people. They are like land mines ready to explode with the right provocation. We all have them, and they have us. They have a will of their own. They constitute repressed, emotionally charged frustrations and memories that exert a dominating influence on us and erupt unexpectedly in response to some event or association that triggers them.

At the core of these reactive complexes are frustrated human needs and old, unresolved distresses that have been repressed or forgotten. All our reactivity is a result of an underlying reactive complex. These wounds are, indeed, the internal demons that possess us, accounting for much of our ugly moods, dark extremes, and childish, foolish, and irrational behaviors.

Our personal experience has no doubt taught us how tenuous and elusive sustained effectiveness is. We can hardly expect that willpower alone will neutralize all our reactive complexes, regardless of how hard we try. First of all, it's not just the reactive behavior that is of concern. For example, I can experience anger overtaking me, count to ten, and bite my tongue for the moment. Then I can moralize with myself on how bad it is to get angry and choose to "forget it" and be a bigger person. But this isn't truly effective, even though I have ostensibly chosen my response based on my values. This type of self-control does not defuse the complex or integrate the emotion. It simply suppresses emotion and denies the unconscious complex and the values it represents—the essential understanding and attention needed to promote wholeness. What we can expect from such a superficial behavioral approach is the assurance that our reactive complex, with all its negative emotions, will emerge again another day to torment our life and the lives of others.

It has been said, "That which does not kill us makes us stronger." Our wounds can, in strange ways, prepare and shape us for our unique callings in life and make us more responsive to the Voice of Necessity that serves our hidden agenda for wholeness and self-realization. However, without proper perspective and healing, our wounds can also block the realization of our life story, or destiny, and make us weak or even dysfunctional.

The emotional, spiritual, and moral strengths and personality traits that develop as we compensate for our wounds do not necessarily make us whole. They merely make us stronger and more able to endure. But, to be healed and made whole requires hard work, great suffering, constant care, and a special act of grace, which I will cover in greater detail in Chapters Five and Six.

What makes destructive wounding especially damaging is that it causes us to avoid the necessary self-examination and legitimate suffering that come with it. This fear of facing our wounds often gets in the way of the inner work we need to do and results in our addiction to:

1. *Controlling behaviors* for getting or doing what we want, such as confrontation, manipulation, criticizing, labeling, judging, threatening, nagging, preaching, shaming, and various types of passive-aggressive behaviors such as patronizing, withdrawing, ignoring, avoiding, pouting, sulking, silence, sarcasm, and so on.

2. *Rationalizing or defensive behaviors* for avoiding personal

responsibility and preserving and maintaining our self-esteem, such as blaming and rationalization.

3. *Mood-altering behaviors* that have life-damaging consequences and seem beyond our ability to control, including typically obsessive or compulsive behaviors such as addictions to work, activities, substances, and self-perfection.

These addictions are not merely problems we need to fix. More significantly, they are symptoms that indicate we are stuck, wounded, and inattentive to the needs of our soul.

The Question of Maturity

Those who have not worked beneath the surface to face and heal their wounds typically seek to defend themselves by avoiding intimacy or dominating others. They take care of others in order to be taken care of, and use others to get what they want. They are driven by the need to be right, to excel, and to win at all costs, without concern for others or for what is right. As we mature to wholeness, we grow in consciousness, wisdom, and spirituality, making us more productive and serviceable *to* others, more interdependent *with* others, and more congruent *within* ourselves.

At low maturity levels we often get stuck trying to satisfy our "dependency needs" for safety, approval, validation, love, and esteem. We instinctively focus on survival and security instead of on the "being needs" of growth, meaning, loving, and transcendence. Our perspective rarely extends beyond self-interest. At this stage we are typically reactive and short-sighted, unable to satisfy our needs, delay our gratification, accept appropriate responsibility, hold ourselves accountable, exercise self-discipline, or live a balanced life. Most of our emotional energy is expended on people pleasing, care taking, role playing, impression management, self-protection, self-gratification, and power struggles. The primary motivator is fear, particularly the fear of unworthiness, rejection, and being alone. We are not differentiated from our original family system, and we find ourselves repeating self-defeating patterns of behavior, or getting involved in destructive or unhealthy relationships. Our capacity to love is retarded, as are our capacities of self-awareness, imagination, discernment, discrimination, detachment, and rationality.

This level of maturity, which some refer to as dependency, is actually a disempowered state of being. Although such a condition does not remove from us the ability or moral obligation to act responsibly, it can limit our ability to act effectively. We have difficulty being in the here and now. We are limited in our capacity to think what we think, feel what we feel, perceive what we perceive, want what we want, or imagine our life differently. Instead, we are dominated by "shoulds" and fears, resigned to live our lives selfishly by controlling others, playing it safe, acting out rigidly defined roles, or trying to be perfect. In this state, we are disempowered in our ability to constructively respond to the demands of the hidden agenda for fulfillment.

Damning the Flow

To be stuck at a low level of maturity means, among other things, that we no longer have access to the essential parts of ourselves that give us the power to live life fully or to grow in wisdom to a state of true effectiveness and abundance. Those needs, capacities, and emotions—which are disowned, weakened, or abused by wrongdoing or neglect—are buried in the unconscious mind where they reside in the darkness as our alter-ego, or shadow, and often express themselves in reactive or self-defeating ways. Robert Bly, in his outstanding work, *A Little Book on the Human Shadow*, from which I have extracted the following excerpts, describes this process of disempowerment using the metaphor of "the long bag":

> When we were one or two years old we had what we might visualize as a 360-degree personality. Energy radiated out from all parts of our body and all parts of our psyche. A child running is a living globe of energy. We had a ball of energy, all right; but one day

we noticed that our parents didn't like certain parts of that ball. They said things like: "Can't you be still?" or "It isn't nice to try and kill your brother."

Behind us we have an invisible bag, and the part of us our parents don't like, we, to keep our parents' love, put in the bag. By the time we go to school our bag is quite large. Then our teachers have their say: "Good children don't get angry over such little things." So we take our anger and put it in the bag. . . . Then we do a lot of bag-stuffing in high school. This time it's no longer the evil grownups that pressure us, but people our own age. . . . [So] out of a round globe of energy the twenty-year-old ends up with a slice. . . .

We spend our life until we're twenty deciding what parts of ourselves to put into the bag, and we spend the rest of our lives trying to get them out again. Sometimes retrieving them feels impossible, as if the bag were sealed. Suppose the bag remains sealed—what happens then? . . . The nice side of the personality becomes, in our idealistic culture, nicer and nicer, . . . but the substance in the bag takes on a personality of its own; it can't be ignored. . . . The man who opens his bag at forty-five or the woman who opens her bag rightly feels fear. . . . Every part of our personality that we do not love will become hostile to us. . . .

But why would we give away, or put into the bag, so much of ourselves? Why would we do it so young? And, if we have put away so many of our angers, spontaneities, hungers, enthusiasms, our rowdy and unattractive parts, then how can we live? What holds us together? Alice Miller spoke to this point in her book, *Prisoners of Childhood*, which in paperback form is called *The Drama of the Gifted Child*. The drama is this: We came as infants "trailing clouds of glory," arriving from the farthest reaches of the universe, bringing with us . . . our 360-degree radiance— and we offered this gift to our parents. They didn't want it. They wanted a nice girl or a nice boy. That's the first act of the drama. It doesn't mean our parents

were wicked; they needed us for something. . . . Our
parents rejected who we were before we could talk, so
the pain of rejection is probably stored in some pre-
verbal place.[1]

The seeds of disappointment and rejection are found in our
spoken or unspoken expectations. When we expect—even
unconsciously—a "boy" or a "girl," or a child who will grow up
in the image of some ideal profile, whether it's the parent's
grandiose self-image ("You'll be just like me"), the opposite of
the parent's degraded self-image ("You'll be everything I'm not"),
or an image of some other great and successful person ("You'll be
a doctor, president, priest, or athlete," or "You'll be just like so-
and-so"), we reject the child from the beginning.[2]

Whoever the child really *is*, if he or she varies unfavorably from
the parents' expectations, then the child will be met with disappointment. Disapproval, and even shame, communicate rejection,
force adaptation, and result in a loss of self-worth that carries forward into the child's adult life. These messages of disapproval and
rejection can be very subtle, allowing the parents to deceive themselves into believing that their rejection is only a form of parental
love or concern. Perhaps it is, but rejection is rejection, and few
children can make such distinctions (which tend to be spurious or
self-serving to begin with on the part of the parents). Bly continues:

> When I read her book, I fell into depression for three
> weeks. With so much gone, what can we do? We can
> construct a personality more acceptable to our parents.
> Alice Miller agrees that we have betrayed ourselves,
> but she says, "Don't blame yourself for that. There's
> nothing else you could have done." Children in
> ancient times who opposed their parents probably
> were set out to die. We did, as children, the only sensible
> thing under the circumstances. The proper attitude
> toward that, she says, is mourning. . . .
> When we have put a lot in our private bag, we
> often have, as a result, little energy. The bigger the
> bag, the less the energy. Some people have by nature

more energy than others, but we all have more than we can possibly use. Where did it go? If we put our sexuality into the bag as a child, obviously we lose a lot of energy. When a woman puts her masculinity into the bag, . . . she loses energy with it. We can think of our personal bag as containing energy now unavailable to us.[3]

In the workplace we find many "repressed monsters" in the bag, "writhing just below the surface of our professional life." David Whyte insightfully identifies a few of these monsters, including: "unresolved parent-child relationships that play out into rigid company hierarchies; . . . unresolved emotional demands individuals may have of fellow workers but will never admit to themselves; . . . the refusal to come to terms with an abused childhood, . . . [and] the subsequent longing for self-protection and the wielding of organizational power and control at any cost to gain that protection." Whyte then accurately observes that perhaps "the parent of all these vulnerabilities is . . . the deep physical shame that we are not enough, will never be enough, and can never measure up."[4] The greater the shame at the core of one's being, the more destructive the shadow forces become, contaminating the work of individuation instead of assisting it.

Such "shaming" damns our growth. It fills our bag with the essential capacities for productive living and personal fulfillment that we received as a birthright, and instead we carry the bag around as luggage instead of using it productively for accomplishing our life's mission or for improving our effectiveness with others.

Perhaps the effects of such disempowerment are best seen in our relationships, which I explore in more depth in the next chapter. In our relationships, we experience how the contents of our bag cloud our vision and set us up for a host of problems. It becomes difficult for us to experience mature love, collaboration, or true synergy. The most troublesome of these relationships are husband-wife, parent-child, and boss-subordinate relationships. Each of these is different, yet the three are clearly related. Let's look at a hypothetical example, inspired by Robert Bly, involving a new marriage. It begins with a little boy and a little girl from two different families:

The little boy's power, or ability, to know and get what he wants when he wants it is preempted by an overly protective mother, who stifles that power to build his "character." She insists on telling him what to want and which of his other wants are bad. She teaches him how wrong it is to be selfish (to want for himself) and how important it is to get permission or to wait patiently to get what he wants.

Dominated by well-intentioned "shoulds" and "should nots," the little boy's power of self-satisfaction, which has been shamed and labeled as "selfishness," goes into his growing bag of undesirables. He learns to adapt and becomes submissive to the sometimes irritable and capricious demands of a powerful woman. When he observes his mother—who somehow, magically, always gets her way, and who gets what she wants when she wants it—he sees her as a witch. Symbolically, a "witch" is an irritable, greedy, sometimes hostile, but often charming woman, who has incredible power to get her way. She makes things happen her way, or else! As Bly suggests, the boy gives his mother his "witchiness"—his power to satisfy himself on his own terms, his power to get what he wants when he wants it.

The process of turning over his "witchiness," or "witch power," to his mother is called "projection." He pulls this rejected power out of his bag and, instead of owning it and using it productively, throws it at his mother or at other assertive women who seem to know what they want, along with his unexplainable feelings of love mixed with resentment, fear, and disgust.

Now let's change scenes: The little girl's power of independence is overshadowed by a domineering, overprotective father. She is raised with the notion that "good girls" are helpless, submissive, and must be protected and provided for by men. Her self-reliance, independence, assertiveness, and sense of adventure are stuffed in her bag. When her father takes charge and protects her, she gives him her power of assertiveness, or her internal "hero" or "giant." When he takes charge and tells her what to do, how to live, and how to feel, she turns over to him her power of authority, discrimination, and restraint—her "tyrant" or "patriarch." Like the boy, this little girl pulls the rejected power out of her bag and throws it at her father, or at other men who try to protect or dominate her or who to try to take charge— along with her unexplainable feelings of love and adulation mixed with resentment, fear, and hatred.

Now let's bring this boy and girl together twenty years later in marriage. At this point I will again let Robert Bly tell the story, since he does it so well:

> While the bride and groom stand in front of the minister exchanging rings, another important exchange takes place in the basement. During a separate meeting, the [groom's] mother passes over [her] son's witch, which she has been carrying, to the bride. An hour after the ceremony the witch is firmly in place inside the bride, though it will take a while for it to show up, because neither the bride, nor the mother, nor the groom knows about this second ceremony. But after a few arguments, a few obstinacies, and a few money fights, it occurs to the groom one day that there is something witch-like in his bride that he hadn't noticed before.
>
> It sometimes occurs to [the bride], too, that something bizarre has happened. During an argument she feels herself more greedy, or more witchy. One woman said to me, "Robert, before I was married I was quite a nice person. But now I've been married for three years, and you know, I'm getting bitchier and bitchier. How can this be?" I said, "Well, you've been eating for two." The husband meanwhile gets sweeter and sweeter, and this enrages his wife still more, and tends to bring out more of her witch side. She is now carrying witchiness—that is, impulsive irritability, abrupt greediness, unfairness, unexplainable hostility, an underground current of rage—for both of them. He feels quite calm, and looks with wonder and pity on her behavior.

During the marriage service a similar exchange takes place between the groom and the bride's father. Perhaps their spirits meet in the garage—their actual bodies being in church—and the bride's father passes over to the groom as much as he can find of the giant or the tyrant that he has been carrying for his daughter. The bride's father leaves the church door lighter, the groom heavier. The groom receives from the bride's father many other transferred projections as well: He may have to carry her spiritual guide, and perhaps her interior bluebeard, some brutal side of the feminine. Besides his childhood witch, the bride receives from the mother of the groom his helplessness, his deviousness, perhaps his Kali-like rage. The bride goes home from the wedding considerably heavier.[5]

Along these same lines it has been said that at least six people sleep in the marriage bed: the husband, wife, and both sets of parents. But, if you add to this the idea that men tend to marry women who are like their mothers and women tend to marry men who are like their fathers, then you increase the number in the marriage bed to eight.

These realities became clear to me some time ago as I was commencing my own midlife journey. During this time I had the good fortune of working with a talented therapist who suggested that perhaps my marriage was being negatively affected by some unresolved issues with my mother. The implication was that I had married someone like my mother to work through these issues, and that until I did I could never be whole and would never be able to fully appreciate and love my wife for who she was.

This suggestion was repulsive to me for reasons that I am, only now, beginning to understand. I remember acting angrily and saying to him with great conviction, "Don't give me any of that Freudian crap!" As I left the session, my therapist requested that I think about his suggestion before dismissing it.

That weekend, Annette and I attended a wedding reception in San Francisco. The son of a close family friend was getting married, and my family had been invited to the celebration. It was a gala affair. The surroundings were elegant; the people were beautiful; the food and entertainment were magnificent, and I was depressed. As we took our seats at the dinner table, my wife, Annette, was seated to my immediate left, and my mother to my right. As I sat between the two most important women in my life I felt closed in, suffocated. Although I wasn't very reflective at the time, I knew it wasn't my tuxedo that was confining me. Something was going on, and I didn't know what it was.

Finally, the breakthrough came. As the band was playing, my mother leaned over and whispered, "Honey, why don't you dance with Annette? She looks so beautiful, and I know she would love to dance."

Instantly, my sense of confinement turned to anger. I looked at my mother and said, "I'll dance when and if I feel like it."

She backed off. Then, a minute later, Annette leaned over and whispered, "Honey, why don't you dance with your mother? It would mean so much to her."

The same anger surfaced again. Then, in what I can only describe as a vision, I saw in my mind's eye the faces of my wife and mother merge into one. The revelation astounded me and has been pivotal in my own healing process.

Projecting Our Lost Power onto Others

Other examples abound. Because our own bag is so full of the split-off sources of our own power, and because we tend to project our lost power onto others, it's not uncommon for us to give our *spirituality* and *internal authority* to bosses, priests, gurus, or "church authorities," our *charisma* and *vision* to leaders, our *creativity* to artists, or our sense of *fun, adventure,* and *heroism* to celebrities or fictional heroes or heroines whom we idolize or seek to imitate.

Therefore, the more our personal power is "in the bag," the more we project what we have rejected or neglected of ourselves onto others and the more disempowered we really are—

although we might believe the remaining portion of our power is sufficient or complete. Knowing this, we can better understand and appreciate how today's common notions of personal empowerment and motivation miss the mark. Such notions and related practices applied to disempowered people, functioning at say, ten percent of their capacity, can rarely result in anything more than better use of the ten percent.

Even the idea of motivating others to "improve" or "get their act together" is highly limited. A person can be highly motivated and highly dysfunctional or disempowered at the same time. The ability to motivate or to be motivated is not necessarily an indicator that those who motivate or those who are motivated are functional, trustworthy, or empowered human beings. Faith, optimism, and enthusiasm alone are no substitutes for the wisdom, maturity, and integrity that come from working beneath the surface. Nor are they precursors to it.

Personal empowerment increases through the process of individuation, or maturity to wholeness, as we strive to reclaim, integrate, and develop the split-off and undeveloped parts of our personality toward a state of healthy interdependence and self-acceptance. This requires us to learn, among other things, how to withdraw our projections and "eat," or assimilate, them. (I discuss how to "eat the shadow" in Chapter Five.) Only by integrating the contents of our "long bag" can we truly empower ourselves to productively fulfill our destiny. Until we do so we will continue to be stuck, and our hidden agenda for wholeness and fulfillment will continue to be frustrated.

The Poisonous Rules of Corrupt Patriarchy

Most of today's organizations, families, and religions instinctively, if not consciously, embrace and perpetuate the poisonous rules of "corrupt patriarchy." Corrupt patriarchy sees people as "things" or "possessions" that are controlled by the authority figure (the bosses, parents, teachers, religious leaders, and so on) to maintain order and accomplish the leader's desired results. This control is accomplished through the authoritarian (or "benevolent authoritarian") enforcement of the following rules:

1. The authority figure is always right.
2. Do what you're told, no matter what.
3. Don't talk back.
4. Don't rock the boat.
5. Don't think, believe, feel, or act in ways the authority figure would disapprove of.
6. Don't need, want, or value anything the authority figure thinks is inappropriate.
7. Don't learn, say, think, or do anything that might threaten the authority figure.
8. Don't screw up or make mistakes; if anything goes wrong, blame yourself, and refer to rule #1.

We communicate or tacitly endorse these rules in many ways. Many familiar statements from authority figures send these messages, along with numerous nonverbal signals such as attitude, voice, tone, posture, facial expressions, and body gestures. Here are a few examples of common, familiar statements ("familiar" meaning, in this case, that they tend to originate from within the family or from people who exercise authority over us, especially paternal figures and authorities, upon whom we tend to project the traits of family members), often made with an attitude of disappointment, disdain, or superiority, which reinforce the eight rules of corrupt patriarchy:

Messages	Statements
1. *The authority figure is always right.*	Don't argue with me.
	That's just the way it is.
	Because I said so.
	Don't do as I do, do as I say.
	What I say goes.
	End of discussion.

2. Do *what you're told, no matter what.*	Do what you're told. I thought I made it clear. If you know what's good for you, you'll . . . Do it or else. When I say, "Jump," you say, "How high?"
3. *Don't talk back.*	Don't talk back. Watch your mouth. Don't give me any back talk. One more word, and I'll . . . Children are to be seen and not heard.
4. *Don't rock the boat.*	Don't fight. Quit complaining and just do it. Can't you ever agree on anything? You're never happy. Don't make waves. Keep it up (said threateningly).
5. *Don't think, believe, feel, or act in ways the authority figure would disapprove of.*	Where did you get a thought like that? Who asked you? What have you got to be sad about? You shouldn't feel that way. How could you think that way?
6. *Don't need, want, or value anything the authority figure thinks is inappropriate.*	Stop thinking of yourself all the time. Why would you want something like that? You're so needy. Don't you ever think about anyone other than yourself? No, and that's final.
7. *Don't learn, say, think, or do anything that might threaten the authority figure.*	Who do you think you are? Don't you ever . . . If you ever say (or do) that again, I'll . . . Don't ever use that tone of voice again. Never worked before. You think (or talk) too much.

8. *Don't screw up or make mistakes; if anything goes wrong, blame yourself, and refer to rule #1.*	Don't screw up. How many times have I told you? I told you this would happen. You never listen, do you? When are you ever going to learn? Get it right. If you can't do it right the first time, don't do it at all. If I want something done right, I've got to do it myself. I should know better than to rely on you for anything. This will teach you. Are you stupid? I give up (on you).

As you review and think about these rules of corrupt patriarchy, consider the following questions:

- Which rules, or similar variations, were present in your family growing up?
- How were you punished or corrected when you broke the rules? How might such corrective or punitive actions have negatively affected or harmed you?
- Which rules have you, perhaps unconsciously, carried into your family or workplace?
- How do you punish or correct others when they break the rules? How might such corrective or punitive actions affect or harm others?

Whenever these rules are violated, the person who violates them is typically shamed in some way and is subjected to various forms of control and power struggle. Any behavior that attacks or insults the individual or attempts to find fault—to discredit, malign, embarrass, humiliate, label, or discount with the threat of rejection, abandonment, or condemnation—is shaming in nature, sending the message that the person is fundamentally defective, "less than," or flawed in some way. As I mentioned earlier, all these things wound and disempower the individual, damning the natural flow of life toward integration and wholeness.

Personal Power Core

As human beings, we all suffer to some degree from destructive wounds and the reactive complexes that come from them. We know that because of such wounds we also suffer from an impaired power core.

The following is a partial comparative list of characteristics of people who have a functional or impaired power core:

Functional Power Core	*Impaired Power Core*
Accepts accountability.	Transfers or avoids accountability through blaming, accusing, or self-excusing behavior.
Values the differences in others and seeks other viewpoints.	Views diversity as threatening or inconvenient.
Accepts personal responsibility for satisfying own needs and for choices and consequences.	Sees self as a victim and as powerless; uses reactive language and controlling, manipulative behavior to meet needs.
Able to identify feelings and use them as signals.	Out of touch with feelings; cannot talk about or label feelings; emotional numbness.
Appropriately open with others.	Politically correct; self-censoring.
Has good personal boundaries as defined by *chosen* values and principles.	Overly rigid, inflexible, or accommodating; lives life according to "shoulds."
Able to "be there" and care for others.	Self-obsessed and self-centered; anxious about survival, covering "backside," and preserving appearances; manipulates and uses people.
Takes appropriate risks; able to tolerate failure or mistakes.	Afraid of taking appropriate risks; inordinate fear of failure and rejection.

Willing and able to conscientiously dissent; encourages and rewards constructive dissent.	Unwilling or unable to dissent; high need for acceptance, approval, and conformity.
Low need for being right and in control; good follower; able to let go of control.	High need for being right and in control; rigid; has difficulty admitting and owning mistakes
Honest with self and others.	Dishonest, self-deluding, and in denial.
Faces and resolves problems; willing to get help.	Avoids dealing with problems; denies problems and refuses to get help.
Able to solicit, accept, and deal with "negative" feedback constructively.	Refuses to receive or solicit feedback; when given, feedback is discounted and disregarded without serious consideration. Or, the person goes into a "tailspin," gets stuck, and can't move on.
Able to think in gray areas: "both/and."	Thinks in "either/or" extremes.
Genuine, truly self-expressive, and authentic.	Excessive approval-seeking; obsessed with image; plays the role.
Able to delay gratification.	Needs immediate gratification.
Self-forgiving and forgiving of others.	Perfectionistic, impatient, intolerant; difficulty in forgiving and in letting go of resentment and anger; moralistic, self-righteous, judgmental.
Guided by a deep sense of meaning and purpose.	Merely existing, without meaning and purpose.

| Able to stand alone in difficult issues concerning conflict of duty. | Overly concerned with safety, conformity, appearance, and societal or group acceptance; difficulty distinguishing moral and ethical demands; weak voice of internal authority. |

None of us is perfect. The good news is that we *can* be healed and become whole. Through the inner work of integration our weaknesses can be made into strengths. This cannot come about, however, without sufficient care and the legitimate suffering and insight that accompany such work. We will, as accountable human beings, always have sufficient willpower to work beneath the surface, if only to reach out for assistance, receive insight, and initiate action toward reconciliation and personal growth. Whatever additional power we lack will be given to us if we sincerely and diligently seek it. We are not helpless victims, and we are not alone.

Chapter Three

LIVING A LIE:

How and Why We Unconsciously Undermine Our Relationships

"He who mistrusts most should be trusted least."
—*Theognius of Megara*

"You are a pain in the neck. To stop you from giving me a pain in the neck, I protect my neck by tightening my neck muscles, which gives me the pain in the neck you are."

—*R. D. Laing*

"To the untrue man, the whole universe is false—it is impalpable—it shrinks with his grasp. And he himself, in so far as he shows himself in a false light, becomes a shadow, or indeed, ceases to exist."

—*Nathaniel Hawthorne*

As a result of being stuck and "out of relationship" with ourselves, we fall out of relationship with others and, in doing so, lose our vital connection to wholeness. We defeat ourselves and jeopardize, or even destroy, the very relationships we need most.

It's common knowledge that, in spite of our need for trust, love, and support from others, we continually damage and even destroy our relationships and then deceive ourselves into believing we are not part of the problem. Paradoxically, our efforts to make things better in our relationships often make things worse.

The Lies We Live

Every day most of us experience some kind of alienating chain reaction that puts us out of relationship with others. Such chain reactions typically begin when an experience with another person acts as a triggering event. It ends with both people locked in conflict. Chain reactions occur in consequence of unhealed wounds and the living of certain lies. The lies we live can be summarized in at least four levels (see Figure 2), which are discussed in this chapter, as well as in Chapters Four and Five.

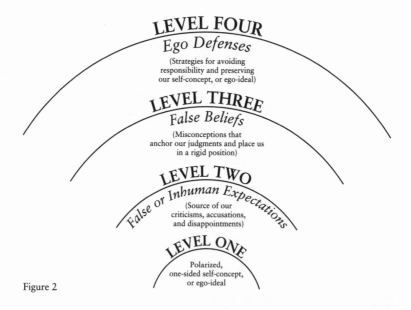

Figure 2

Level One lies involve our misconceptions about who we think we are. These are the lies associated with our "ego-ideal," or our one-sided, polarized self-concept. They exist because we are undifferentiated and unintegrated. These lies, which result in the projection of our rejected parts onto others, will be dealt with in Chapter Five.

Level Two lies include our inhuman expectations of ourselves and others. These lies can be recognized by our beliefs that "good" people "should," "ought to," and "always will" behave in certain ways. The list of these lies is endless. Examples include: "Tell the whole truth," "Keep your word," "Be one-hundred percent supportive and loyal," "Show appreciation for the good things I do or say," "Treat me with consideration and respect," "Act 'normal,' " "Obey the rules," "Play fair," "Reciprocate in fairness," "Put the needs of others above your own," "Be nice and considerate," "Be pleasant and cooperative," and so on. These expectations become inhuman when prefixed by "always." They have become poisonous lies that form the basis of our criticisms and accusations of others.

Level Three lies are false beliefs that anchor our judgments of others and place us in a rigid position. They include well-accepted notions such as, "I am right; you are wrong," "You make me feel . . . ," "This is different," "It's always the same," "I can change you," "There's no way out," "If I wait long enough, the problem will get better (or go away)," and "The way I see you is who you really are." These lies enable us either to avoid responsibility or to accept too much responsibility.

Level Four lies involve ego defenses—the lies we tell ourselves to get our egos off the hook and quiet our consciences. These lies include behaviors of denial, rationalization, and shifting blame, to name just a few. They form a hard outer shell that protects all the other lies we live.

Reactive Cycles: Fulfillment of a "Death Wish"

The hidden agenda brings us together and tears us apart. It contains idealistic images and expectations, lurking beneath the surface like seductive promises, separating us from those who do not, and cannot, live up to those expectations or embody all the characteristics and ideals we project onto them. Even in our closest relationships, the hidden agenda acts out an unconscious "death wish" and desire for a new way of relating that would better satisfy our needs and fulfill our quest for wholeness. This unconscious death wish often becomes a self-fulfilling prophecy that plays out in an ugly interactive process I refer to as the *reactive cycle*.

Reactive cycles merely carry out a self-fulfilling prophecy. Technically, these cycles are known as "deviation amplifying processes."[1] Commonly, they are known simply as "vicious circles." Their function as the "operative mechanism" of self-fulfilling prophecy is effectively described and illustrated in a hypothetical example by Paul Wender, who writes:

> The self-fulfilling prophecy and its ["deviation amplifying feedback chain"] play a frequent role in interpersonal relations. Let A, for whatever reason, approach B with the expectation that B is a "son of a bitch." A will then select from B's behavior those aspects that are consistent with this hypothesis and discount those that are inconsistent with it. If B is friendly, he is being deceptive; if B is angry, he is showing his true colors. A will treat B as an S.O.B., and B in general will react in kind. It is necessary to note that A need not be conscious of his expectations or set. In fact, he often is not. A's conscious report then, that people are "no damn good," need not be a distortion. His report may be an accurate report of people's behavior toward him. What A does not notice is that he is the generator of this behavior.[2]

Also known as "advocacy loops," "reinforcing processes," and "games," reactive cycles are a common phenomenon that exist as a result of being stuck in life and out of relationship with ourselves.[3] They are a natural outgrowth of our chain reactions to one another, engaging all four levels of untruth in the systematic destruction of the relationship.

Reactive cycles often begin as a natural reaction to being disappointed, threatened, or offended by the other person in some way. When one person feels minimized, humiliated, or compromised, the natural instinct is to criticize, shift the blame, strike back, or merely withdraw or "rise above it" as a disguised means of control or retribution. Such reactions, of course, usually provoke counterreactions, and the downward spiral continues, with both parties triggering the reactive behavior of the other. In advanced stages, this destructive dance takes on a malignant intentionality, with one person acting deliberately to provoke the other person, unconsciously obtaining evidence to justify punishment of the other person or to justify his or her own behavior.

It's easy to fall into such reactive cycles. Some years ago, I was on the road 175 days of the year, teaching and consulting. Often, I would arrive home on a Friday night and leave again on Sunday. The more I was away, the more out of touch I felt with my family. Although I would call home each night and speak at length with Annette and each of the children, I still felt disconnected and was always glad to come home.

I remember driving back from the airport one Friday night, tired and eager to get home, fantasizing about a warm and enthusiastic greeting from my entire family who would be waiting eagerly at the door for my arrival. What a wonderful scene it was in my mind! And well-deserved, I might add. After all, I had been out there in the cold, lonely world working for them.

What I didn't factor in was the fact that all my children were now old enough to have lives of their own, filled with friends, sleep-overs, dates, and exciting weekend activities. So, instead of a greeting party of five, I was met by a greeting party of one. At least Annette was home. Oh yes, and Corky, my faithful dog— he was the first to greet me, carrying a sock in his mouth.

On this particular weekend the children were gone with friends Friday night and most of Saturday. They came home for a couple of hours on Saturday afternoon and then left again Saturday night. On Sunday morning, as I was packing to leave again, I slipped into the "darkness" and my hidden agenda took over in a destructive way. I began to feel sorry for myself and to accuse my family: "They don't care about me. If I died, they would never miss me. They only want me around to make money. I'm a meal ticket, that's all."

As I was packing and wallowing in self-pity my family was upstairs interacting with one another, laughing, and having a good time together. And there I was, alone. My dark thoughts continued: "The least they could do is come downstairs and spend a few minutes with me before I leave again. Is that asking too much?"

As I accused my family in my mind for gross crimes of neglect, abandonment, and ingratitude, I spawned a plan. I would simply finish packing, sneak out of the house, and leave without saying goodbye. When they finally realized I had left, they would feel guilty about how selfish and cruel they had been. They would seek my forgiveness, and I would pardon their sins and be whole. It would be wonderful. But it never worked out that way. When I awakened from my trance, I was still packing. Finally, my consciousness dawned, and I saw where I had been and what I needed to do. I was not a victim. This was not about my family; it was about me.

When we are out of relationship with ourselves, we are often out of relationship with others. To be out of relationship with another person is to be defensive and alienated in the relationship. To be out of relationship with ourselves often involves acting the part of the victim or the rescuer.

The "Victim" and the "Rescuer"

Our natural tendencies to judge or criticize others negatively—to accuse them and then assume the role of "victim" or "rescuer"—form the basis of reactive cycles that undermine our interdependence and, subsequently, our interpersonal effectiveness. For the purposes of this discussion, a "victim" is someone who feels neglected, unappreciated, deprived, offended, provoked, used, harmed, betrayed, threatened, abused, or violated in some way. Victims typically feel innocent in their own mind, and are undeserving of such treatment. Although true victims certainly exist, those who pick up the "victim role" are really victims by choice.

At the core of a victim's psyche are seemingly inhuman expectations of others, along with deeply rooted beliefs of powerlessness, inadequacy, and unworthiness. According to one explanation, the inferior aspects of a victim's personality are commonly projected onto others in the form of accusing, blaming, or cynical behavior. Another persuasive explanation involves seeing other people falsely, due to unrealistic expectations, or improper framing of the relationship. This sets up the victim to be deprived, disappointed, or offended.

A "rescuer" is someone who feels the need to fix broken, defective, or misguided people and relationships. On the surface, rescuers seem motivated by genuine, selfless love and concern for others. But, in reality, rescuers are motivated primarily by the need to be needed, appreciated, and esteemed.

It is not always easy to tell the difference between a "rescuer" and a truly charitable caregiver; both are motivated by needs—the rescuer by the need for acceptance and esteem, the charitable caregiver by the need to love and serve. Both can exist, to some degree, in the same individual, and both can trigger chain reactions that result in reactive cycles. Also, rescuers tend to become victims when they don't receive sufficient compensation in the form of appreciation and acceptance.

Victims and rescuers are, essentially, two sides of the same coin in the ongoing cycle of life experience. Victims often despise or are cynical toward rescuers (or even toward truly charitable caregivers) because hidden within each victim is an unacknowledged rescuer, with all the same shameful neediness and insecurity. Even showing genuine love and concern requires wisdom in order to avoid the appearance of pity, accusation, and rejection.

As I discussed in the previous chapter, the wounded soul naturally tends to assume the role of either a victim or a rescuer. This tendency resides in the shadow regions of the psyche. When such tendencies are "triggered," consciousness decreases, reactive complexes are mobilized, and we fall out of relationship with one another, entering a vicious cycle of reactivity that results in intolerance, contention, and alienation. Such a cycle is usually (if not always) unconsciously motivated and the people involved feel perfectly justified in their judgments and reactive behavior toward one another. In my experience, telltale signs include being critical, assigning blame, making accusations, and finding excuses for personal behaviors.

Falling Out of Relationship

The following is a true story involving two individuals I will call Tim and Alan:

> Alan and Tim are both senior executives in a large organization. Tim reports to Alan. One day, Alan sees a need in Tim's department and addresses the need in a way he believes is right. But the action affects Tim's area of responsibility and disrupts Tim's plans. So, when Tim finds out what Alan did, he takes offense and gets angry. Tim sees Alan's action as wrong, and sees Alan as "in over his head," uninformed, controlling, and disrespectful. In retaliation, Tim reverses Alan's action.
>
> When Alan finds out that his decision has been overturned, he takes offense and gets angry. He sees Tim as overreactive, territorial, power hungry, childish, disrespectful, and "not a team player." Alan and Tim are now alienated from each other and in a power struggle. Alan believes Tim is out of line, so he begins to assert greater control over Tim's department. He starts getting more and more involved in Tim's business: attending more meetings, asking more questions, challenging more decisions, and making more directives to Tim and his people in the guise of "suggestions." Alan feels perfectly justified in his behavior because, after all, he does have a vested interest in the business, and Tim does report directly to him. And besides, Tim needs to be reminded of who's in charge.
>
> Alan's behavior triggers a counterreaction in Tim. Consequently, Tim avoids Alan and basically disregards his suggestions. He tells Alan to back off, and tells his department not to bother with Alan's directives. He makes himself "unavailable" to Alan for any meetings, busying himself with "urgent" matters that require his immediate attention. This is how Tim controls Alan, by keeping him out and intimidating him with the urgency and importance of his (Tim's) work. After all, anybody as busy and in demand as Tim must be important and powerful.

Likewise, Tim's reactive behavior triggers another counterreaction in Alan. Both executives feel perfectly justified in their behavior and judgments toward one another. Both feel they are doing the best they can. However, in reacting to each other, Tim and Alan provoke the very behavior they find objectionable in the other. They continue in this reactive cycle, pretending to be partners, each hoping the other will change. They maintain cordial relations and get along most of the time. Sometimes they even believe the relationship is getting better—when asked, one or both may say that everything's fine, but it's not. Deep down, though they may never admit it, they don't trust each other.

The judgments and behaviors of Tim and Alan toward each other are like a small ax wedge left between the large limbs of a tree. Over time, the tree limbs grow over the wedge, hiding it from view, but the wedge is still there. No one thinks about the wedge. Like so many other hurts we suffer, it's best just to "forget it" and move on. Besides, says Alan, "Tim will never change." "Neither will Alan," says Tim. When the strong winds of adversity come—and they always come—the hidden wedge will take its toll. The weakened limbs will one day break, and the relationship will die. The death wish will be realized. There will be no "winners." Even if one stays and one goes, they both lose, and the cycle will continue once again with someone else.

I went through a similar experience with my younger brother wherein I was not aware of my own part in a longstanding problem between us. It's hard to say when it began, but I believe it was about twenty years ago, when my decision to pursue a more religious life changed our relationship. My emotional and spiritual immaturity resulted in extremism; I was dedicated to my newfound religion to the point of being dogmatic, rigid, and judgmental. My excessive zeal put many people off, particularly my family. My brother felt he had lost his older brother—I had pretty much been a "hero" until then, but no more. I had fallen from his graces, and I knew it. I could feel his disapproval of me. Sometimes it would hurt. I would respond by righteously turning the other cheek. After all, what could I expect from a younger brother who was so self-centered and immature, and whose priorities in life were so meaningless and empty?

In my own way I disapproved of him, too, although I would have called it "Christian concern." I'm sure he felt my disapproval. An interesting dynamic soon emerged between us. Whenever we got together, he would behave toward me in ways I felt were rude, disrespectful, and insulting. It really bothered me, but I never showed it or admitted it to myself or others; such a reaction was beneath me. So I just took it righteously—like a martyr—thinking to myself, "Poor guy, how sad. It must be hard for him to live with himself." My love and concern were genuine, but so were my accusations. He was the offender, and I was the offended victim. This pattern continued over the years. We rarely got together or even spoke to each other; it was just too hard.

Some time ago my other brother and his wife decided to have a surprise birthday party for my mother, who was turning 70. We would all meet in Carmel, California, to celebrate. Among the various activities, my brothers had scheduled a formal dinner that would require a suit and tie.

I remember packing to go: As I entered the closet to pick out my clothes, I knew my brothers would be wearing nice suits and ties. I also knew they expected me to dress accordingly. I passed by my suits and picked out a blue blazer with gray slacks and a pink shirt—not exactly formal. Then it came time to pick a necktie. My eyes passed over all my nice silk ties and rested on my Western bolo tie. That was the one I wanted. I reached for the tie, but as I did so, I had a feeling that I was making a mistake. Now there's nothing wrong with bolo ties, but I knew my brothers would disapprove—particularly my youngest brother. I hesitated, then took it off the rack.

"You're not going to wear *that,* are you?" Annette asked.

"Why not?" I replied.

"Because your brothers will think you look too informal."

"That's their problem," I said. "They can think what they want."

As I parried Annette's warning, I remember feeling indignant, but also very justified and independent. As I dressed that evening before dinner, I wondered what abuse my younger brother would dish out. I felt uneasy about the bolo tie, but I was also determined not to let it bother me. I would rise above my brother's immaturity and rudeness.

The evening was not a disappointment. From the time we met to go to the dinner I could tell my brothers were looking at my bolo tie, and I knew what would be coming. That night, several snide comments were made about my clothes and my tie. I felt persecuted and unappreciated, an outcast. But, as Annette and I returned to our room after dinner, I felt strangely victorious.

This was a classic example of a self-inflicted wound. It didn't even dawn on me until over a year later, when Annette and I were packing to go to San Francisco to celebrate my uncle's 75th birthday. Again, I needed to bring a suit and tie. And, as I searched for an appropriate tie, I saw my bolo tie and asked Annette with a smile, "What do you think, shall I bring my bolo tie again?"

We both laughed, and then Annette said, "I never figured out why you brought that tie to your mom's birthday dinner when you knew what would happen."

Without hesitation I replied, "That's simple. I wanted to provoke my brother to get the evidence I needed."

"Evidence for what?" she asked.

"Evidence to justify my judgments of him."

Even now, as I write this admission, tears come to my eyes. Without intending to do so, I had set my brother up. Sure, he could have responded differently, but that wouldn't have excused me from provoking and accusing him on that occasion or in years past.

Although at the time I had been unaware of my reasons for doing so, I *knew* when I was packing that I shouldn't bring the bolo tie—my conscience had warned me. But I packed it anyway because I needed to fulfill my prophecy and justify my ego in accusing and resenting my brother. Additionally, at a deeper level, I realize now that I'd had a death wish for the relationship. Feeling that true relatedness with my brother was hopeless on my terms, I sought unconsciously to destroy our current way of relating and somehow start over. I was willing to suffer his abuses to get my evidence and my "wish." I was also willing to put him through his own hell by unnecessarily provoking him. So, when I got what I wanted, I felt victorious. It was worth the emotional beating. Not only did I feel justified in my judgments of him, I also felt validated in my sense of Christian long-suffering and righteousness. After all, martyrs are always saints when they die innocently. And I was an innocent victim. Such was the lie I lived.

We live many lies, and we live them in many ways, when:

- We go against our consciences.
- We take offense.
- We blame others, insisting that we are right.
- We believe that the way we see others is the way they really are.
- We resent others for hurting us and assume we are innocent victims.
- We think we can change people or impose our will on others "for their own good."
- We refuse to acknowledge how we are part of the problem by provoking others to abuse or attack us.
- We expect others to take care of us or be good or fair to us.
- Our expectations of others are inhuman.
- We project our ideals of unconditional love and perfect loyalty onto others.
- Our instincts to love and atone through apology and forgiveness are eclipsed by our instincts to save face or "get even."

These and other lies are forms of control that alienate us from others and from our own souls. They contaminate and frustrate the work of individuation, keeping us away from the truth about ourselves and others. They also separate us from the joy of real love that could protect and enhance our self-concept or self-esteem, which is also a lie or, at best, only a partial truth.

Again, we live these lies because as human beings we are wounded and imperfect, and our values and beliefs are incomplete or incorrect. We value perfection and competition—an unholy alliance, indeed. In connection with these values, we have been deeply scripted to believe that our performance equals our worth, that being right equals being good, that winning is the "only thing," that success means being "Number One," and that flawlessness equals worthiness. These lies constellate into our inhuman expectations and rob us of compassion.

Additionally, our capacities for love and self-awareness are impaired, while our needs for power, validation, acceptance, approval, and loyalty increase. Such is the human condition. Add to this our inflated egos and our denial of all the lies listed earlier in this chapter, as well as our fears and disguised feelings of powerlessness, inadequacy, and unworthiness, and we have a psychic culture which is a natural seedbed for dishonesty and reactivity. It's time we face all this and begin the healing process.

How Reactive Cycles Begin

Almost anything can trigger a reactive cycle. It begins with an accusation or criticism formed in the heart, a negative judgment that might not even register in the person's awareness (if it registers at all) until long after the negative feelings associated with it have been experienced. Others pick up our negative, critical feelings and react in turn.

The accusations of the heart are often communicated, loud and clear, in very subtle ways. A simple, familiar gesture, word, inflection, posture, touch, facial expression, or attitude can do the trick, as well as any number or combination of circumstances and situations that disclose true feelings without any verbal or nonverbal clues from the person. When these reactive cycles are triggered, our hidden agenda takes over and we fall out of relationship. We go into a reactive "trance" that results in power struggles, passive-aggressive behaviors, or even aggression. No one is totally immune from such cycles. Any one of us can be "hooked" the moment we take offense, make a negative judgment, blame or accuse another person in our heart, or assume the role of "victim" or "rescuer."

These negative judgments are often formed as a result of violated expectations. The problem with expectations is that they are often unrealistic and uncommunicated—or, if they are communicated they are not agreed upon. When this happens, we set ourselves up for disappointment and alienation in our relationships.

Reactive cycles are particularly evident in relationships involving an "authority figure," in which the inappropriate or inconsiderate exercise of authority, counsel, or direction are laced with shaming overtones of superiority, accusation, criticism, or judgment. Such tones open the wounds of authoritarian abuse—which we all have suffered to some degree—and trigger the natural reactivity that leads to alienation and contention.

Authority figures in any institution cannot escape the high probability that they are complicit in the downward spiral of mutual offense, reciprocal criticism and accusation, divisive dissent, overt or passive resistance, and deep-seated resentment. Further, when these authority figures are seen by others as infallible or somehow beyond reproach, the problem is intensified, provoking shamelessness or self-righteousness in the leader. Such leaders then make constructive dissent wrong and diversity of thought and belief threatening, instead of making them essential to real unity and true commitment. Insecure leaders, or leaders who lack sufficient consciousness, maturity, and wisdom, often do more damage than good.

Large Scale Cycles

Finally, it's important to know that reactive cycles can and do exist among groups, including families, teams, and entire organizations. A group can contend with a single individual or with other groups. Many times a "fix-it" mentality interferes with our ability to recognize the reactive cycles that undermine our best efforts and intentions. This narrow-mindedness produces a host of perplexing paradoxes that taxes everyone's patience and causes a return to control and further disempowerment.

For example, in a merchandising status meeting, the senior management team of a large retail organization was severely chastised by the chairman, who couldn't understand why the prices reflected on merchandise racks weren't correct. The racks in the stores showed one price, but the prices in the computerized registers indicated different prices. This was a simple problem that had been brought up before, yet no improvements had been made. When confronted, the executives and senior managers were embarrassed and elusive. No one had any answers. No one owned the problem.

Senior management took the problem to the employees at the store level, and finally, the apparent problem was fixed. Rack prices were audited and corrected each day, and the computer systems and pricing processes were cleaned up and refined. But the systemic organizational problems remained. Like dependent children waiting to be told what to do, these employees had gotten quite good at provoking the same directive behavior that they accused management of using too frequently.

And so, after this particular problem had caused enough suffering and damage, it went away. But another would soon take its place, then another, and another. That's the way it has been, and that's the way it will be. The prevailing *modus operandi* in this company has become "management by plugging holes in the dike." Meanwhile, the real problems—the reactive cycles and the death wishes behind them—are missed entirely. These cycles multiply like rabbits, while reactive managers exhaust themselves and their resources with incessant meetings, discussions, strategy sessions, and threats—trying to fix the wrong problems time and again. As organizational psychologist Karl E. Weick states, "Most managers get into trouble because they forget to think in circles."[4]

In another organization the cycle took on a different form. The production supervisors chronically complained of the heavy-handed management style of the production manager. When a new CEO entered the scene with an "empowered style," the production manager resigned and was not replaced. Now the oppressed production supervisors reported directly to the CEO, who gave them charge and authority to do what needed to be done. They had experience, so the CEO released them to take charge. This was exactly what they wanted, right? Wrong.

Instead of leading, the supervisors began complaining again. Only now they said, "Tell us what you want us to do." The CEO refused and dug in his heels, informing them that telling them "what to do" was contrary to his philosophy. He insisted they take the lead. The production supervisors saw this partly as a weakness, but mostly as a threat. If the CEO continued with this "empowerment crap," as they called it, they would no longer be justified in accusing senior management of being heavy-handed. The prophecy would not be fulfilled, and the death wish would not be realized. Instead, they would have to face their own accountability and the fact that their accusations and reactions were part of the problem.

Having invested in their lies for too many years, the production supervisors began to provoke senior management. Productivity dropped, costs escalated, and profits began to decline. Finally, the CEO couldn't take it anymore. He intervened and took over. He began telling the supervisors what do and how to do it, accusing them in his heart of being unreasonable malcontents who were immature and incompetent as leaders. In doing so, he gave them what they wanted. When they continued to demand direction and act unresponsive to his control, they in turn gave him the justification he wanted.

Both parties were strangely satisfied in their torment and committed to their provocation of each other. Each blamed the other. Each felt justified. Each wanted something more. And each was living a lie. It took an outside intervention to break the cycle. In nearly twenty years of consulting, I have not found one organization that did not need help to identify and break these reactive cycles. It's a phenomenon of epidemic proportion in organizations of all types and sizes, which erodes the very fabric of trust, unity, and commitment to excellence.

From Reactive Cycles to Interdependence

With sufficient consciousness and integrity, a group can break these cycles and move toward greater unity by engaging in processes designed for this purpose. In my work I sometimes assist individuals and groups within organizations to break reactive cycles and face the lies they are living. The process I developed relies on honesty and helps others deal respectfully with one another to establish mutual understanding, accountability, and a common direction. Both groups work beneath the surface of their own perceptions to explore judgments, accusations, and reactive behavior patterns on both sides. I help them see how their reactions to each other result in counterreactions that keep the cycle going.

After gaining all the pertinent information, everyone meets together. The reactive cycle is diagramed and discussed. The truth is told. Then, under strict rules of order that require adult communication skills and mutual respect, both groups go through a highly structured, facilitated process of establishing mutual understanding and accountability in context of their interdependent roles and responsibilities. Conflicts are resolved and behavioral guidelines are established by mutual agreement, along with specific performance suggestions offered by each to the other and to themselves, in consideration of the other. The process might vary according to specific circumstances, but in my experience it has always been effective—when both groups were willing to work—in breaking reactive cycles and in helping the groups get back in relationship with each other.

The key to this process is honesty, empathy, and ownership, as one group accepts responsibility for its own negative judgments, reactive attitudes, and unproductive behaviors and resolves to break the reactive cycle—all without blaming the other group.

This is not a process of airing past grievances and negotiating compromises, but of honestly owning one's part, both individually and as a group, in triggering the reactivity of the other party. It involves seeking to find and reestablish one's own integrity and accountability, rather than expecting or demanding that the other group "shape up" and become more trustworthy. The process demands, as the Bible suggests, that we remove the beam from our own eye before trying to remove motes from the eyes of others.

Whether they are found on an interpersonal or group level, reactive cycles can be broken to fulfill the hidden agenda for wholeness through authenticity, honesty, and mutual respect. In the next chapter we will learn what is required to channel our inner forces of individuation in a constructive way to break these destructive cycles and get "in relationship" with others.

Chapter Four

BREAKING REACTIVE CYCLES AND GETTING "IN RELATIONSHIP" WITH OTHERS

"For there is but one veritable problem—the problem of human relations. We forget that there is no hope or joy except in human relations."

—Antoine de Saint Exupery

A significant sign of maturity is the deep realization that we need others in order to be whole. I personally believe our relationships are not accidental, nor merely coincidental. Relationships are formed for a reason, and that reason, apart from the obvious practical or social functions, is to work the soul's hidden agenda of individuation. Understanding this and becoming more aware of our own developmental needs can help us discover why we need the people we have relationships with. In this process we come to discover that those we dislike, don't care about, or even hate are just as important to our growth as those we like, respect, and love. Embracing the real value of the "other person" to our own quest for wholeness can be a powerful motivation to break free from our reactive cycles and get "in relationship."

Breaking Free

So, how do we break free from reactive cycles and get in relationship with others? We impatiently ask this question in our desire for a quick, practical cure or solution. But the solution is not in a "cure" at all. There are no success formulas or habits to master.

Breaking free of reactive cycles and cultivating more mature and productive relationships involves six essential requirements. Four additional requirements help us avoid unnecessary conflict and stay in relationship with others—they are more preventive in nature. These ten requirements enable us to cut through many of the lies we live and allow us to work our hidden agenda for wholeness and fulfillment in a *constructive* manner, rather than through destructive power struggles and game playing.

The way of life these requirements represent is not easy, particularly if we are "out of relationship" with ourselves and functioning at a low level of maturity. In fact, I believe none of these requirements can be *completely* fulfilled or sustained without doing the necessary work beneath the surface of our ego, fears, wounds, and insecurities prescribed in Chapters Five and Six. With this caveat in mind, let's move forward.

First, we must have sufficient self-awareness to recognize when we have broken out of relationship and have slipped into a reactive complex. James Redfield and Carol Adrienne suggest, "In order to begin to unhook ourselves from the need to control, the best thing we can do is focus on our feelings in the moment we feel caught or anxious. We need not analyze other people or try to change them. All we need to do is ask, 'What am I feeling right now? What do I need here?'"[1] Some basic symptoms might include feeling critical, offended, or defensive, as well as blaming and accusing others. Feeling resentful, vindictive, jealous, and envious are also telltale signs. The symptoms reveal the condition and needs of the soul and are always negative and alienating.

Second, we must mature to the point where we value the truth more than we value being right. This enables us to examine and challenge how we process reality, remembering that as human beings we are fallible, and that our judgments are always subjective, and as such, imperfect or incomplete. Our judgments are formed unconsciously—either through projections or through a series of steps that begin with observable data or sensed perceptions—and progress toward the adoption of derogatory or accusatory assumptions, conclusions, and beliefs about others. Chris Argyris calls this process of making judgments the "ladder of inference," which deals with how we typically process reality. It involves the following steps or "rungs":

Step 7: I take action based on my beliefs.
Step 6: I adopt beliefs about the world.
Step 5: I draw conclusions.
Step 4: I make assumptions based on the meanings I added.
Step 3: I add meanings.
Step 2: I select data from what I observe.
Step 1: I observe "data" and experiences (first rung of the ladder).[2]

Recently, I experienced the ladder of inference as I arrived home one Saturday afternoon after completing some errands. Before leaving that day, I had asked one of my sons to rake the leaves in the front yard. When I returned I could see that the leaves had not been raked. In the time it took me to park the car in the garage, I moved from the observation that the leaves hadn't been raked to the selected fact that the job didn't get done. From there, I inferred that my son had had plenty of time to rake the leaves. This progressed to the assumption that "he never does any work around the house," and finally to the conclusion, based on my assumption, that he wasn't going to do the work at all. This conclusion, of course, reinforced my belief that "teenagers are worthless." By the time I entered the house I was disappointed, angry, and ready to let him have it.

It wasn't until after I confronted him that I discovered how wrong I had been. He had intended to do the job later that day and was not aware of any specific time requirement for completion. He was right: I never told him the leaves had to be raked by a certain time; I only asked him to do it that day, *assuming* he would attend to it right away. There was no urgency to the task, except in my mind—and even that wasn't necessary. This same scenario has occurred to me numerous times both at work and at home. It's as natural to all of us as breathing.

We need to give ourselves permission to be human and to admit mistakes, seek for understanding, and ask for help. Practically speaking, we can avoid reacting to erroneous conclusions by taking the time to check our facts, challenge our beliefs, and verify our thinking. This can be done simply by sharing what we have heard or observed, following with our conclusion, and then verifying whether our thinking is correct. For example, with my son I might have said: "T. J., I noticed the leaves weren't raked and concluded you weren't going to do the work. Is my thinking right or wrong?" Another obvious approach might be to simply state what we have heard or observed and then ask, "What's going on?" These are simple, yet effective ways to avoid unnecessary conflict.

We do not see things and people as they really are, but as *we* are. In addition to "jumping to conclusions," it is also common for us to see our own undesirable traits in others. This is known as "projection." When we project our own personality weaknesses onto others we usually feel a sense of disgust or repulsion. We are immediately turned off, become critical, and feel like we "can't stand" the other person. But our feelings betray us. It is precisely because we have not faced, understood, and integrated our own undesirable traits and powers that we project them, with *negative emotion*, onto others. Hence, perception is often (if not always) projection. Understanding this, we are always wise to withdraw and reverse our projections. This helps us defuse the criticism and focus on our Level One lies about ourselves and our self-concept, instead of on the personality traits of others.

Third, we must examine our Level Two lies, or inhuman expectations of others, and align them with reality. In aligning our expectations with reality, we can expect virtually anything. We may still trust in the fundamental goodness of people and in their inherent desire to do the right thing and perform as effectively as they can, but such trust need not take the form of ideal or inhuman expectations. By allowing ourselves to expect anything, we acknowledge our own humanity and the humanity of others.

With compassion, we understand that as human beings we all labor with emotional or psychic wounds, imperfections, ignorance, misconceptions, and subjectivity, and that we are moved upon by unconscious needs and forces more powerful than we can imagine. Although these truths do not necessarily lower our standards or excuse us or anyone else from wrongdoing, they enable us to avoid the self-abandonment and reactivity that come from inhuman expectations.

Embracing these truths of human nature also helps us learn how to protect our boundaries and to assist or correct others without feeling the disappointment, blame, and rejection that come from projecting inhuman or ideal expectations onto others. Such disappointment rarely, if ever, results in increased responsibility.

As we have learned, blame usually begets blame, and blame is the avoidance of responsibility. Even communicating real disappointment toward others for their misdeeds—a common tool for "motivating" people by applying behavioral rewards or punishments—often results in unhealthy outcomes, causing defensiveness and alienation. Disappointment, as an emotional shaming tactic, does more harm than good. But, by learning to manage our expectations we not only break and avoid reactive cycles, we also make room in our hearts for genuine care, compassion, and concern.

Aligning expectations with reality can be done in many ways. Noted author, lecturer, and therapist John Bradshaw suggests one helpful approach, which I have broken into three stages[3]: First, identify what you believe are the characteristics of an "ideal" person in your relationship. For example, if you are examining your relationship with your boss, list what you believe are the characteristics of an "ideal" boss—the "boss from heaven" who anyone would die to work for. Your list might include some of the following characteristics: *always* in a good mood, *always* generous, *always* supportive and loyal, *never* talks about me negatively, *always* praises my work and recognizes my accomplishments, *always* gives me raises and bonuses without my having to ask, *always* tolerant with my mistakes, *never* gets angry, *always* solicits my opinion, *always* involves me in decisions that might affect me, and so on.

Next, identify the "degraded" accusations that would result from a violation of your ideal expectations. Let's return to your boss: When your boss shows up in a bad mood, trust is broken and the bubble of idealism is popped. After only a few unexplained mood swings, your boss moves from *always* in a good mood to *always* moody and unpredictable. So it goes with all the other ideal expectations; when they don't stand the test of time, the "boss from heaven" becomes the "boss from hell." In addition to *always* moody and unpredictable, your degraded boss now has the following degraded characteristics: *always* stingy or cheap, *always* manipulative and self-serving, *never* tells you when you're doing well, only when you screw up, *always* makes you grovel for a raise, *always* expects perfection, *never* happy, *always* critical, *always* has to be right, *always* quashes dissent, *always* humiliates people in public, *always* threatens poor or marginal performance, *never* asks for your opinion or involves you in decisions that affect you, and so forth.

You have now listed the inhuman expectations for your ideal boss and the related accusations associated with your degraded boss. Notice how often the words "never" and "always" crop up. You might consider these lists to be ridiculously overstated or exaggerated and deny that you ever had such inflated expectations of people. Well, they *are* ridiculous standards, but I think we would all be very surprised by what we would find in our unconscious mind. Can you think of a time when you *weren't* disappointed that someone did not live up to your expectations? I believe such lists are exactly what many of us use to judge others. Such characteristics represent inhuman expectations and are part of what Bradshaw terms as being "mystified" in our relationships.[4]

In reality, human beings are neither "ideal" nor "degraded." They are both ideal *and* degraded. As Maslow has rightly suggested, we are at once gods and worms. This leads us to the third and final stage of the exercise: Create a list of real characteristics that pertain to a *human* being who has both a light side *and* a dark side. When these two sides come together in polarity, what realistic expectations emerge? If, for example, your ideal boss is *always* honest and tells the truth, then you can be sure you will be disappointed at some point in your relationship. On the other hand, if your degraded boss *never* tells the truth, then you might as well quit—why would you work for such a person? As you blend the two sides, you can see that neither set of characteristics is real. Somewhere in the middle you find your boss, besieged as we all are by outside pressures and working to do the best he or she can. Hopefully now you feel admiration for your boss's struggles and can empathize with his or her weaknesses.

One woman I know struggled with her disappointment in her father, who had taught her to "always be honest," but who had been caught several times lying or misrepresenting the truth as she saw it. As a child she had worshiped her father, and so her adult experiences with his humanness were very difficult to bear. She felt betrayed and let down. Her father sensed her disappointment and reacted to her resentment either by demeaning her goodness or by avoiding her. Their once-close relationship was now strained, and they felt alienated from each other. Because her father had been caught telling a few lies, she saw him as dishonest and hypocritical. This was now her degraded image and accusation of him.

In reality, no one is *always* one-hundred percent honest. A more realistic expectation might be, rather, that people *often* tell the truth but *sometimes* don't, at least not the whole truth—perhaps because of fear, competition, self-interest, or out of genuine care and concern for others. This is a legitimate, human expectation. Even saints lie on occasion, and with valid motives. Although the standard for honesty is not compromised and the natural consequences of dishonesty are not abated, the meaning of honesty might profitably be reevaluated and our expectations realigned with human limitation, including our limited understanding of right and wrong.

If you find that someone you trust has lied to you, you might take extra precautions to allow for such possibilities in the future. You might inquire of the person's motives with an open mind. Perhaps you might choose not to trust the person completely, and yet do so with compassion for his or her humanity. You might even choose to chasten the person or, in extreme cases, sever the relationship for the welfare of both people, without picking up the victim role or feeling the resentment or disappointment that come from inhuman expectations.

Betrayal is often, if not always, a self-inflicted wound born of idealism and naivete, and it usually leads to reactive cycles. This process of demystifying our expectations is critical in helping us stay in relationship with others, even if we disagree with their choices.

We have examined the "boss" role. Now go through the same exercise for the other roles the people in your life have, such as spouse, parent, child, sibling, friend, employee, client, and so on.

Fourth, in addition to cultivating greater self-awareness, withdrawing our judgments, and humanizing our expectations, *we must work consciously to convert the Level Three lies, or the false beliefs we embrace, to truth.* These lies, together with our inflated self-concept and inhuman expectations are all—pardon the expression—bullshit. I suppose there is no end to the list. We embrace false beliefs selfishly to protect our self-image, get what we want, and evade personal responsibility. When we buy into them we are self-deceived. Here again are a few of these Level Three lies. Which ones do you like best?

- I am right; you are wrong.
  —Being right means being worthy.
  —Being wrong means being flawed and unworthy.

- You make me feel . . .
  —I feel . . . ; therefore, . . . must be true.
- If only you would change . . .
- This is different.
- I can change you.
  —If I change or treat you well, you will change and treat me well.
  —If I cooperate and play fair with you, you will do the same with me.
  —I can change (or save) you by loving you.
- If I leave it alone, the problem will get better (or go away).
- There's no way out.
- The way I see you is who you really are.

"I am right; you are wrong" has probably been my favorite lie over the years. Our insistence on being right is a form of grandiosity. One psychologist I know defined grandiosity as "believing your own bullshit." Since most of us suffer from this malady, we need to clean up this lie fast. I think it's at the root of all the other lies we live. The truth is, right and wrong are often subjective judgments based on different perspectives. Being right (correct) or wrong (incorrect) has nothing to do with self-worth. In fact, a person can act with complete integrity and still be incorrect. Living this lie, we often fight—even to the death of the relationship—to be right. Our inability to acknowledge the possibility of being wrong, morally or otherwise, is rooted in pride, which is not only a hatred of truth but, at its deepest level, is a hatred of self.

"You make me feel . . ." is a lie because, in living it, we fail to acknowledge our own part in creating the feeling. Feelings do not exist independently of our judgments or interpretations; our interpretations trigger our complexes and feelings. We are, in large measure, responsible for our own feelings and emotional reactions by the way we think. We are also responsible for the *interpretation* of our feelings. Contrary to popular belief, feel-

ings do not provide self-evident truths. We provide the meanings to our feelings, usually in ways that validate or confirm what we want to believe or that justify the interpretation or projection that produces the feelings to begin with. The lie "You make me feel . . ." and its corollary, "I feel . . . ; therefore, . . . must be true," can result in numerous problems with others and harsh consequences in our personal lives.

"If only you would change . . ." erroneously places the responsibility for our success, effectiveness, or happiness on someone or something else, outside of our control. We alone are responsible for doing what's right and meeting our needs. That responsibility doesn't depend on others doing likewise. Perhaps a truer statement might be, "If only I would attend more to my own needs, and stop selling out to fear and expecting others to take care of me."

The problem with *"This is different"* is that *everything* tends to be different, and therefore, nothing is really our fault or responsibility. In any relationship problem wherein we feel alienated, hurt, defensive, or critical, we can be sure that we are part of the problem. At least in these cases, nothing is different.

My favorite lie, next to "I am right; you are wrong" is, *"I can change you."* (I guess that's one reason I chose to be a consultant.) This lie is a common one for managers and leaders worldwide: "How can I get so-and-so to do such and such?" At times I have found, much to my dismay and frustration, that I don't have the power to change anyone, nor would it be morally right to do so even if I could. Who's to say my way is right or best?

It might be argued that we have the power to influence others toward change, but we need to be careful here, too. In its truest form, I believe the power to influence is the gift of an open mind and heart given to one who is perceived as trustworthy. This takes the power of influence out of our complete control. A variation of this lie is, "If I change or treat you well, you will change and treat me well," or, "If I cooperate and play fair with you, you will do the same with me," or, "I can change (or save) you by loving you." The list is endless.

How many times have we unwisely backed away from necessary confrontations because we bought into the lie, *"If I leave it alone, the problem will get better (or go away)"*? Maybe we've deceived ourselves into believing it's too small an issue to worry about—perhaps it is. But we often sell out to fear and revert to complaining, quiet resentment, backbiting, or some other form of passive-aggressive behavior that makes things worse. Further, though we need not be petty, I have found that if we let the "little things" slide too often, they turn into big things over time.

When should an issue be confronted? Whenever it becomes an issue that, upon calm reflection, bothers or concerns you. Reactive cycles, as we learned, often begin with little offenses and grow over time. They don't die of natural causes, and time alone won't kill them. A change of heart is required, and that usually requires meaningful interaction.

One of the most damaging lies we live is the one that tells us we have no options: *"There's no way out."* This lie springs up from our deep sense of powerlessness and inadequacy, grips us in fear, and, ultimately, leads to apathy or despair. When we are unwilling or too frightened to consciously seek an option, the hidden agenda usually provides one. The unconscious forces of the soul move us to resolution, even if the outcome could be painful, or possibly lethal. It's far better to work *consciously* with these inner forces toward freedom and reconciliation and seek for a new solution, even if that means walking away and starting over.

One poignant example of this last lie comes from the movie "Dead Poets Society": One of the characters, a young man named Neal Perry, is the only child of a domineering father and a weak, enabling mother. Neal, inspired by the words of his English teacher, Mr. Keating, seeks to find his own way in life and be free. He discovers his love for the theater and tries out for a part in a Shakespearian play. When his father finds out, all hell breaks loose. Mr. Perry had made it very clear that Neal was to concentrate only on his studies so he could qualify to go to Harvard and become a doctor. Neal disobeys his father's wishes, forges his father's signature in a consent letter, and tries out for the part. He gets the part but never tells his father, even after Mr. Keating counsels him to do so.

On opening night, Neal performs brilliantly, only to find out that his father had been informed and had been in the audience. After the performance, Neal returns home with his father. In the presence of Neal's mother, Mr. Perry confronts him. Neal tries to assert himself, but he is overwhelmed by his father's dominance. Hopelessly realizing, "There is no way out," Neal sits down, withdraws, and yields in despair to his father's wishes. Later that evening the force of resolution comes—resulting in Neal's suicide. Once such a lie takes root in our soul, we set ourselves up for tragedy. For most people this amounts to, as Henry David Thoreau put it, living lives of "quiet desperation."

Once, after conducting a one-day seminar for nursing students, I received an anonymous note from a participant that read, "Thanks to your teachings today I've decided to leave my husband . . ." I sat down to read the rest. She went on to say, "After ten years of continual abuse toward me and my ten-year-old son, I've come to the conclusion that I will not be a victim any longer." This woman's way out was to walk *through* the fire of separation and divorce. In many other cases, the way out might be to consciously remain *in*, with different eyes. In any event, there is always a way out, if we have sufficient faith, hope, wisdom, courage, and internal security to see it through.

The last lie in this list asserts, *"The way I see you is who you really are."* This lie, of course, is related to the first one: "I am right; you are wrong." When we embrace the lie that others are only who we see them to be, we avoid the responsibility of questioning our perceptions that would lead to our accepting those perceptions as projections of ourselves onto others. Remember, the second requirement for cultivating mature, productive relationships is to realize that we don't see others as *they* are, but as *we* are.

All these lies are sustained by hidden needs for validation, power, acceptance, and ego protection. Until we sufficiently heal the wounds behind those needs and integrate our personality, we will not likely choose to convert the lies to truth. They serve us too well. Meanwhile, our attempts to become more effective by learning new skills or modifying behavior will only produce counterfeit results. We simply learn and adopt more sophisticated ways of control and manipulation. The lies live beneath the surface of our new behavior, ultimately undermining our conscious intentions to do what's right.

The first four requirements of breaking reactive cycles and cultivating mature and productive relationships involve performing various types of personal work on a continuous basis. However, the *fifth* requirement involves *interacting with the person we are out of relationship with. It involves getting honest and "starting over" with the other person.* We can do this by first taking ourselves out of the victim role. This requires that we stop abandoning ourselves and accusing the other person in our heart. When we do this, we begin to reclaim our personal power and see the other person differently. Finally, we can break the cycle, start over, and stay in relationship by:

1. *Being authentic about our personal feelings, observations, and concerns.*

This means honestly acknowledging and owning our feelings and expressing or dealing with them appropriately. For example, we might say, "I'm feeling . . . (defensive, pressured, threatened, criticized, rejected, etc.). In my mind I'm accusing you of being . . . (insensitive, uncaring, inconsiderate, etc.), and I feel I'm being accused of . . ." Make sure you state the judgments both ways.

Other examples include: "I can tell you're angry with me: Why?"; "I feel like you're trying to make me feel guilty. Are you?"; "Are you withdrawing from me?"; "Are we in a fight?"; "I feel like you're trying to intimidate me. Am I right?"; or, "Why are you raising your voice at me?" James Redfield and Carol Adrienne refer to this first step as "naming the drama," meaning that we are "staying in the truth of [our] feelings and taking steps to disengage by getting the truth out in the open."[5]

2. *Listening empathically to the other person, then respond-*
ing honestly to clarify needs and boundaries, negotiate
solutions, and communicate natural consequences.

It has been said that the deepest need of the human soul is to
be understood. Understanding validates us and gives us greater
emotional security and psychological freedom to be who we are.
Deep, empathic listening comes from a genuine desire to understand, and is one of the highest expressions of care for others we
can make. When we listen with the heart, we give the person
talking "someone else" to respond to. When this occurs the other
person often responds differently, usually more honestly, allowing
us to see him or her with the eyes of true understanding. This can
be a powerful way to break a reactive cycle and get in relationship.

Often, what interferes with listening from the heart is our
tendency to control. We often use one of four common control
strategies to interpret information, while we pretend to listen:
First, we listen with the intent to reply, correct, entrap, prove a
point, or win an argument. In doing so, we might judge what
others are saying and feeling as right or wrong, good or bad,
appropriate or inappropriate. Second, we play the role of detective
by asking probing questions. Third, we act like a parent by giving
advice. Finally, we sometimes listen for hidden messages or
motives, interpreting what others *really* mean or what is *really*
bothering them.

But listening from the heart is not about control. It is about
seeking to understand the feelings and messages of others—to
enter into another person's reality without bias, prejudice, or
preconceived notions. It is not about agreeing or disagreeing; we
can understand other people without agreeing with them. But
we cannot give adequate advice, nor can we take someone else's
advice, until we have first paid the price to understand.

After our understanding has been confirmed, we might need
to give constructive feedback. We give such feedback not with
the intent to change others, but to be understood by them—to

help others while we ask for what we need. Giving constructive, corrective feedback requires first that we check our inferences (listen to understand) and then follow a basic process in which we: (1) describe the behavior that is bothering or concerning us, (2) express our feelings using "I" messages, (3) specify or negotiate what corrective actions need to be taken to accommodate the needs of both parties, (4) state the consequences, or reasons, why such changes or actions are important, and (5) confirm the other's understanding, feelings, and commitment.

The *sixth* requirement for breaking reactive cycles and staying in relationship involves *resisting the provocation to return to the fray.* Relationships are systems, and, as individuals, we do not function wholly independent of these systems. Understanding this can help us avoid reentering reactive cycles after attempting to break free. Thinking "win-win" is usually not enough when the provocative forces of reactivity are active and strong. These forces act like a strong undertow that can easily pull the most "proactive" person back into reactivity. Knowing this is an essential step to avoiding the trap.

It is not enough for us to merely go through the process of starting over, nor is it enough for us simply to "do the right thing." We must also be conscious of this reactive system, which is activated by unconscious motives and dependency needs. When we attempt to break free from the reactive cycle, we disturb the reactive cycle and place the system in a state of imbalance. Even diseased social systems seek for homeostasis. The family system is an excellent example of this.

People who are stuck in the reactive system will seek homeostasis by provoking "defectors" to enter back into the cycle. Consider a dysfunctional marriage in which one spouse gets professional counseling while the other spouse refuses to get help. As the one spouse gets healthier and more independent, the other spouse feels threatened, becomes critical, withdraws, or becomes offensive or defensive to provoke the now-healthier spouse to reenter the old cycle. This also happens when managers go to off-site retreats to learn how to become better leaders. When they return to the workplace, they are quickly provoked to return to their old ways.

This may explain some of the backsliding that occurs after people try to apply new principles or processes in the workplace or at home. In both cases, those left behind lose their proof—their evidence—that justifies their reactive behavior and relieves them of the responsibility to change. Although reactive cycles are painful and unproductive, we are strangely addicted to our suffering. Without it we could never be "right" about other people.

Dealing with this undertow effect involves honesty on an interpersonal level, and mindfulness on an intrapersonal level. A shared understanding of what's happening can also be helpful. Interpersonal honesty has been described as authenticity about our personal feelings, observations, and concerns. Too often, we treat reactive behavior as though it doesn't exist. We internalize the negative energy of others' reactivity toward us and take offense, becoming defensive and alienated in the process. We suppress it, or try to "forget it," but it just doesn't go away. Instead, we need to deal with it honestly and directly with courage, wisdom, and consideration, and with faith that the truth will cut its own way—that whatever happens will be right, even if that means the relationship does not continue.

Intrapersonal mindfulness involves the inner work of observing and dialoguing with our reactive emotions as they arise within us. We honor our reactivity by experiencing it, understanding it, and reasoning with ourselves without moralizing or self-shaming. Such inner work is facilitated by developing methods of self-observation and self-interaction, such as reflection and active imagination.

Reflection is simply the act of conscious observation or introspection. It's like walking into a room and observing and experiencing everything in and about the room: smell, temperature, air, colors, brightness, design, sounds, furnishings, decorative objects, function, and overall feeling. At a deeper level, reflection involves observing and thinking deeply about our judgments and experiences as we observe the room. Our reactive mind is like this room. Taking time to reflect in this way increases patience and enables us to respond according to the wisdom of the soul.

Another approach to intrapersonal mindfulness is the technique of active imagination. A powerful technique developed by Carl Jung, active imagination involves both self-observation and interaction. By using our faculty or imagination, we personify our moods or complexes into human form and dialogue with them in our minds to obtain a deeper understanding of our wounds and needs. This enables us, among other things, to understand and defuse our reactivity through empathic interaction, reasoning, and resolution. This technique will be presented in more detail in Chapter Five.

Avoiding Unnecessary Conflict

So far, I have presented what is required to break free from reactive cycles. But, how can we keep conflict from happening in the first place? Although there certainly are no foolproof formulas, I can suggest at least four requirements for staying out of "trouble."

A *first* requirement, described earlier, involves *aligning our expectations with reality*. A *second* requirement, also described earlier, is to *make our assumptions and reasoning visible to others and give them the opportunity to confirm or correct our thinking*. This simple process can begin with you saying, "I'm concerned about something and wanted to check my thinking so I don't jump to the wrong conclusion." Then, simply explain your thought process: "I heard (or observed) . . . and because of these things, I assumed. . . . Then, based on my assumptions, I have tentatively concluded. . . . Am I correct in my conclusions?" Checking our inferences in this way shows respect for others and can prevent misunderstandings from happening.

A *third* requirement for avoiding conflict is to *get into proper relationship with others*. To be in "proper" relationship is to interact as mature adults, one adult to another. This means seeing the other person as an adult and treating him or her with respect and consideration while holding our own authority and remaining open to the person's point of view. In the workplace, adult interaction requires leaders to give up the "authority" role and, instead, become resources that serve others and respect their roles as final decision makers.

Years ago, while I was working as a manager at Digital Equipment Corporation, I had the good fortune of working with a leader who instinctively understood his "proper" relationship with others. I remember approaching him with a particular problem after he had been on the job for only two weeks. After I sat down in his office, I explained that I needed his help on a difficult issue. Before I could begin describing the problem, he pulled out a plaque and asked me to read out loud what was written on it. As I recall, it read:

> At no time, while I am helping you with this or any other problem, will your problem become my problem. The moment your problem becomes my problem, you no longer have a problem, and I can't help someone who doesn't have a problem.

I was struck by how it ended:

> When you leave this office your problem will go out exactly as it came in—on your shoulders.

He then looked at me and asked, "Do we have an understanding?" I nodded. Then he said, "Good, now what is your problem?"

His role was clear, and his expectations were clear. My ownership of the problem was clear. I proceeded to explain the problem in detail. Instead of rushing in to solve my problem, he simply asked, "Do you mind if I ask a few questions?" He was getting in proper relationship. Even though I reported to him, with respect to this problem I was the boss—it was *my* problem. He was simply a resource, a coach. I consented to his asking questions, and after I did my best to answer them, he remarked, "You know, I don't think you've identified the real problem here. Maybe you could give it some more thought, and we can talk again?"

I left and returned a couple of hours later with some additional insight. He listened carefully and respectfully. After securing permission to ask a few more questions, he began his inquiry again. I answered, and he responded, "Tom, I still don't think you have defined the problem correctly."

Perplexed, frustrated, and challenged, I returned to my office and spent six hours digging in, looking at the problem from different angles and trying to see what I was apparently missing. At 4:30 p.m., I went back to his office—tired and frazzled, but victorious and proud. It took me twenty minutes to present my analysis. Afterward, I sat back and said confidently, "There, that's the problem."

My boss acknowledged the hard work I had done by remarking, "This is an impressive piece of work." He then looked at me and asked again, "Do you mind if I ask a few more questions?"

I said, "Fire away," confident that I could handle any questions he might ask.

After three or four questions he remarked, "I know you've worked hard on this, but I still don't think this is the core problem."

That was the last straw. Exasperated and humbled, I remember putting my pencil on his desk and saying, "I give up! I don't know what the problem is. Please help me."

This wise leader stayed in proper relationship with me. Rather than take the "top dog" authority role with all the wisdom, instead he shared with me a process for identifying problems that I remember to this day. He didn't "rescue" me by telling me what my problem was or how to solve it. He didn't try to fix me or my problem. He coached me. He kept his place. We avoided conflict, and I was empowered in the process.

Whenever we insist on being right in our relationships—whenever we believe we have the only right answer, or feel it is our duty to save or rescue others from the error of their ways—we run the risk of provoking a reactive response. Our "rightness" can become an implicit, if not explicit, accusation of their "wrongness." Our directives, usually in the guise of advice or suggestions, demand agreement, obedience, and loyalty. The other person's response often becomes a struggle for power, even if the resistance is silent or disguised. We, acting as the "authority," feel betrayed and unappreciated and accuse the other person of stubbornness, rebellion, ingratitude, or just plain incompetence, while the other person feels violated and accuses us of being controlling, inconsiderate, and intrusive. The unreasonable demand for loyalty has been breached, and both parties are out of relationship.

The *fourth* requirement for avoiding conflict involves *aligning our behavior with our values in order to respond more effectively to difficult, or "triggering," situations.* Such alignment promotes greater consciousness and integrity. To help you become better aligned, I suggest a process of mental mapping, or "imaging," to identify acceptable and unacceptable behaviors in certain stressful situations:

- When I am behind and under pressure to achieve results.
- When a person I am relying on violates my expectations.
- When I feel unfairly and incorrectly judged by someone who can harm me.
- When I feel unreasonably resisted by an authority figure in getting what I want.
- When someone disagrees with my best ideas.
- When someone I supervise doesn't do what I ask.
- When someone in authority makes a demand on me that I don't want to do.
- When I feel offended or abused by another person.

As you review this list, read each situation separately and ask yourself, "What do I feel, in my heart, would be acceptable behavior in responding to this situation?" "What do I feel is unacceptable?" To help answer these questions, you might want to invoke the "Golden Rule": "How would I want to be treated in this situation?" "How would I *not* want to be treated?" By thinking through, feeling, and reflecting on acceptable and unacceptable behavioral responses—and by writing them out—we become more aware of our values and better prepared to respond with integrity to those values. This, in turn, helps promote greater trustworthiness and assists us in avoiding conflict.

The Power of Heartfelt Apology: A Personal Story

In very close relationships, sometimes the wounds are very deep. It seems the more we love someone, the more hurtful reactive cycles can be, and the harder they are to break. In such cases I have found the need for special assistance—a special dispensation of grace, if you will—so both can experience the necessary sorrow to stop hurting the other and to sincerely apologize, forgive, and begin loving again. This has become very evident in my own life on many different occasions. One very significant experience involved my father.

My father was a very powerful man. His intensity and presence were captivating. Aside from being physically large and strong, he was also very passionate and charismatic. Like all of us, his strengths were also his weaknesses, and one of his greatest strengths was his capacity to love. There is a dark side to love that involves control, domination, possessiveness, jealousy, enmeshment, and even cruelty. I'm not sure how aware Dad was of this dark side of his love for me, but I was aware of it, and it was sometimes confusing to me. I even experienced it in my love for him.

I am the oldest of three sons. I don't know that a father could be more proud of his children than my father was of my brothers and me. Even so, my relationship with Dad was often stormy. I often saw him as controlling, unreasonable, and selfish, and he saw me as rebellious, unreasonable, and selfish. I coped by resisting him, avoiding him, and ignoring him. He reacted by controlling, demanding, threatening, punishing, and shaming me.

Dad saw in me the worst that was in him, and he wanted to save me from myself—even if it meant beating it out of me, which he tried to do on rare occasions. I saw in my father someone I never wanted to be, but he is someone I since have become. We were locked in a reactive cycle for many years until shortly before he died. And yet we loved each other very much.

Our conflict came to a head when I was twenty-two years old. I had plans to get an apartment with a buddy of mine and to spend a relaxing summer between terms at graduate school. But Dad had different plans. He wanted me to live at home and work in his company for the summer. I resisted and tried to stand up for myself.

I remember it well: We were alone in the living room of my Aunt Sophie's home. The subject came up just before I was about to leave. He asked me what my plans were. When I told him, he got angry and said they were out of the question. He made it very clear that I didn't have a choice in the matter. I was to live at home and work in the business—and that was final. I got angry and dug in my heels, refusing to give in one more time to his unreasonable demands.

The argument escalated. We were standing toe to toe in the living room when finally my father informed me, in no uncertain terms, that if I walked out of the house I could never come back. As far as he was concerned, I would no longer be his son, and he would never want to see me again. He was angry and dead serious. At the time I really believed he meant it.

Before I could respond, he spoke again. This time he told me I could not keep the car he had given me as a college graduation present, and I could not take any clothes with me—all I could leave with were the clothes on my back. I was stunned. As he spoke, I could feel the rage come up through my body from the soles of my feet. I was trembling with anger.

I remember throwing the car keys on the floor, looking my father in the eyes, and saying, "You can keep the car and the clothes. I'm leaving and never want to see you again. I've had it. I won't take this from you." I stormed out of the house filled with anger and hatred, determined never to go back. I was free. My father would never tell me what to do again.

I got an apartment and a summer job. It was an important summer for me: I met my wife, Annette, that summer. She was living in the same apartment building. One day toward the end of the summer, while I was sitting in my apartment alone, the screen door opened, and my two younger brothers walked in. When I saw them, I jumped up off the sofa and asked coldly, "How did you find me?"

Dean, who was nineteen years old at the time, told me how they had been searching all summer to find me and tell me that Dad wanted to meet. I told Dean to tell Dad that I didn't want to meet with him—ever. I was angry all over again, and found that my hatred for my father had made me cold toward my brothers as well. I was poisoned inside.

When I told Dean, he got tears in his eyes and said, "For God's sake, Tommy, he's your father!" My heart softened, and I agreed to meet.

The meeting was scheduled for the next day at Dad's office. As I walked into the office, my brothers were seated against the wall, and my father was seated behind his desk, looking down. I was so defensive and sensitive that if he had even looked at me the wrong way, I would have been gone forever. As I entered the office, I glanced at my brothers and approached my father's desk. He would not look at me. As I stood before him I coldly said, "What do you want?"

There was silence. I didn't know what was happening or what to expect. Then it happened. Dad looked up at me with tears in his eyes and said, "I wanted to give back the keys to your car and tell you that I don't blame you for never wanting to see me or talk to me again. I was wrong. Please forgive me." With that, this big, strong Greek patriarch bowed his head, put his face in his hands, and wept from the depths of his anguished heart.

As I saw my father sobbing with contrition, every ounce of anger left my soul. I raced around the desk and embraced him. As we cried in each other's arms, I asked for his forgiveness, and our hearts were healed. How kind God was that day, and how He must have wept with joy to see father and son reconciled, perhaps for the first time. My father died several years later, and to this day, I am so thankful that he cared and was humble enough to apologize so we could be whole together.

I have thought about this experience many times and cannot tell or write about it without crying. I share this story to emphasize the power of a sincere, heartfelt apology and plea for forgiveness in healing the wounds of the heart and breaking reactive cycles. Nothing is more powerful. As Aaron Lazare said, "A genuine apology offered and accepted is one of the most profound interactions of a civilized people. It has the power to restore damaged relationships, whether on a small scale, between two people, or on a grand scale, between groups of people—even nations."[6] I am a witness of this truth.

Breaking free from conflict and forgiving others is very difficult for those who are determined to be victims. That's where I was with my father. It is usually the more mature person who will take the initiative to get back in relationship. As I discussed earlier, a more insecure, codependent personality will unconsciously try to perpetuate the reactive cycle by provoking the one who is breaking free to get back in. Again, this happens because it affords the reactor a type of security upon which she or he depends.

Although there are no guarantees that the person not taking the initiative will agree, or be ready, to break the cycle and get back in relationship, it is possible to break the reactive cycle even if only one person breaks free. A positive reaction often occurs as one person gets honest, stops accusing, apologizes, and thereby gives the other person "someone else" to respond to. Given this new perspective, the other person responds differently—usually more honestly—allowing both to see each other as they really are, and enabling honest evaluation and choice in the relationship.

Moving from codependence to interdependence requires that we strive to reclaim and integrate all aspects of our personality, including the lost or impaired elements of our personal power that reside in the shadow. This process of personal empowerment, or individuation, enables us to become truly trustworthy in our relationships. This will be explored in more depth in Chapter Five.

The Snare of Self-Deception

Perhaps the greatest challenge people face in breaking reactive cycles and cultivating more mature relationships is breaking free from the Level Four lies of self-deception. In reactive cycles, both parties are self-deceived, each believing that they are innocent victims and that the other person is the problem. Even in making mistakes or personal acts of wrongdoing, we live a lie by justifying our behavior in some way.

To break free from self-defeating and relationship-damaging accusations, attitudes, and behaviors requires a level of humility and honesty that, for most of us, is difficult to muster, especially in the heat of battle. Breaking free becomes more complicated by the fact that we can do the right things in the wrong way, thus at once performing an act of integrity and transgression.

Reactive cycles can be confusing as we struggle internally between our conviction that we acted in truth, while we were guilty of being reactive or selfish, without sufficient regard for others. Daniel Goleman points out: "Information that threatens the self—that does not support the story one tells oneself about oneself—threatens self-esteem. Such threats are a major source of anxiety."[7] At this point, any attempt at direct self-analysis carries the possibility of further self-deception or, more accurately, ego-protection. However, we can confront ourselves indirectly by examining certain behavioral indicators of self-deception. If we are sincere, we will see what we are doing and repent.

My studies of the literature on this subject, as well as my own experience, have resulted in the following list of suppressive, ego-protective, or deceiving behaviors, which are indicative of being in a state of denial, and which constitute the Level Four lies we live. This list is not intended to be all-inclusive, but it serves as a useful overview of behavioral indicators that can help us get honest.

Ego-Protective/Self-Deceiving Behaviors
(Level Four Lies)

- Refusing to face the implications and consequences of behaviors.
- Avoiding self-reflection.
- Disregarding inquiries.
- Minimizing seriousness, underestimating harm done ("Big deal! It wasn't that serious").
- Victim derogating ("He or she had it coming").
- Raising consensus that others would have behaved similarly because of the difficulty of the task, bad luck, coercion, and so forth.
- Blaming and accusing others.
- Disavowing ("It wasn't me," "I'm not responsible for what I did," "I was in a bad mood," or "I was under stress").
- Explaining away.
- Manipulating, distorting, and twisting evidence.
- Inventing excuses to justify actions.
- Evading or ignoring relevant facts, neglecting their import.
- Refusing to sincerely examine or seriously consider opposing evidence, opposing viewpoints, or the possibility of error.
- Hiding behind feelings ("It can't be wrong because it feels so right").
- Justifying self on the basis of adherence to some belief, principle, or voice of external authority.
- Seeking to convince others of correctness or justification of actions, for any reason.
- Avoiding professional evaluation.

Any of these behaviors, along with feelings of defensiveness, guilt, irritability, or even numbness, can signal a condition of self-deception. In the final analysis, however, it is only when we sincerely and wholeheartedly face the truth—which includes the real possibility that we have been or have done wrong—that we can free ourselves from the lies that bind us.

Clearly, self-protection is not necessarily bad. It can be beneficial whenever the ego is not strong enough to face the whole truth. I would even argue that we are not able to face more truth about ourselves than we can handle. The whole truth can sometimes destroy what is good along with what is not. Ultimately, however, the truth about who we are and what we have done, or not done—and why—must be known if we ever hope to be whole and experience the joy of being right and at peace with ourselves.

Many methods—including the process of "shadow work" presented in the next chapter—can help us see the truth we need to see. However, regardless of what methods are used, the process remains difficult and painful, and for this reason very few people embark on it. The truth about ourselves, it seems, is only of limited value to most of us. Understanding this, we must continually strive to keep our own house in order by working beneath the surface toward greater personal wholeness.

As I have stated, to get into and stay in relationship with others, we must first be in relationship with our Self—we can't have one without the other. And, to be in relationship with our Self—to rise above our lies, wounds, and reactive complexes—we must face and work with our own demons in the darkness, and then learn to listen and attend to the needs of our soul.

Chapter Five

RISING ABOVE BY DESCENDING BELOW[1]:

The Personal Quest for Self-Knowledge and Wholeness

"At the bottom of the abyss comes the voice of salvation. The black moment is the moment when the real message of transformation is going to come. At the darkest moment comes the light."

—*Joseph Campbell*

"Each of us contains a darkness within, a darkness with which we will have to come to terms, for within the darkness is a new light. In order to do so, we have to confront our fears, accept our alienation, and find a bridge to the new."

—*Robin Robertson*

"And I will bring the blind by a way that they knew not; I will lead them in paths that they have not known: I will make the darkness light before them, and crooked things straight . . ."

—*Isaiah 42:16*

The ideal of being or acting "normal" is a virus that infects the Western mind. It joins the ranks of other damaging ideals such as perfection, fairness, selflessness, consistency, love, and goodness, as they are commonly understood. In my view, much of what we call "normal" is psychologically undesirable— even unhealthy. As we have learned, everything about us that is considered by significant people in our lives as "not normal" is pushed into the darkness, into the "long bag" of the unconscious, leaving us split, fragmented, disempowered, and dis-integrated— "out of relationship" with ourselves.

The previous chapter addressed some of the requirements for getting "in relationship" with others, acknowledging that to fulfill such requirements we need to be in relationship with ourselves. When we are in relationship with ourselves, the requirements are fulfilled as a natural expression of who we are. When we are not, they are mere contrivances of the ego that usually miss the mark. We may have relationships with others, but they are merely different relationships with our Self. Like the pagan Greeks who worshiped an unknown god, we relate to the unknown "other," searching for our unknown Self, not realizing that what attracts or repulses us is merely a reflection, in part, of who we are.

We get in relationship with ourselves as we expose the Level One lies of the false self and work toward individuation, or wholeness, which is the hidden agenda of the soul. The completion of our personality is not fully attained in this life. As Aniele Jaffé writes, " 'Successful individuation' is never total, it is only an optimal achievement of wholeness."[2] We can only approach it by deliberately working beneath the surface. As we know so well, life has a way of teaching us the lessons we need to learn.

To work toward individuation is to consciously assist nature in its formative work by continually: (1) differentiating and integrating all aspects of the personality, (2) attending to the needs of the soul, (3) clearing the past, and (4) responding ethically and faithfully to the call of the soul. This process enables us to manage the inner forces of the Self toward completion or fulfillment, making us fully human and fully alive. It involves reaching into the very depths of our being to reclaim, accept, and embrace all of our Self—our energy, vitality, and power—that has been lost through neglect, taboo, ignorance, and the disabling forces of traditionalism, wrongdoing, and abuse. This work assists in redeeming these lost parts of our personality—bringing them from the shadows into the light, where they are differentiated, integrated, and made useful in benefitting ourselves and others. It transforms our weaknesses into strengths and our suffering into wisdom and mature spirituality.

In contrast to other approaches that advocate affirmation, performance, or behavior modification as a way to increase self-esteem, this work involves reflection, healing, caring, and reconciliation through the wise and dedicated pursuit of truth and wholeness. It is an ongoing discipline that is foundational to all other efforts toward personal development. And, in the final analysis, it is the work of forging true leaders from the unconscious mass of humanity.

In this chapter I help you cut through the Level One lies of the false self by exploring the processes for integrating the personality and attending to the deeper needs of the soul. This chapter is lengthy and the work will become somewhat dense and difficult. Please take it slowly, read the material carefully, work through the exercises, and review the notes. The concepts in this chapter and the accompanying notes are critical to your understanding and appreciation of the depth and scope of inner work.

Self-Knowledge, Self-Deception, and "Group Think"

> "Therefore . . . it is the greatest of all disciplines to know oneself, for when a man knows himself, he knows God."
>
> —*Clement of Alexandria*

Self-knowledge, like wholeness itself, is a pearl that loves the deep. Oscar Wilde insightfully observed, "Only the shallow know themselves." Joseph Joubert adds, "How many people eat, drink, and get married; buy, sell, and build; make contracts and attend to their fortune; have friends and enemies, pleasures and pains; are born, grow up, live, and die—but asleep!?"

So much of what we do, whether in our relationships with others or by ourselves, is motivated by forces we are not even aware of. Our capacity for self-awareness is limited by our self-knowledge, and self-knowledge depends on experience and self-reflection, or the sincere pursuit of self-understanding. Such a pursuit can be problematic since most people confuse self-knowledge with only that small part of their personality they are conscious of. According to Carl Jung:

> Most people confuse "self-knowledge" with knowledge of their conscious ego-personalities. Anyone who has any ego-consciousness at all takes it for granted that he knows himself. But the ego knows only its own contents, not the unconscious and its contents. People measure their self-knowledge by what the average person in his social environment knows of himself, but not by the real psychic facts, which are for the most part hidden. . . .
>
> What is commonly called "self-knowledge" is therefore a very limited knowledge, most of it dependent on social factors, of what goes on in the human psyche. Hence, one is always coming up against the prejudice that such and such a thing does not happen "with us," or "in our family," or among our friends and acquaintances. . . . In this broad belt of unconsciousness, which is immune to conscious criticism and control, we stand defenseless, open to all kinds of influences and psychic infections.[3]

Self-knowledge, beyond what we think we know about ourselves, requires first the *differentiation* of all parts of our personality. To be differentiated means to be clear about who we are and who we are not. It also means to be clear about who it is within us that is acting, reacting, and responding at any given point in time: *Who* believes what, *who* wants what, *who* values what, *who* feels what, *who* judges, moralizes, thinks, reacts, interacts, and responds. Differentiated people know when they are responding or reacting in their own name or in someone else's, when they are being genuine or authentic and when they are not. They know who's who in their interactions and life experiences.

These notions are not strange to us. We have all experienced internal conflicts in which "part" of us wants one thing and another part of us wants something else. When this happens, we say we feel conflicted, split, or torn. Perhaps we also can relate to feeling "beside" ourselves with some emotion, or to reacting out of character and wondering what "got into" us. Then there are those almost uncanny moments when we recognize that we're talking or acting "just like" our mother, father, friend, or some other significant person in our life. Finally, how many times have we observed that someone we knew wasn't acting like himself or herself, or admitted that our own feelings, desires, attitudes, or behavior, were "not like me"? All these occurrences testify that "I" am many. Self-knowledge means, "I know who is who within me; I am clear about who *I am* and aware of the inner powers and subpersonalities or complexes that guide, move, and overtake me when they are operating in my life."

One related and essential aspect of differentiation is the ability to recognize the difference between the voice of internalized *external* authority—father, mother, guardian, priest—and the voice of *internal* authority. The first voice tells us what we "should" do or how we "ought" to live our life. It is the voice of general counsel, social conscience, moral code, or Freud's concept of the "super ego." The second voice tells us what we "must" do. It is the internal, moral imperative—or voice of true conscience—imprinted within us as part of the hidden agenda that shapes our destiny. Differentiating between these two voices is critical to our necessary growth upward *and* downward to wholeness.

Differentiation enables us to be conscious of the various aspects of our personality without necessarily identifying with them. In this context, to be differentiated also means to be clear about the fact that, though these inner realities are part of us, they do not *define* us. For example, I can be overtaken by a dark mood and not only know *what* is happening to me, but *who* the mood is and what she or he wants. I can react to another with deep feelings of attraction or repulsion, or with a strong emotion

of anger or rage, and know I am in the grip of some complex—
an inner "angel" or "demon," which is part of me and which
has a separate identity—that needs to be acknowledged and
worked with. Through the process of knowing all our psychic
parts more fully, we begin to differentiate our essential character
from the parts, and thereby avoid identifying ourselves solely
with them. This, in turn, helps us avoid the perils of inflation, or
pride, which are characteristic of the undifferentiated personality,
or "false self."

Self-knowledge also requires the *integration* of all our parts.
The process of integration, which begins with differentiation,
puts us in proper relationship with our Self. Through integration,
we begin to see and feel the intrinsic value of each part of us in
the evolution of our soul to wholeness. We begin to understand
the value of our feelings, emotions, and complexes. We embrace
them and learn how to relate to them so we can better relate
with others toward greater fulfillment and joy in life. Integration
means taking back, or reclaiming, the essential parts of our Self
that we have split off and disowned in order to "adapt," "succeed,"
or "fit in."

Self-deception. Closely related to our quest for self-knowledge
and self-awareness, as discussed in Chapter Four, are the Level
Four lies of self-deception. These lies are a natural response to
the anxiety produced by irrational, reactive behavior and acts of
wrongdoing that threaten our self-image. We are all familiar, for
example, with the uneasiness that accompanies certain "selfish"
actions, motivating us, often quite unconsciously, to reduce our
discomfort by leading us to rationalize that such actions are
right. Concerning our efforts to disguise our selfishness,
Langdon Gilkey insightfully observes:

> Rarely does self-interest display itself frankly as self-
> ishness. More often it hides behind the very moral ide-
> alism it is denying in action; a legal, moral, or even
> religious argument is likely to be given for what is at
> base a selfish action. And what is more, the moral dis-

guise usually deceives even the self who has donned it. For no one is more surprised and outraged than that self when someone else questions the validity of his [or her] moral concern. For this reason . . . idealistic intentions are not enough; nor is a man's idealistic fervor the final yardstick of the quality of his character. We commit most of our serious sins against our neighbor— and these are the serious sins—for what we regard as a "moral principle."

Most of us, in spite of whatever harm we may be doing to others, have long since convinced ourselves that the cause for which we do what we do is just and right. Thus teaching high ideals . . . will not in itself produce better men and women. It may merely provide the taught with new ways of justifying their devotion to their own security.[4]

To persist in a belief, action, or course of action in the face of evidence that could reasonably indicate error or falsehood is to be in a state of self-deception *if* such persistence involves: (1) stubborn refusal to admit honestly or face the possibility of wrongdoing or one's capability to commit such wrongdoing; (2) an absence of due diligence in the pursuit of truth; (3) an absence of good conscience as evidenced by peace and quiet assurance, or the presence of bad conscience as evidenced by feelings of uneasiness, defensiveness, irritability, and aggression; and (4) the presence of certain strategies such as blaming, accusing, or self-excusing behavior—or, more dangerously, the manipulation of evidence or the contrivance of interpretations of that evidence— that justify one's beliefs or actions. Self-deception also involves the avoidance of legitimate suffering and self-honesty in the face of conflict or confrontation.

Self-deception, or perhaps more accurately, ego protection, at times presents a natural barrier to the pursuit of self-knowledge. Few people are willing to sacrifice their "ego-ideal" on the altar of truth. Most of us want to hide from the revelation of our "dark side." Many do not have sufficient ego strength to face and embrace their shadows. In such cases, ego protection can serve an important developmental purpose by deferring the full realization of the shadow until we are able to assimilate it and not identify ourselves with it. Knowing how we deceive or protect ourselves, however, is essential in helping us become aware of our unconscious efforts to evade the truth. It can also help us resist the temptation to do so.

When we run or hide from the truth about ourselves, we become complicit to a variety of possible ills. Out of our false self, we might live at a low level of fulfillment or prolong and repeat our trials and suffering. Conversely, we might "soar too close to the sun," like the mythical Icarus, only to have our spiritual wings of wax melt from the heat while we fall to our deaths because of pride or foolhardiness. We might cheat ourselves out of the happiness we seek, or deny ourselves the depth and richness of soulful lives filled with meaning, purpose, and a sense of destiny. We might become numb, living from pleasure to pleasure as though they were narcotic fixes. Or we might become obsessed with "success," "performance," "perfection," or "effectiveness" as the gods we worship, who somehow will validate our worth or existence. The list goes on and on.

Further, by avoiding the work of individuation, we lose ourselves to the mass and add to the collective evils of our world through our own blindness, wounds, and lack of "depth" integrity. Perhaps this is most evident today in our organizations and institutions. Here, the "I" becomes the "we" and those with limited self-knowledge and self-awareness extend individual ego protection to *collective* self-deception.

Evidence of this phenomenon can be found everywhere. Reactive cycles between and among countries, political parties, churches, companies, governments, departments, and families are an ongoing fact of life. These reactive cycles, as discussed in Chapter Three, are created and fed in large part by the projections of each group's dark, inferior, or sinister qualities onto other groups or individuals.

"Group Think." As further evidence of collective self-deception, there is the well-known phenomenon of "group think,"
which can infect even the most intelligent, well-intentioned,
inspired, and "righteous" of groups or councils. Daniel
Goleman, in his book *Vital Lies, Simple Truths*, effectively illustrates this phenomenon in describing John F. Kennedy's worst
fiasco, the Bay of Pigs invasion.

The attack calculated to overthrow Fidel Castro was a dismal
failure from beginning to end. "How," Kennedy asked himself,
"could I have been so stupid to let them go ahead?" The dynamics
of Kennedy's inner circle of advisors provided the answer. In
studying the situation carefully, Irving Janis identified several
ways in which Kennedy and his advisors went wrong[5]:

First, there was the illusion that anything they planned was
"bound to succeed." Kennedy was charmed; he could do no wrong.
There was a sense of invulnerability and feelings of power,
euphoria, and righteousness in being part of such a powerful group.

Second, there was the illusion of unanimity. "Along with the
sense of invulnerability," writes Goleman, "comes the illusion of
unanimity. Both stem from group coziness. Once the group
adopts a belief or decision, individual members are likely to feel
it must be right. After all, the members are such great people—
how could they be wrong?"

Other forces at work included the suppression of dissenters'
personal doubts, who likely experienced a subtle fear of being
"soft" or "undaring" in the eyes of colleagues. These rationalizations happen in the quiet quest to justify group actions, just
as the phenomenon of "stereotyping" does, which solidifies the
group against common enemies. Goleman writes, "Stereotypes
are self-confirming . . . [and] tenacious; members will stick to
them despite all evidence to the contrary."

Finally, and perhaps of greatest danger, was what Goleman
refers to as "ethical blinders":

> The group's schema includes an unstated belief in its
> rightness and morality. This glib assumption allows
> the members to ignore the moral status and conse-
> quences of their decisions. This belief flows from the
> group credo that "we are wise and good," an aspect
> of its self-image of invulnerability. And, after all, if we
> are good, then whatever we do must be good. These
> ethical blinders help the group avoid feeling ashamed
> or guilty about what otherwise might be questionable
> means or goals. Their actions can go on cocooned in
> a comfortable sense of righteousness.[6]

Whether we confront "group think" in the White House, the
board room, the presiding councils of Church and State, or a
local street gang, it is all the same, dark side of unity.
Unconsciousness eclipses the conscience; truth becomes what we
make of it, and effectiveness is defined by whatever we think is
appropriate. Even so-called righteous "principles" become allies
to the lie and protect the self-deceived from the light of truth.

Here we have, ironically, the coming together of select, talented individuals, who perhaps are effective and even distin-
guished individually, but who are ineffective and even dangerous
as members of an "elite" group. I have witnessed this phenomenon
many times in the workplace and in the religious sector—and,
regrettably, I have even been party to it on occasion—where people
are wrongly wounded by those who wield their sword of power
out of fear, greed, and prejudice, while they hide behind the
shield of "principle," the veneer of moral "rightness," or the
mantle of "higher authority."

Our greatest protection against such self-betrayal, self-deception, and "group think" is self-knowledge and the insight, wisdom,
maturity, and character strength gained through virtuous living,
coupled with honest self-examination, the integration of our personality, and a clearing of the past. According to Aniela Jaffé:

> The individuation process [and the protection it
> affords] requires a ruthlessly honest confrontation
> with the *contents of the unconscious*. . . . Evil as well

as good is given to man along with the gift of life. It can never be completely conquered, yet man has a chance to hold it in check through self-awareness and struggle, and through confronting it directly. The more conscious he is of his proclivities for evil [or wrongdoing], the more he is in a position to hold out against the destructive forces within him.[7]

Understanding and Integrating the Shadow

Before we begin learning how to work beneath the surface, we need to understand more about the human shadow. I have been using the term "shadow" in a limited sense to represent certain contents of the personal unconscious. This includes those emotionally charged memories (or complexes) that account for our reactivity, as well as unacceptable or unknown needs, beliefs, emotions, values, and goals which operate within us in ways that might surprise, concern, shame, or even frighten us. These inner forces can help the work of individuation or hinder it.

Also included in the personal shadow are repressed memories of negative or traumatic experiences, as well as those capacities and characteristics—both constructive *and* destructive—which we are either unaware of or have disowned because their existence has, at some time, embarrassed us or threatened our acceptance by others. Additionally, the shadow includes the scripts and lies we live that alienate us from ourselves and others.

Often referred to as our "inferior personality," or "the disowned self," the personal shadow in many ways is the opposite of our ego-ideal, or alter-ego, that needs to be understood and integrated if we are to grow toward greater wholeness and self-acceptance. We need the personal shadow to fulfill our hidden agenda and bring us to ourselves. The workings of the shadow help us learn life's lessons and grow in strength with the humility and meekness needed to guard against the nemesis of pride. Further, by bringing our darkness to light we experience greater power and joy. We also become more productive with our talents and strengths and more serviceable to others.

As I carefully lead workshop participants through their own personal shadow work, I find that their initial reaction is often one of fear and resistance. As Jung has indicated, our attitude and preparedness are crucial in this work. We simply are being reunited with a dark friend who can be a powerful ally and who will only become our enemy if shunned.[8]

In consequence of false Christian tradition, our shadow has been disowned and the Western mind has been split, divided against itself and made one-sided. Such one-sidedness represses and denies the dark side of the personality, elevating an unreal idealism that damns our growth, deadens the soul, and disempowers the human spirit, alienating us from ourselves, others, and God.[9]

When we identify only with the "good," or seek to conform or identify ourselves with narrowly or traditionally defined attributes of ideal "goodness," we become polarized, or one-sided. Who we think we are is not who we really are. Our psyche is split, and we are living a lie. The shadow, which is a complex of all that we think we are not, and which is a part of us, compensates for our one-sidedness through various revelations of our own darkness—through dreams, fantasies, slips of the tongue, reactive or compulsive behavior, humor, secret obsessions, or projections. Our hidden agenda for wholeness seeks the integration of the shadow, and our true Self unconsciously enlists the powers in the darkness to ensure that such wholeness ultimately takes place.

The work of consciously integrating our shadow toward greater wholeness is essential to personal empowerment and trustworthiness, as discussed in Chapter Two. It is also essential for us to cut through the Level One lies of the false self and to face the whole truth about who we really are. This process of integration includes four continuous steps:

• *Step One: Facing the Shadow.* We can't integrate what we can't see. The first step of integration is differentiation. In this step we can employ various methods to enlarge our knowledge and understanding, of who we really are and what we really value, beyond the boundaries of our self-image or ego-ideal. Part of facing the shadow involves identifying and clarifying those parts of our personality that we have disowned or lost access to, as well as those countervalues that complement the light side of virtue as an essential part of the wholly ethical conscience.

• *Step Two: Experiencing the Shadow.* Integration is experiential. I can't integrate my anger unless I experience it. "Feeling" the shadow makes it real and creates a tension that we must hold and work with consciously to become more conscious and productive.

• *Step Three: Embracing the Shadow.* Understanding the broader context of our shadow's contents, including family secrets and the system dynamics that created them, fosters greater self-acceptance, compassion, maturity, and wisdom. This step brings us into intimate contact with our history and our wounds.

• *Step Four: Bringing the Darkness to Light.* This step involves methods of self-interaction and active imagination in the effective and ethical employment of our shadow contents toward a more productive and fulfilling life.

The benefits of this work are of great worth. According to Connie Zweig and Jeremiah Abrams, editors of *Meeting the Shadow*:

> The aim of meeting the shadow is to develop an ongoing relationship with it, to expand our sense of self by balancing the one-sidedness of our conscious attitudes with our unconscious depths. . . . When we are in a proper relationship to it, the unconscious is not a demoniacal monster, as Jung points out. "It only becomes dangerous when our conscious attention to it is hopelessly wrong."
>
> A right relationship with the shadow offers us a great gift: to lead us back to our buried potentials. Through *shadow-work*, a term we coined to refer to the continuing effort to develop a creative relationship with the shadow, we can:
> > • Achieve a more genuine self-acceptance, based on a more complete knowledge of who we are;

- Defuse the negative emotions that erupt unexpectedly in our daily lives;
- Feel more free of guilt and shame associated with our negative feelings and actions;
- Recognize the projections that color our opinion of others;
- Heal our relationships through more honest self-examination and direct communication;
- Use the creative imagination via dreams, drawing, writing, and rituals to own the disowned self. . . .

Perhaps we can also, in this way, refrain from adding our personal darkness to the density of the collective shadow.[10]

Additionally, by facing, experiencing, and embracing the shadow—instead of suppressing or denying its contents—we acknowledge the dark side of our personality and thereby prevent its destructive, negative energy from enlarging as a compensating complex that can wreak havoc in our lives.

Step One: Facing the Shadow—"The Hero's Quest"[11]

"Furthermore, we have not even to risk the adventure alone, for the heroes of all time have gone before us. The labyrinth is thoroughly known. We have only to follow the thread of the hero path, and where we had thought to find an abomination, we shall find a god. And where we had thought to slay another, we shall slay ourselves. Where we had thought to travel outward, we will come to the center of our own existence. And where we had thought to be alone, we will be with all the world."

—*Joseph Campbell*

The process of "shadow work" begins with courageous confrontation. Here is where we expose the lies of the false self and see ourselves as we really are. These Level One lies include identifying with our ideal self-concept, or "ego-ideal," while refusing to accept the dark side of our personality. They also include believing that our behavior or performance defines us, denying the masculine or feminine aspects of our psyche, and insisting that our perceptions of others—which are really projections of ourselves—define who others are. These lies, and others like them, embrace a polarized, one-sided view of Self and discount or deny the existence and significance of the unconscious. They result in a hopelessly wrong attitude toward ourselves and others, which leads to alienation, hardship, and even tragedy.

In George Lucas's film "The Empire Strikes Back," there is a classic scene wherein Luke Skywalker, during a break from his training regimen with Jedi Master Yoda, looks toward a dark and dreary swamp and tells Yoda that "something's not right here. I feel cold . . . death."

Yoda informs Luke that the place is strong with the "dark side of the force" and is a "domain of evil." Then he says, "In you must go."

Luke asks, "What's in there?" to which Yoda responds cryptically, "Only what you take with you." The symbolism is rich with the archetype of the "hero's quest"—the inner journey to greater consciousness, during which the hero is initiated into the mysteries of personal darkness and becomes humble, wise, and powerful.

Luke then arms himself with his weapon, and Yoda tells him that his weapon will not be necessary. Luke disregards Yoda's words. After all, who goes into the darkness unarmed, especially when one senses danger? Protected by his psychic defense mechanisms—for that is what the light saber symbolizes—Luke begins his fateful journey. Into the swamp he goes, and down into a dark cave below the surface. It is a God-forsaken place— dark, misty, cold. Down he goes until he gets to the bottom. Then, from out of nowhere, it seems, enters Luke's archenemy, Darth Vader—large, imposing, threatening, and dressed in black, his face covered by a dark, hideous mask—who approaches Skywalker in a menacing way. I remember sitting in the theater and feeling threatened and startled.

Luke pulls out his weapon. Vader draws his, and the two begin a dual to the death. Luke fights for his life. The light sabers clash again and again. Finally, with a mighty swipe, young Skywalker strikes Vader at the neck and decapitates him. Vader's head rolls off his shoulders onto the ground. When it hits the side of the cave it explodes, and the mask blows off. When the smoke clears we see the face behind the dark mask of Darth Vader: It is Luke Skywalker's face.

When I saw this years ago, I was stunned. I didn't know what it meant. Now I do. This scene is richly symbolic of the first step toward integrating the shadow. I see Yoda, Luke, and Vader as metaphors of the higher Self, the ego (who I think I am), and the shadow (the alter-ego, or inferior personality), respectively.[12] The dark cave represents the unconscious mind, or Robert Bly's "long bag."

As I mentioned, Luke's weapon seems symbolic of those ego defense mechanisms that are used for the protection of the ego-ideal, or self-image, and Luke had been told by Yoda that he would not need his weapons. (Imagine what Luke might have learned if he had not brought his weapon and had not tried to defend himself.) It would follow that the fight between Luke and Vader is symbolic of the inner conflict associated with the integration of ego and shadow. This struggle, of course, results in Luke facing his darkness—his shadow.

Clearly, the process is not complete. Other dark encounters are sure to come in subsequent stages of the integration process. To continue this example, Luke must now begin his development to wholeness that he might fulfill his destiny. For Luke to become a jedi knight—to realize his potential and help save the galaxy— first he needs to plumb the depths of his own soul and face his shadow. The person he hates and fears most—Darth Vader—is really himself. All his defenses could not ward off the truth.

As it turns out (with my apologies to those who have never seen the movie), Vader is actually Luke's father, who, many years earlier, had been seduced by the dark side of the force and had given himself to it. This truth had been hidden from Luke from an early age. But the key tension in the film is: If the father could fall, so could the son. This would be Luke's destiny if he does not—or will not—complete the process of integration—a sobering caution to us all, particularly if we fail to understand that such a fate is merely the consequence of self-evasion.

Although Luke has taken the first step, he succumbs to fear. He emerges from the cave still polarized, albeit shaken by the self-revelation received in the cave. Later, as he is about to abort his training to save his friends, Yoda reminds him of his "failure" in the cave. If we go no further than to face the shadow and then try to destroy it, we fail. I will return to this story in step four of this process to show how Luke completes his hero's journey and becomes a jedi knight—a whole, individuated person.

If we would become whole and empowered, we must do as Luke did. We must embark on the "hero's quest" and face our shadows. There are many ways to do this. What follows is a discussion of several methods I have found effective in my own life. They include: eating the shadow, discovering the "flip side" of our strengths and weaknesses, soliciting and honoring feedback, analyzing dreams and applying active imagination, reviewing "slips of the tongue" and what makes us laugh, and learning from reactive episodes. Also, I introduce the important concept of "conceiving the inconceivable," and discuss how to identify and clarify the "countervalues" of the soul.

Eating the Shadow. In Chapter Two we discussed how, through projection, we give away the rejected powers we have placed in our "long bag," and in Chapter Three we continued the discussion, learning how our negative projections toward others alienate us and provoke reactive cycles. Then, in Chapter Four, we learned that by reversing the arrow of projection, we can face our shadow and avoid reactive cycles and alienation. "Eating the shadow," or this process of reversing our projections, seems like a simple concept to understand, but in reality it is difficult to accomplish. For example, if I get turned off or emotionally upset about someone whom I see as rude, arrogant, fake, or deceitful, I need to own those labels, for they represent parts of me that remain unintegrated as part of my personal shadow complex. Such is not always easy. In short, whatever we admire, hate, or despise in others, we unconsciously identify with. Whatever we hate or admire in others, we are.

I experience this with my children from time to time, especially my teenagers. On one occasion, it was my job to prepare a "chore chart" that would evenly distribute the household work among the six members of our family. I finished my task, presented it to Annette and the children, and we all agreed to the schedule.

One Saturday, after a busy work week, it was my turn to clean the kitchen. It was a mess, and I didn't want to do it. Everyone else was gone except T. J., my then 15-year-old boy, who was upstairs playing video games. Even though it wasn't his job, I wanted T. J. to clean the kitchen. After all, I thought, it was my "right" to exercise such parental prerogatives. I felt that I had worked harder than he had during the week, and I deserved a break. An exception to the schedule was in order. So I called to him from the kitchen.

"T. J.?"

"Yeah, Dad?"

"Would you come down and help me with the kitchen?" I was being deceitful here. I didn't want help. I wanted him to do the whole job.

He responded, "Sure Dad, in a minute."

I started to clean, at least to show I was doing something. I could handle a token display of effort for a minute.

Ten minutes later, T. J. still hadn't come down. I called to him again: No answer. I decided to take the garbage out. As I went outside, I saw T. J. in the back yard with his friends hitting golf balls. I couldn't believe it—how could he do this to me? I was disgusted and disappointed. I looked at him, and he saw me and waved.

"Hi, Dad."

I said nothing. I was so disappointed that I could not even dignify him with a response. I walked back into the house and proceeded to clean the kitchen. Somehow, the work went faster while I was accusing T. J. in my mind. "He is so selfish, inconsiderate, and lazy. He's spoiled rotten," I thought to myself. Then, just as I had deduced that he must have inherited these traits from his mother's side of the family, he walked in.

"Hey, Dad?"

"Yeah."

"Why didn't you say hi to me when I said hi to you?"

"I didn't see you," I lied again.

"Yes, you did. You were looking right at me. You ignored me on purpose."

Busted. It was time to tell the truth. He needed to hear it. "To tell you the truth, Son, I didn't say hi because I was so disappointed in you. You said you'd help me with the kitchen, and you lied to me. Then you went out and selfishly began playing with your friends."

"Yeah right, Dad," he said, with anger in his voice. "You just wanted me to do your work for you. You're the selfish one, not me." With that, he turned and left, leaving me standing in the kitchen with a broom in my hand. Part of me wanted to run after him, grab him, and tell him to never talk to me like that again. Instead, I looked inward and reversed the arrow of projection. Where did he learn to be this way? Could it be that I had been selfish, inconsiderate, lazy, and dishonest? Instances came to mind that proved it so beyond any doubt. The very traits that disgusted me about my son were within me.

When I realized this in my heart, I was humbled to the core and my anger was gone. I went back to work without a complaint. Just as I was finishing, T. J. came back in. I'm sure he wanted to see if he'd gone too far.

"Hey, Dad."

"Hi, Son." Then I paused and said, "T. J.?"

"Yeah?"

"I'm sorry for calling you selfish. You were right; I'm the one who was selfish." Facing it wasn't easy, but it needed to be done—for me, for T. J., and for our relationship.

He came over, put his arm around me, and said, "That's okay, Dad; I was selfish, too."

Sometimes genuine honesty begets honesty, and, as Carl Rogers has taught, "Self-disclosure begets self-disclosure."

Without honestly facing our own shadows, we risk laying them on our children. This is a terrible legacy. Our projections become so intense that a child's personality splits or fragments. Children lose touch with themselves and carry the weight not only of their own shadow, but of the collective shadow of their entire family system, especially that of their parents.

Somewhere in the system, a member of the family will eventually bring the darkness to the surface and act it out, or become the family "oddball," "black sheep," or "prodigal." Such an individual is either treated as a "scapegoat," or the person may somehow play a redemptive role that, ironically, saves the family from its one-sidedness and prods the family on to greater integration and consciousness. In this role, the wayward family member becomes the incarnation of the shadows of parents, siblings, and other close relatives. The key, again, is in the family members' willingness to face their own personal shadows. Refusal to do so can result in further cumulative contamination for generations to come.

Repression is no protection, and even love and nurture are often insufficient antidotes. "Toxic shame," unresolved neuroses, and psychic wounds are passed on, it would seem, at the cellular level, regardless of how positive the family environment might be. Further, the typical loving concern of "normal" family members, and particularly of "righteous"parents, often takes the form of pity, which is easily interpreted as further shame.[13]

Merely shining the light of such loving concern on the darkness does not redeem and integrate it, unless such love is sufficiently empathic and unconditional. At this level, pity is replaced with a transforming compassion and acceptance that can be given only by those who have descended below their own egos into the darkness, who have performed some of the essential inner work, and who have experienced the journey of the soul toward individuation along the strange, often painful paths it takes. How important it is for parents to do this work.

Not all that is in the shadow, of course, is negative, and not all projections are bad. In many instances, we encounter positive projections that attract us to people who seem to have qualities we admire. These positive qualities in others represent the same unrealized qualities in ourselves. Often, this establishes a real basis for unrecognized interdependence. Nor are our projections completely wrong: Usually, any projection will convey at least some truth. This is one reason why any feedback from others, including so-called negative feedback, must be carefully considered.

The five-step process of eating our shadow, or integrating our projections, involves making a conscious effort to examine our attractions and repulsions toward others. One effective way to do this involves, first, asking ourselves what we see in the other person that affects us. Clearly, some kind of projection has taken place if we feel affected by a particular attitude or behavior. Second, we need to label the traits or characteristics that affect us by asking, "How am I seeing this person? How would I describe him or her? What is it about this person that affects me this way?" Third, we must look for the same traits and characteristics in ourselves, just as I did with my son, T. J., in the earlier example.

Fourth, we need to look for our lost power that we have projected. For example, if I feel a favorable attraction, such as admiration, I might ask myself, "What power does this person have that I have lost or given away?" Perhaps the answer is the power to be "in control," or "even-keeled," or "level-headed" under pressure. Or, if I feel a negative emotion, I might ask, "What power is this person *not* using that could account for seeming rude, obnoxious, irresponsible, or extreme?" With some thought I might conclude, if I were behaving in a similar fashion without a good reason, it would be because I had temporarily lost access to my ability to think clearly, exercise intuition, use common sense, or feel empathy. These powers help us keep our strengths balanced and stay in the middle of unconscious extremes. They also relate to the basic functions of the psyche.

The fifth and final step of the process involves reflecting on how we might have lost our powers and how we can reclaim them. Sometimes this can be done, as Robert Bly suggests, by playfully acting out the negative image of the lost power—like playing the "witch," the "patriarch" or "giant," the "intellectual" or "bleeding heart," and feeling what it's like. Or, we might engage in some form of harmless but meaningful ritual or exchange to adopt or redeem the lost part. Such rituals could be as simple as making a toast to the return of the lost power or celebrating its homecoming. Perhaps a valuable or symbolic piece of jewelry could be dedicated as a token of honor and remembrance, and so on. There are numerous possibilities.

Sometimes, after we have actually felt the diminishment of our personality due to our loss of power and have sensed deeply the value of what we have rejected or neglected, we might ask for such powers back at 100 percent. For example, according to Bly again, we might ask the person to whom we have given our powers to give them back: "I want my witch back," or "I want my patriarch or giant back." Or, we can make the demand vocally to ourselves and reflect on how to use our reclaimed powers productively.[14]

The "Flip Side of the Coin." Another way to face the shadow, similar to the process of eating the shadow, is by identifying the negative poles of our strengths. Examine your strengths. List the qualities you feel have been most responsible for your success and then ask yourself what their shadow side is, or what it might become. For example, a "determined" person is potentially stubborn and inflexible; the "assertive" person can become aggressive, overbearing, and obnoxious; and the "caring" or "loving" person can also be controlling, smothering, domineering, and possessive.

While polar shadow extremes potentially exist within every person, they become increasingly dominant in the unintegrated personality. Thus, the more unintegrated the personality, the more artificial, duplicitous, one-sided, rigid, and self-protected the individual becomes, and therefore, the more frequently the person enters into the shadowlands of otherwise positive or productive characteristics while falling out of relationship with others. I have found this to be the case with people who identify themselves with effectiveness, success, or moral "rightness" or righteousness.

Both the negative poles of our strengths and the positive poles of our weaknesses are in the shadow. Often, we fail to understand that many of our so-called weaknesses have redeeming value and represent strengths that have been taken to an extreme in response to stress, excitement, or anxiety. When we seek to eliminate our weaknesses, we must be careful, for doing so likely will also weaken the strengths. Likewise, when we are critical of others' weaknesses we can inadvertently dissempower their strengths. John O'Neil refers to the "flip side of the coin" as the basis for what he terms the "Paradox of Success":

> Every positive, success-producing trait has its shadow side, revealed under certain conditions. Just as every admirable human quality can be used badly, *the gifts and habits of mind that lead to achievement can become counterproductive.* When we keep problems and inconvenient desires in the shadow, when our goals remain too narrowly focused for too long, when the rarefied air of winning seems to set us apart from ordinary mortals, our natural gifts may be exhausted or perverted. Even the strong, healthy ego can become overinflated, leading to personal or organizational disasters if not diagnosed and checked early enough.
>
> Examining these success traits and their flip sides illustrates the paradox of success in detail. Here is a quick reference list:
>
> | | |
> |---|---|
> | Confidence | Sense of infallibility |
> | Quickness | Overhastiness |
> | Sharp wit | Abrasiveness |
> | Alertness | Narrow focus |
> | Dedication | Workaholism |
> | Control | Inflexibility |

Courage	Foolhardiness
Perseverance	Resistance to change
Charm	Manipulation
Thriftiness	False economy
Commitment	Blind faith[15]

Identifying these complementary opposites is not easy. It requires a different kind of thinking. For example, the negative shadow side of self-confidence is not insecurity, but might be arrogance, impatience with others, or a sense of infallibility. The positive shadow side of procrastination is not hastiness, but might be carefulness or cautiousness, just as the positive side of impulsivity, or "shooting from the hip," might be decisiveness. One way to help identify the complementary opposite is to ask yourself, "If this strength were taken to an unhealthy extreme, what would it look like?" or, "If this weakness could be developed to a positive or constructive quality, what would it look like?"

Once you identify the "flip side of the coin," try it on, and ask yourself—honestly—if it fits. If you do it right, you'll learn a lot about yourself and help others learn a lot about themselves as well. Analyzing the flip side of negative attitudes and projections toward others can be another way to discover unintegrated personality strengths, as well as the lies, associations, and complexes that turn those strengths to the "dark side."

Recently, I found myself out of relationship with several people, and thus, out of sorts with myself. This isn't an uncommon experience for me. I personally wrestle with being impatient, cynical, critical, judgmental, and intolerant. All these weaknesses are the flip side of some of my greatest strengths, provided I'm not engaged in some form of twisted thinking or in the grip of some reactive complex. Whenever I find myself feeling negative toward someone else, I try to label my attitude.

In a particular instance during this time, I found myself standing in line to buy theater tickets. I had called ahead to find out when the box office opened. The recording had said 6:15 p.m., and the newspaper had said 6:15 p.m. But, at the theater, the sign said 6:30 p.m. I made a judgment: "These people are *incompetent*." And, since I have no tolerance for incompetence, I soon became impatient. It was now 6:15 p.m., and the show was to begin at 6:45 p.m. I still needed to go home to pick up my wife and return in time for the show.

As I stood in line, I noticed a group of young, teenage theater attendants joking around and shooting the bull inside the theater, while the line outside the theater was getting longer and people (mostly me) were losing patience. I became critical and began to accuse them in my mind of being *inconsiderate* and *insensitive*. So, by now, my "attitude" involved being judgmental, intolerant, impatient, critical, and accusatory. My projections involved seeing these young people as incompetent, inconsiderate, and insensitive.

Later, as I reflected on this episode, I determined that my negative emotions toward the young theater attendants were indicating to me that something worthwhile about me was being revealed. First, I reviewed my attitude characteristics and projections. Then I tried to determine the "flip side" of those traits in myself. Soon, I began to identify several personality strengths that had become dark and self-defeating. I could now see how my bias for action had turned into impatience; my strong sense of appropriateness had turned to criticism; my effectiveness and competence had turned to intolerance, and my results-oriented thinking and strong desires for honesty had turned to blunt, insensitive, and inconsiderate behavior. Further, I could see how my experience, which I viewed as another strength, had led me to "assuming" that the show was supposed to begin at 7:15 p.m. (After all, I thought, all shows begin after 7 p.m.—because, why would they begin any earlier than that?), and had turned to incompetence: I had failed to attend to the simple detail of checking the newspaper or listening to the theater's phone message for the show's starting time. I had only checked what time the box office opened.

So there it was: Not only had I acted incompetently, inconsiderately, and insensitively—which is what I had been accusing the theater attendants of doing—these weaknesses, along with my negative attitudes, were also revealed as the flip side of my strengths, which had somehow turned against me.

This kind of realization leads us to the next step in facing the shadow, which involves seeking to understand how we fall victim to the extremism that turns our strengths into weaknesses. What moves us from the positive pole to the negative pole? What "flips the coin" and causes us to "flip out"? Part of the answer lies in our faulty and inflated expectations and beliefs, the Level Two and Level Three lies discussed earlier. These lies, or false scripts, distort our thinking and perceptions of reality, resulting in anxiety and distress. Another part of the answer lies in the emotionally charged memories, or reactive complexes, that are set off through the unconscious association of the present with the past, which creates a "reactive episode."

Later in this chapter I discuss how we can get to the unconscious root of such episodes as another way to face the shadow. In the meantime, suffice it to say that our character strengths do not exist in isolation, away from their dark counterpoles. Instead, every positive capacity, strength, quality, and virtue that we aspire to exists on a continuum with light on one end and darkness on the other. We move back and forth on this continuum, usually without awareness until after the fact. As one friend and colleague has suggested, this continuum can also be seen as a circle, and even a spiral, of life experience as we move from light to dark extremes and either learn and grow—in an upward spiral—or unconsciously repeat self-defeating patterns until we ultimately are awakened by more severe consequences.

The continuum of light and darkness, fundamental to both the circle and spiral of life experience, is real, making the quest for greater self-knowledge and self-awareness essential to our personal growth and welfare. The more split-off we are from all aspects and capacities of our personality, either through ignorance or denial, the more unconscious we will be of our movement into the dark regions of the continuum, and the more we will seek to justify ourselves or blame others when we realize how we've been acting and what we've done.

The Importance of Feedback. Another window to the shadow is feedback, especially from those who live with us, work closely with us, and know us best. When similar feedback comes from more than one source and reveals a pattern over time, we have sure insight into ourselves, particularly if we are surprised by the feedback. One way, then, to face our shadow is to solicit feedback and seriously consider it. This is not always easy.

On one occasion several years ago I decided to ask my wife, Annette, for feedback regarding my performance as a husband and father. I had been making a real effort for two or three weeks to get home from work sooner and to be more interactive and attentive. I was sure I would get a glowing report. On a Saturday morning, while the children were out playing, I came into the kitchen and found Annette eating breakfast alone. I kissed her, sat down, chatted with her for a while, and then said, "Honey, I'd really be interested in knowing how you think I'm doing as a husband and father."

There was silence for a moment. Then, Annette looked up at me and asked, "Are you serious?"

Something in the way she asked unnerved me. I wanted to bail out and tell her I was just kidding. But I didn't. Sensing that all was not well, I said, "You seem to be concerned."

She pushed herself back from the table and said, "Since you asked . . ." Then she continued, "I can tell you that the children and I have noticed how you have been making an effort to get home earlier and spend more time with us, but . . ." Here it came. I was waiting for it: the big "but." I could feel my whole body tense up. She continued, "You're still not really present when you're here, and you insist on loving us on your terms, not ours."

I did not want to hear this. I disagreed and insisted that she give me just one example to support her ridiculous allegation.

After three or four examples, I admitted to myself that she was right. I was just going through the motions to win points and prove to myself and my family that I was being a "good" husband and father. The feedback hurt, but I found out something important about myself that I needed to know.

How easy it is to slip into denial when we come face to face with our shadow. The late psychiatrist R. D. Laing poetically describes the mind's denial reflex:

> The range of what we think and do
> is limited by what we fail to notice.
> And because we fail to notice
> *that* we fail to notice
> there is little we can do
> to change
> until we notice
> how failing to notice
> shapes our thoughts and deeds.[16]

"If the denial holds," as Laing continues, "then we may not even notice that we fail to notice."[17] This state of denial can seriously undermine personal trustworthiness and the quality of our relationships with others. If we persist in such a state, our hidden agenda will eventually employ more severe measures to awaken us to the truth.

I am always impressed by people who can accept negative feedback and own their weaknesses, especially when they are visible, successful leaders who seem to have few, if any, faults. Once, while I was facilitating an executive team-building session, I encountered a very sensitive feedback exchange involving the senior management team of a *Fortune* 500 company. The chairman and CEO, together with his staff, engaged in a 360-degree profiling exercise, providing comprehensive feedback to one another on various aspects of leadership. After I had distributed the feedback reports to the participants, the chairman called me over to his seat. He was a powerful man, as most people at that level are: My experience in working with senior executives of large companies has exposed me to men and women of remarkable ego strength, intelligence, competence, and charisma. With their tremendous strengths they tend to cast equally large shadows. This chairman was no exception.

When I arrived at his seat, he invited me to look at his feedback scores. I had seen the scores of many executives over the years, but none lower than this man's. My heart went out to him. He had been hit hard. Momentarily letting my guard down, I responded without thinking: "This is awful!" And then I quickly caught myself. Fortunately, my client had a sense of humor. He smiled, told me not to be concerned with my slip, and then made a very unusual request. He asked me to make a transparency of his feedback scores and put them on the overhead projector for all to see.

I reacted. Afraid of what might happen, I advised against it. After seeing his scores, I didn't know what to expect. His profile placed him in the same leadership category as Genghis Khan. I envisioned myself becoming a referee in a brawl, and I could see my own career being damaged as my "team-building workshop" resulted in mass firings. Still, beneath my fears I sensed the importance of his request. I made the transparency.

When the group reconvened, I began by announcing that the chairman had asked me to put his feedback on the screen. I placed the transparency on the projector, and I tell you, never did any group of vice presidents squirm more! There it was, in all of its glory: the worst scores I had seen in years. And the ones who gave the scores were all sitting in the room. You could cut the tension with a knife. Finally, after a few moments of dead silence, the chairman cleared his throat and began to speak. "I want you all to know," he said, "that what you see on the screen is mine. I own it. I've had these problems all my life. Please help me."

I couldn't believe my ears. My entire view of this man completely shifted. He was, in my eyes, more powerful than ever. With courage, he had faced his shadow and had admitted his weaknesses. With humility, he reached out for help, asking his colleagues to be a part of the solution. I sat down and let the team do its healing work. Truly, feedback can be a wonderful window to the soul if we will receive it with courage and humility, an open mind, and a receptive heart.

Dreams and Active Imagination. As you sincerely begin working beneath the surface, be prepared to dream. Your *dreams* are another way to face the shadow. They are also windows to the soul that can reveal much about your current condition and your ongoing journey to wholeness.

The sources of our dreams are often the hidden forces within us seeking conscious attention to satisfy our needs for healing, self-acceptance, actualization, transcendence, and integration. To ignore our dreams is to neglect our internal call for care, development, resolution, reconciliation, and transformation. Such neglect can bring severe consequences that might be difficult to bear.

Although dream analysis is certainly not a science, there are many excellent resources for helping us interpret our dreams. A qualified dream analyst or therapist, for example, can be of great value. In our dreams, the personal shadow usually appears in the form of others of the same sex as ourselves, and the soul image in the form of the opposite sex. With respect to the shadow, I quote from William Miller:

> When shadow appears in our dreams, it appears as a figure of the same sex as ourselves. In the dream we react to it in fear, dislike, or disgust, or as we would react to someone inferior to ourselves—a lesser kind of being. In the dream we often want to avoid it, frequently sensing that it is in pursuit of us, when it may or may not be. Shadow may also appear as an indistinguishable form we intuitively fear and want to escape.[18]

I have analyzed many of my own dreams, particularly those that have affected me, stuck with me, or recurred over time. These dreams have had a powerful transformational effect on my life. One dream in particular occurred at a time when I was just beginning to face my own shadow. In this dream a large, angry-looking man was alone in a park watching with a scowl as I engaged in fun and innocent recreation with a close, childlike friend. The man, irritated at the good time my friend and I were having together, began to hurl steel-encased razor blades at us, wounding my friend in the arm. As the angry man continued to throw more razor blades at us, we ran. I escaped injury and helped my childlike friend to a nearby medical center. The male administrator at the center was not wearing a shirt. He had a youthful torso and was busy talking on several telephones, too busy to attend to my friend. We then left to seek other help.

The first step of my dream analysis involved amplifying each significant dream image through association and then diagraming my spontaneous associations for each dream symbol. In this dream, I initially identified ten significant dream images: the park, my childlike friend, "fun recreation," the angry man, the steel-encased razor blades, my wounded friend, running to escape harm and get help, the medical center, the youthful administrator, and leaving to seek other help.

My associations for the park included a playground, a safe and fun place, freedom, nature, recreation, childhood, and family togetherness. I associated these feelings, impressions, words, and ideas with a park. My childlike friend conjured images of friendship, trust, closeness, intimacy, reunion, love, innocence, and being with myself. The image of "fun recreation" brought to mind thoughts of playfulness, relatedness, light, freedom, joy, absence of worries, and being lost in our own world. The angry-looking man symbolized the words lonely, unhappy, menacing, anger, hatred, jealousy, and "wanting to stop us and hurt us," and his steel-encased razor blades seemed to be associated with words such as dangerous, lethal, sharp, and cutting. The sixth image, my wounded friend, I connected with the words hurt, weak, bleeding, sad, disabled, dying, dependence, and loss of strength, and I associated our running to escape harm and get help with emotions of fear, escape, worry, and avoiding harm. The medical center represented help, a safe place, refuge, a place to heal, salvation, and traditional "Band-Aid" solutions, while the administrator seemed to typify intellect but lack of wisdom, distractions but lack of care for important things, logic, efficiency, "the arm of flesh," and failure to observe. Finally, leaving to seek other help brought forth associations of disenchantment with current options, desperation, and the need for creative new solutions.

An essential part of this first step of analysis was to find associations that resonated with me, that affected me or hit home in some way. In my dream, the associations with the most energy were fun, freedom, togetherness, closeness, intimacy, being lost in my own world, loneliness, unhappiness, anger, hatred, jealousy, "wanting to stop us and hurt us," danger, cutting, hurt, bleeding, disability, escaping harm, getting help, finding a safe place, salvation, traditional solutions, "the arm of flesh," efficiency, failure to observe, and disenchantment with current options.

The second step in my dream work involved connecting each dream image to an inner part of myself. To do this, I needed to go back to each dream image and ask, "What part of me is this?" This is perhaps the most difficult part of dream analysis. I had just begun the process of healing my wounds and reconnecting with my true Self—the part of me that was free, innocent, spontaneous, and full of light. Some authors refer to this part of the Self as the "inner child." I felt joy at this reunion and was losing myself in it, unaware that another part of me was being neglected. This, I soon realized, was my shadow, my inferior personality or alter-ego. I still had not come to terms with this part of my personality, which had many aspects that seemed ugly, menacing, and unacceptable to me. I found out later that I had rejected my anger, hatred, and jealousy—critical emotions that I needed to reclaim, integrate, and honor to be whole. My shadow was wounding my spirit, and my fear sent me to the masculine, rational, efficient, problem-solving part of me to be "taken care of." But it wasn't working.

The third step of my analysis involved interpretation. In my dream it had become apparent to me that my traditional, rational,

"Band-Aid" solutions and my patriarchal, religious, salvational beliefs were not enough. I needed to move to the next level of shadow work. I needed to face, experience, and embrace my shadow and learn to use my anger, hatred, and jealousy in a productive way as essential parts of my personality. I needed to enter the realm of the irrational to integrate the light with the darkness. I needed to return to the earth and befriend my demons. And I needed to realize that only my soul—my *anima*, including the feminine aspects of my psyche—could heal me

The fourth and final step in the process involved active imagination, in which I generated a dialogue with the large, angry-looking man from my dream. My dream analysis helped me immensely in the task of facing and embracing my shadow.

In addition to what I call "shadow dreams," such as the one I had, we also can experience "bigger" dreams that come from the deepest levels of the psyche, or collective unconscious, which are archetypal in nature. The collective unconscious affects our dreams differently. Because it is universal and impersonal in nature, the collective unconscious works in our dreams through symbols that have a somewhat mythological motif. These universal symbols go beyond personal experience, creating a transformational effect in the soul either through the revelation of evolving wholeness at the deepest level of the psyche, or through the representation of instinctual patterns and prescriptions of behavior or experience that lead to wholeness and transcendence. In dreams that include these symbols, we are not dealing with personal complexes, repressed emotions, or unresolved neuroses. Rather, we are dealing with archetypes that are common to the entire human race. These archetypes are the imprinted agenda of the soul that may function as harbingers, confirmations, or even prophetic calls to completion, or they may serve as records of our present condition or past experience. According to Anthony Stevens:

> There are archetypal figures (e.g., mother, child, father, God, wise men), archetypal events (e.g., birth, death, separation from parents, courting, marriage),

and archetypal objects (e.g., water, sun, moon, fish, predatory animals, snakes). Each is part of the total endowment granted us by evolution in order to equip us for life. Each finds expression in the psyche, in behavior, and in myths. Again writing figuratively, Jung summed it up: "The collective unconscious is an image of the world that has taken aeons to form. In this image certain features, the archetypes or dominants, have crystallized out in the course of time (and eternity). They are the ruling powers."[19]

These "ruling powers" reveal and connect us with the Self, or divine center within us. Whatever you do, welcome and attend to your dreams with an open mind and heart. They are the voice of the soul, calling you to your Self and to God. Take time to record your dreams and to reflect upon them, being careful not to be too literal. Although some dreams lend themselves to a literal interpretation, most are highly symbolic. If our minds favor literalism, then we should seek help from someone who might enlarge the possibilities of interpretation.[20] (See the endnote for more information on dream analysis and interpretation.)

Active imagination is a powerful process of self-discovery that enables us to consciously interact with the unconscious and get in relationship with our Self. As such, it is a vital part of working beneath the surface, considered by many analytical psychologists to be even more effective than dream analysis in facing and integrating the shadow.

Developed by Carl Jung, active imagination involves talking and interacting with the various shadow images that are influencing or even controlling our lives. On a deeper level, it connects us with the transpersonal realities that reveal our fate and enable us to care for our soul. Robert Johnson elaborates:

> This experience, to be sure, is symbolic. The images with whom we interact are symbols, and we encounter them on a symbolic plane of existence. But a magical principle is at work: When we experience the images, *we also directly experience the inner parts*

of ourselves that are clothed in the images. This is the
power of symbolic experience in the human psyche
when it is entered into consciously: Its intensity and its
effect on us is often as concrete as a physical experience would be. Its power to realign our attitudes,
teach us, and change us at deep levels is much greater
than that of external events that we may pass through
without noticing. . . .

In active imagination I am not so much "talking
to myself" as talking to one of my selves. It is in that
exchange between the ego and the various characters
who rise up from the unconscious and appear in my
imagination that I begin to know, and learn from, the
parts of myself I had never known before.[21]

According to Johnson, active imagination involves four steps:

1. Inviting the unconscious.
2. Dialoguing with and experiencing dream figures.
3. Adding the ethical element of values.
4. Making it concrete with physical ritual.[22]

Foundational to inner work, particularly dream work and
active imagination work, is an understanding that the human psyche
is made up of many parts. Our language affirms this understanding
at some level when we speak of one part of our self feeling one
way while another part feels another way: "Part of me wants X
and another part Y," or, "Part of me feels X, another Y, and yet
another Z." The differences and even conflict among these various
parts of us constitute the creative tension that becomes the crucible which promotes wholeness. Reconciling or integrating these
parts is the primary objective of inner work. It is also the basis of
personal integrity and empowerment.

One common way to invite the unconscious is to close your
eyes, clear your mind of distractions, and re-enter a past or recent
dream that has been unresolved. Perhaps there were images or
personalities in the dream that will come to mind. Another
approach is to quietly and patiently wait for some image to

appear. Still another approach is to personify a mood, obsession, emotion, feeling, impression, intuition, or stirring. Once an image appears in the mind's eye, invite interaction by asking it questions: "Who are you? What do you want? What do you have to say to me?" The dialogue begins. If the image does not respond, don't control it. Wait, listen, and if you feel like doing so, keep asking. "Please talk to me. I want to listen. I want to learn from you. I want to understand who you are and what you want."

Don't try to control the conversation. Relax. When the personality or image speaks, listen empathically. This induces intrapersonal healing and facilitates getting in relationship with oneself. Perhaps the imaginal personality will say nothing, but might instead reflect a mood, a feeling, or an emotion. Or perhaps the image will do something, communicate symbolically through action, or beckon you to go on a journey or to look. If you sense something the image is feeling, reflect it and ask for a confirmation. "I sense you're very sad; am I right?" If you don't understand, say so. "I don't understand. Please help me understand." As the dialogue commences, you might find yourself exchanging viewpoints, questioning for clarification or information, arguing, or simply responding. Be careful to record the dialogue as it occurs. The image will wait for you to write.

Part of this experience will involve the expression and understanding of what these imaginal parts of you want. "What do you want from me? How can I care for you?" As the images make their needs and wants known, or even request or demand your cooperation or action, you must add the ethical element of values and seek for a new alternative that is ethically acceptable to you. If what the image wants is not appropriate in its requested form you might choose to negotiate a way to fulfill the need. This stage of the process involves ethical evaluation, including debate, negotiation, and creative resolution.

Once a resolution or understanding has been reached, it is best to solemnize it with a token in the form of some ritual. Perhaps you have made a covenant with some neglected part of the shadow to better care for some need. Perhaps you have been enlightened by some realization that has changed or transformed you in some way. Perhaps your new understanding has resulted in a new commitment. Whatever the nature of the outcome, some physical ritual helps make it concrete. Such rituals are private and harmless to self and others. A commitment to stop accusing others, for example, might be solemnized and concretized by a ritual such as preparing a list of all accusations toward self and others, followed by an oath to banish them, a burning of the list, and a burial of the ashes. A ritual might be as simple as taking a walk, writing a contract and signing it, saying a prayer, or celebrating in some way.

My experience with this technique has been very fruitful. The following example of active imagination involves a dialogue I had with the angry-looking man in my dream, which was the fourth and final step of my dream analysis. I wanted to know who this lone, angry man was, why he hurt my friend, and what he wanted. My role in the dialogue is designated as "E" for ego. The angry man is referred to as "S" for shadow. The following is the actual transcript of the dialogue I had, followed by a description of the ritual I used to solemnize my commitment to myself. Try to identify all four steps of the process.

E: Who are you?

S: I am he who is never happy.

E: Why are you never happy?

S: I'm never what I seem to be.

E: Saintly?

S: Yes.

E: Why were you so angry with me and my friend?

S: I was not part of you. Your happiness tormented me and reminded me of what I don't have. I wanted you to go. I wanted to hurt you so you would hurt as I do.

E: What do you want from me?

S: I want peace.

E: Peace from what?

S: Peace from the constant reminders of what I'm not, and acceptance of who I am.

E: What else do you need?

S: I need to be loved. I need to be included in your life. I don't want to be alone as an outcast anymore.

E: Help me to know how to do this for you.

S: Invite me. Affirm my presence. Ask for my involvement in your decisions. I am your energy. Don't be afraid of me.

E: But I am afraid. I'm afraid I won't be able to control you and that you'll get me in trouble.

S: I'll only get you in trouble if you ignore me and treat me with disdain.

E: How do I involve you?

S: Ask me about my feelings. Don't provoke me.

E: How do I provoke you?

S: By silencing me and shaming me. When I speak to you, listen. Honor me, and I will honor you.

E: Like when I write in my journal about my preferences and feelings?

S: Yes. You honor me when you give me expression. Then I can listen. I am your shame. I am everything about you that you're ashamed of. I'm the ugly, unattractive part of you. And I will wound you as you have wounded me. Teach me to be useful. My energy will work for you for good.

E: What energy is that?

S: Anger, jealousy, hatred.

E: How can these work for me for good?

S: They are powerful forces of love. Use your anger to protect, your jealousy to possess yourself and others in truth, and your hatred to eschew evil. I will respond to light. I will comprehend the light. I am the fourth part of you. I will make you whole. Command me, and I will obey. Reject me, and I will wreak havoc in your life.

E: So I need to honor you by involving you, by asking what

you're feeling, by writing about you, by asking what you want, and by giving you wisdom and keeping you in the light of consciousness?

S: Yes. Talk to me. Don't ignore me. Don't shame me. Don't dismiss me. Include me. I'm not a monster. But sometimes I feel ugly, and then I strike out. Share me with others when it is wise. I am your passion.

E: Who did you wound?

S: That part of you who is my opposite. I wounded your innocence, your purity and righteousness. He cannot live without me. I will wound him if I'm ignored.

E: You said you were the fourth, but there were only two of us, and you were the third. Where is the third if you are the fourth?

S: The third is the connection between the first and the second. The first is the ego, the second is the Self, the third is the soul, and I'm the fourth.

E: Who was the administrator of the hospital?

S: The arm of the flesh. He cannot heal you. You are the healer. You look and find no one. [By "arm of the flesh" I understand that it is the rational, analytical, masculine part of me, which is of no healing value to me.]

E: And how will I heal myself?

S: By accepting me—not by running away from me. Come back to me, and I will help you heal your wounds and will wound you no more.

E: So I am healed by self-acceptance?

S: Yes. God has accepted me. Why won't you?

E: I will. Please help me.

After this experience I solemnized my commitment to myself with a ritual that set apart my wristwatch as a token of that commitment. My watch, which was my father's before he died, represents those parts of my father which are part of my personality and which I have disowned over the years. Most of my life I tried to avoid being like my father, and yet, of all my brothers, I am told that I am most like him. He has been symbolic of my shadow, and so his watch, which is now mine, was a most appropriate token. It is also 18-karat gold, which further affirms its appropriateness as my shadow, making it an item of great worth to me.

Through active imagination I have been able to connect, in a meaningful way, with moods, dream images, and neglected parts of my personality that required greater understanding or needed special attention. Before attempting active imagination work, I strongly suggest that you study the book *Inner Work* by Robert Johnson. This readable book provides detailed procedures, examples, and necessary cautions that need to be observed while doing this work.

Slips of the Tongue and Humor. Insight into the shadow can also come by observing our language or *slips of the tongue.* Reactive language such as "I can't," "I have to," "You make me . . . ," or "If only . . . ," and so forth, can reveal a shadow tendency to be a victim. Similarly, slips of the tongue can lead to invaluable sources of insight. Addressing someone with someone else's name is one example. In the film "Ordinary People," a suicidal son who is alienated from his mother is encouraged by his psychiatrist to ask for his mother's forgiveness. The son, wanting to say, "She will never forgive me," slips and says instead, "I can never forgive her." He catches himself, and the slip of the tongue becomes a source of great insight for the young man. We tend to laugh at certain slips of the tongue and pass over them without any thought or reflection. In doing so, however, we might miss valuable opportunities for insight.

Humor is another avenue of personal insight. What we laugh at can reveal much about our shadow side. Consciously, we might abhor racial prejudice, yet find ourselves laughing at Archie Bunker in "All in the Family." We might not approve of vulgarity, yet certain off-color jokes or remarks might make us laugh, even against our will. What can we learn from our sense of humor? Perhaps we can learn that we are capable of racial or religious bigotry, or that there is part of us that is, in fact, prejudiced, crude, or vulgar. Hard to face? Perhaps. Important to face? Undoubtedly. Why? For one reason: We can then stop unconsciously projecting our darkness onto others.

Reactive Episodes. Perhaps the most difficult way to face the contents of the shadow is through actual reactive episodes. When someone intentionally or inadvertently hits a "sore spot," or complex, and the complex takes over our consciousness, a transference takes place, and we regress back to our prior wounds. The person who triggers this transference becomes the person who wounded us initially. We fall out of relationship with ourselves and the other person and into a reactive trance, often saying and doing things we later regret. These episodes, though disrupting, can be a source of great insight and transformation. Sometimes our hidden agenda sets us up for such episodes to provide the impetus for greater learning and integration.[23]

Such a reactive episode once happened to me in an encounter at the airport. Earlier that day, for some reason I had deliberately delayed leaving home on time to catch a flight to Phoenix. I had looked at my watch, acknowledged that it was time to leave, and then ignored my better judgment. I then rushed to the airport with barely enough time, and, after being delayed at the security check due to a carry-on bag inspection, I arrived at the gate three minutes before my departure time. I checked in at the gate and was informed by the gate attendant that my first-class seat had been given away. The policy was clear, and I had known it in advance: I had to be at the gate at least ten minutes before departure in order to be sure I could keep my seat. Still, I protested, challenging the gate attendant to make an exception.

This behavior was uncharacteristic of me for three reasons: I knew it was my fault, I knew the policy, and it was a short flight. Normally, I never would have protested under such circumstances, but this time I chose to push it. The gate attendant stood her ground. I persisted. Finally, she dismissed me, insisting,

"That's our policy, and that's final." The moment she said this, I exploded. She had stepped on a "land mine," or rather a deep-seated complex. I made a scene, enlisting support from others nearby who were, inwardly, as "mad as hell" as I was at such airport abuses. I was angry and enraged. It was not a pretty sight.

It took me about half an hour to work through my anger, and several hours more to understand what happened. This unfortunate flight attendant had triggered one of my reactive complexes. When she had said, "That's our policy," in her tone and in her way, I had seen my father dismiss me in the same way with a disrespectful wave of the hand. I had heard the words: "No, and that's final!" come out of his mouth, not hers. She had, in that moment, become my unreasonable, authoritarian father. I had transferred my anger for my father to her. She had inadvertantly played the role of a good therapist, bringing me in touch with one of my wounds. Hopefully, her counter-reaction had been just as revealing to her. Of additional interest to me was how my hidden agenda had unconsciously set me up for this experience. Apparently, this part of my personal shadow required revelation through transference to be integrated.

Considering the Inconceivable: Clarifying the Shadow's Countervalues. In my workshops on personal empowerment, I ask participants to answer the following questions:

- What choices or actions are inconceivable to you? (To answer this question I ask them to complete the stem, "I could never . . ." with as many completions as possible.)
- Under what circumstances might the inconceivable become consciously conceivable to you?
- Identify a serious past or recent accusation or criticism that someone has made toward you, and then answer the following question: What character flaws associated with such an accusation or criticism are you unwilling or resistant to own or seriously consider?

Usually, the more answers we have for the first question and the more completions we have for "I could never . . . ," the larger and denser our shadow is; the shorter the list of answers we have for the second question, the larger our shadow is. Finally, the answers to question three are self-revealing, particularly if accompanied by an emotional conviction. Whatever we are adamantly unwilling to own is part of our nature.

The discussion of traditional values also provides an excellent springboard for facing the shadow. While teaching the virtuous side of traditional values, I often ask: "Aren't there situations that might justify the opposite value?" The value system of the ego is very different from the countervalues in the shadow that so often motivate our decisions without our awareness. Our one-sided emphasis on traditional values forces us to become hostile to those countervalues that are essential to our individuation, true effectiveness, and ethical behavior. Further, since integrity is a function of integration, the more integrated our values become, the more potential we have for integrity.

The ethical aspect of conscience embraces both traditional "ego" values and countervalues as *whole* ideals that are necessary, virtuous, and good when applied consciously, maturely, and wisely. The "dark" values of the shadow are complementary to the "light" values of the ego, not contradictory. Thus, we have honesty-dishonesty comprising a whole, as well as cooperation-dissent, obedience-disobedience, loyalty-disloyalty, mercy-ruthlessness, love-hate, peace-war, and so on. Wisdom dictates, "To everything there is a season, and a time to every purpose under the heaven."[24] There is great strength in flexibility when we take a stand for truth, instead of a set of one-sided values or virtues.

To clarify countervalues, it might be helpful to answer the following questions:

1. Under what circumstances might the following countervalues be ethically justifiable: harshness, disobedience, dissent, dishonesty, ruthlessness, disloyalty, jealousy, hatred, aggressiveness, contention, and so forth?

2. What might the consequences be in employing these countervalues?
3. How might such values be employed in good faith?
4. How might self-deception be involved and avoided in the
decision-making process?

Although we certainly should not seek artificial opportunities to apply countervalues, particularly when doing so would
hurt others, it might be wise to experience the ethical tension of
dealing with opposing values in situational exercises designed
for that purpose. "Ethical isometrics" is a powerful way to work
beneath the surface in developing ethical consciousness and
obtaining invaluable insights into our countervalue system. I will
discuss this concept later in this chapter under the heading of
collision of duty.

In our society we are conditioned to value and esteem only one
side of virtue. This conditioning creates a reinforcing loop wherein
the more one-sided we are, the better we feel about ourselves and
the more socially affirmed we are as being morally "good." Such
reinforcement, however, can limit the development of our ethical
conscience and personal effectiveness in dealing with complex
social and ethical issues. We also delude ourselves into believing
that our one-sidedness makes us *wholly* virtuous and good, which
is not so. Paradoxically, to employ only one side of virtue, when the
other side is called for, is to be less than virtuous.

Facing the shadow is the first great step in the process of personal wholeness and empowerment. With it comes increased
self-knowledge, self-awareness, and humility, without which
there can be no real progress, no lasting success, and no effectiveness in its truest sense.

However, facing our shadow is not enough. We must also
experience it, embrace it (without identifying with it), and subject it appropriately to consciousness and to our conscience.
Finally, we need to learn to care for and reconcile ourselves
internally, with others, and with God, for all acts of wrong-

doing that remain unresolved in our lives. All this encompasses what I have been referring to as "working beneath the surface" and getting "in relationship" with Self.

Step Two: Experiencing the Shadow

Jolande Jacobi informs us, "The concept of integration [individuation] involves more than a mere [conceptual] knowledge of the shadow's qualities. . . . For, 'a content can be integrated only when its double aspect has become conscious and when it is grasped not merely intellectually, but understood according to its feeling value.' "[25]

It is not enough merely to acknowledge our weaknesses or shadow qualities intellectually. In fact, such intellectualizing can be a subtle form of denial. There is, rather, a "feeling value" that needs to be experienced to make it real. When someone has been rude or offensive to one of my children and I envision or *feel* myself angrily punishing that person, whether physically or verbally, I am experiencing my shadow. When someone is disrespectful to me and I *feel* like retaliating in an angry rage, I am experiencing my shadow. When I *feel* like putting someone down, I am experiencing my shadow.

Essentially, to truly own our shadow we must experience it internally and acknowledge our dark feelings, thoughts, urges, and impulses for what they are. To repress, deny, or explain away such feelings is to live a lie and to forego the opportunity to integrate the shadow and benefit from it. One way to experience the shadow is to listen and observe ourselves *in silence*. Quiet meditation can be very helpful here. Our souls have much to say if we will listen without judgment or response.

In experiencing the shadow, we must not identify with it or give ourselves license to act out our feelings, to misbehave, or to act irresponsibly or without conscience. Rather, we must give ourselves the opportunity to observe, understand, and care for ourselves toward greater health, wholeness, and relatedness with others. Additionally, through feeling the internal workings of our complexes and destructive shadow forces, we can more easily engage the conscience as the primary evaluative function, rather than the ego, which determines what is right or wrong from a self-centered viewpoint. In this way, we develop what Jung refers to as an "imagination for evil." Without such an imagination, "Evil has us in its grip," and we are powerless to beat the devil at his own game. We are also less able to make truly ethical decisions and resist temptation.[26]

Step Three: Embracing the Shadow

Embracing the shadow is about loving ourselves, not self-indulgence. Imagine finding a neglected child locked in a dark closet of an abandoned house. As you open the closet door and see the gaunt, deranged, and ghostly child, you are startled, repulsed, and frightened. You bring the child into the light, and, after the initial shock wears off, compassion sets in. Imagine now that this child is you. What then? That's simple, we might say. Perhaps. Yet, according to Jung:

> Simple things are always the most difficult. In actual life it requires the greatest art to be simple, and so acceptance of oneself is the essence of the moral problem and the acid test of one's whole outlook on life. That I feed the beggar, that I forgive an insult, that I love my enemy in the name of Christ—all these are undoubtedly great virtues. What I do unto the least of my brethren, that I do unto Christ.
>
> But what if I should discover that the least amongst them all, the poorest of all beggars, the most impudent of all offenders, yea, the very fiend himself—that these are within me, and that I myself stand in need of the alms of my own kindness, that I myself am the enemy who must be loved—what then? Then, as a rule, the whole truth of Christianity is reversed: There is then no more talk of love and long-suffering; we say to the brother within us, "Raca," and condemn and rage against ourselves. We hide him from the world; we deny ever having met this least among

the lowly in ourselves, and had it been God himself who drew near to us in this despicable form, we should have denied him a thousand times before a single cock had crowed.[27]

We need to experience the soul to truly understand it, learn from it, and love it. Genuine wisdom, compassion, concern, and empathy, which are the basis of all loving and trusting relationships, extend from the intimate contact we have with our own soul—with our own history, feelings, wounds, dreams, values, and experiences. Cognitive understanding alone is not enough. Nor is knowing we are unconditionally loved by God or others. Deep, personal contact with ourselves and our history is essential.

We cannot obtain a meaningful understanding of ourselves without making an intimate contact with our history and our wounds—including the deeply programmed dynamics of our family system—as well as all else that lies in the shadow. Understanding through personal contact is essential to the transformational process. Humility, empathy, wisdom, and compassion deepen, and the more we know about ourselves, the more serviceable we become to others and to God, and the more intimate we are with ourselves and with forces that come from within.

As stated earlier, the shadow has great value. The forces of the shadow move us toward the realization of Self, even by derailment. We all reach a point in our lives when what worked before won't work anymore. We get stuck. The shadow helps us move forward if we listen to it and work with it. The shadow is not dangerous; only our attitude toward it is dangerous. If we are afraid of it—of ourselves—and do not acknowledge it, it will have power over us.

Getting Back to Our Roots. Perhaps the first and most productive place to start looking for understanding is in our family of origin. Here is where we were most vulnerable and most impressionable. Here is where we placed most of our Self and our personal power in the "long bag" of the unconscious. And here is where we inherited the collective shadow of the family system. Nowhere is the pull on the heart stronger than in the family. Nowhere, then, will the defenses of denial, reversal, rationalization, and selective inattention be stronger than in examining our family system and, in particular, our relationship with our parents or primary caregivers.

This is "sacred" and "secret" ground for many. Hidden in the shadow of our family system is rich soul "stuff," the stuff that makes us who we are and brings meaning and perspective to our lives, our work, and our relationships. We need to approach it with imagination, honesty, and compassion.

It is unfortunate that the good work of so many qualified family systems therapists and authors has been so misunderstood and criticized. Some revisionist psychologists suggest that working beneath the surface to acknowledge and heal the wounds of the past, inflicted in our family of origin, somehow extinguishes our unique individuality and makes us victims, content to abdicate our lives and life callings by blaming our parents. But this work is not about blaming parents or shifting personal responsibility for one's life to other people or circumstances. Those who characterize family systems work or the "recovery movement" in this way simply show their ignorance or fear of the process through their uninformed criticisms. The fact is, we all need to differentiate in order to return honorably to ourselves and to be whole. Such work is a fundamental call of the soul. I am continually amazed by how limited we all are by our family wounds and scripts, even if we have attained great success and respectability.

This point has been reinforced many times in my own life. Even when rereading this manuscript as I prepared to send it to my editor, I had occasional thoughts such as, "A Riskas would never write a book like this." My authorship became, in some strange sense, a betrayal of my family culture: "Riskases don't think this way or get involved in this kind of stuff." Occasionally, the shaming voice would speak, "Who do you think you are?"

My family is very patriarchal. We value family, friendship, love, power, and loyalty. To be esteemed, the men had to be tough, determined, strong-willed, decisive, dominant, courageous, and successful. All these qualities, to some degree, are part of me, and I can conform well to family expectations when I need to. But my work, my passion, my values, and my highest meaning and purpose in life are, to me, very "un-Riskas-like."

Granted, my parents and family played a significant role in preparing and shaping me for my work. Nevertheless, to find my work and to grow personally *through* it and *into* it, I have needed to "leave home." Now, after years of personal work beneath the surface, I am able to return home and love and accept my family for who they are—an essential part of me—without being critical or trying to change them or over-identify with them. Through all this, I have begun to understand the deeper significance of "honoring" my mother and father.

Leaving home is very difficult. It requires demystifying the family, particularly parents or primary caregivers. It requires ongoing shadow work and usually some form of original pain work in grieving childhood losses. My own work has been very painful, yet very rewarding. There has been a lot of crying over the years, with a lot of anger and sorrow as I have honestly faced myself and my family relationships—and I come from what might be termed a solid, intact family with a lot of love and affirmation! We all need to leave home, and it is hard for everyone. It might be more difficult for some than others, but it is always a heart-wrenching stage of maturation. Some of us never leave home; some start earlier than others, and some don't begin until they are well into the second half of their lives.

Occasionally, I meet "well-adjusted" individuals who come from healthy, loving, affirming families and who insist or imply that they are exempt from such work. What these good people are saying, in essence, is that they (and their families) are not human. The more we resist this work, the more we need it. I know; I resisted parts of it for years. I say again: As human beings, we all need to leave home in order to truly become whole and fulfill our destiny. As one friend aptly put it: "Everyone gets thrown out of the 'garden' at some point."

Many wonderful methods can help us embrace the shadow, leave home, and integrate our personality. This part of the individuation process helps us heal the wounds in our personality through understanding, accepting, and loving those parts of us that have lived in the darkness for so long. In doing so, we must be careful not to identify with the negative, antisocial parts of our personality or with their opposing virtues. To do so is to take a one-sided ego position that invites derailment, and even disaster. Instead, we need to embrace the shadow without ego attachment and subject it to the light of consciousness and conscience, allowing all of our power to serve and follow the truth of the self in its journey to wholeness.

One excellent exercise for both facing and embracing the shadow was adapted from the work of Hal Stone and Sidra Winkelman by John Bradshaw in his book, *Healing the Shame That Binds You*, which I include here, along with Bradshaw's concluding comments:

"Making Peace with All Your Villagers"

1. *Think of people you dislike* [these can be family members]. Rank them in order according to the intensity of your feelings, the number one person being the most reprehensible and the most worthy of contempt. Write a line or two under each person, specifically outlining the character and moral defects that repel you.

2. *Read over each name on your list.* Pause and reflect on the reprehensible aspects of that person. Be aware of your own feelings as you do this. Which one trait brings out your feeling of righteousness and goodness most intensely?

3. *Reduce the people to their one most reprehensible character trait.* For example, on my [Bradshaw] list are:

a. Joe Slunk, grandiose egomaniac.
b. Gwenella Farboduster, aggressive and rude.
c. Maximilian Quartz, hypocrite (pretends to help people, but does it for the money).
d. Farquahr Evenhouser, uses Christian facade to cover up phoniness.
e. Rothghar Pieopia, wimp who has no mind of his own.

4. *Each of these personality traits represents one of your disowned parts*—an energy pattern that you do not want to integrate into your life under any circumstances. You have now externalized a personality trait that you have disowned.

5. *Every disowned part has an opposite energy with which your Protector/Controller [i.e., ego] is identified.* It takes lots of energy to keep this part disowned. This explains the intense energy we feel about our enemies. Hal Stone compares this energy to a dam that has been built to stop the flow of this energy. Behind the dam is an accumulation of dirty water and all kinds of debris. It is important to integrate this energy and use it more creatively.

Ask yourself these questions about each person on your list: "How is this person my teacher? What can I learn by listening to this person?" This person whom you feel aversely toward can help you look at the parts of you that you are over-identified with.

On my list, Joe helps me see that I'm over-identified with being humble. In my case it is really more like appearing humble. Gwenella helps me see that I'm over-identified with people-pleasing. Maximilian helps me see that I'm over-identified with being a total helper without wanting anything in return. Such helping is inhuman. It's a product of toxic shame trying to be more than human. Farquahr helps me see that I'm over-identified with having to be a perfect Christian (which at times keeps me from being one at all), and Rothgahr helps me see that I'm over-identified with my "be strong" driver. Being strong is a way I try to be more than human—refusing to accept normal

human weakness. This is the way I reject my
healthy shame.

6. *As you go through your list, talk to the disowned
part directly.* Ask it what it thinks. Ask it how it
would change your life if you owned it. Let this
part talk to you. Listen to what it has to say. See the
world through its perspective. Feel any new energy
that it brings you. It's bound to be a source of new
ideas. Maybe it can offer new solutions to old
problems. "After all," Sidra Winkelman writes, "its
views have never been available before."

You may be surprised at the new energy you
receive from this exercise. You are bringing a part of
you out of hiding and secrecy. You are turning your
shadow into the light. You do not have to become
the disowned self. That would be doing the same
thing you did before—identifying with one part to
the exclusion of another. In this exercise you learn to
speak and listen to a shamed and disowned part of
you. By so doing, you free up an energy that has
been bound in shame."[28]

So the person, for example, who despises her "neediness"
might discover that her needs have been shamed, that she can't
feel okay about herself if she feels need. She compensates by
over-identifying with being independent and self-sufficient. Her
neediness degrades to frustration, cynicism, and resentment as
she picks up the victim role and becomes either a "loner," "care-
taker," "people pleaser," or "martyr." By facing and accepting
her neediness, she can learn how to ask for what she needs or
reach out for help without feeling weak and vulnerable. She is
not defined by her needs, but her needs are part of her. Only
when she neglects her needs does she become "needy." This is an
example of some of the powerful insights that can come when
we strive to "make peace with all our villagers."

This part of the integration process also involves understanding the basis of our reactivity. Three questions help us do

this: (1) How do we typically react to or control others? (2) What triggers such reactive or controlling behavior? (3) Why are we affected by such triggers?

A simple way to answer the first question is to list the various reactive behaviors that you commonly use to control others. Which ones fit you best? Perhaps you tend to please, flatter, ignore, avoid, withdraw, give the silent treatment, become a martyr, pout, criticize, use sarcasm, interrogate, demand, insist, beg, nag, complain, murmur, whine, threaten, issue ultimatums, label, shame, rebel, patronize, intellectualize, moralize, preach, become dogmatic, yell, go into a rage, attack, and so on.

Our favorite control strategies are usually triggered whenever we take offense, get defensive, or in some way feel threatened by or disappointed in another person. So the next question is: What typically offends you, makes you defensive, disappoints you, or makes you feel threatened? Much of your list can come from memory and feedback from others, and some items on the list will be added in the future as new situations arise.

One way to identify your triggers, if you are not sure exactly what triggers your reactive behaviors, is through sentence completion work. For each of the following sentence stems, write 10 to 12 completions. Don't censor your responses. Take each one separately. Write down whatever comes into your mind:

- I am at my worst at work when . . .
- I am at my worst at home when . . .
- Generally speaking, I am at my worst when . . .

Your responses represent those things that tick you off, set you off, put you off, or turn you off. After you complete this exercise, review your sentences and place a checkmark by the ones you personally identify with. The ones you mark indicate that you have some awareness of these triggers and how they work. The ones you did not check are perhaps triggers of which you have little or no awareness. These are deeper in the "long bag" of the unconsciousness.

The third question in this exercise explores the deeper roots of our reactivity—the emotionally charged memories or complexes that often become the lenses through which we interpret reality. Why do these triggers affect you the way they do? The general answers that apply to all of humanity must be personalized through intimate contact with our own psychic history if we are to be healed and become whole, well-rounded, and truly serviceable to others. To answer this question, we need to understand our family patterns and characteristics, as well as the emotional, intellectual, spiritual, physical, social, or sexual abuse that wounded us. This takes us back to our family system and early childhood experiences.

Discovering the truth about our family system can provide powerful insights and perspectives while helping us differentiate ourselves from our family systems and deal with our reactive natures in the proper context. The ways to do this work range from interviewing extended family members to performing assisted family systems work under the guidance of qualified counselors or therapists.

Step Four: Bringing the Darkness to the Light

Finally, we need to find ways to effectively deal with these triggers of our reactive behavior—ways that acknowledge the shadow and defuse our tendency to pick up the "victim" or "rescuer" roles. Dealing with these triggers helps keep us out of reactive cycles and in relationship with ourselves and others, and is the next phase of the integration process which, like the previous phases, continues on throughout our lives.

Returning to the "Star Wars" saga, we reconsider how Luke Skywalker failed in his encounter in the cave in "The Empire Strikes Back." He failed by seeking to destroy his shadow instead of experiencing it, embracing it, and consciously working with it. He drew his weapon first. He was afraid and repulsed by Darth Vader, the father from whom he came, the unconsciousness from which he—his conscious self—emerged. He went into the cave split, or polarized, and came out essentially the same as he went in. He had faced his darkness but hadn't integrated it. Vader seems to have defeated Luke by the end of the movie.

At the end of "Return of the Jedi," the third movie in the trilogy, Luke confronts Vader in a final encounter, knowing now that Vader is his father and, therefore, a significant part of him. (Again, my apologies to those who have not seen the movie.) In a burst of rage, Luke makes a valiant attempt to destroy Vader in order to protect his sister, Leia, who represents Luke's innocence and goodness. Evil looks on, personified by the Emperor.

Just as Luke is about to prevail over Vader, he realizes what he is doing and stops. He realizes he is giving in to evil and is about to destroy an essential part of himself. He withdraws his weapon, faces the evil that is within him, and refuses to destroy Vader or give himself over to the dark side. He now stands unarmed and independent before Vader and the Emperor, in the midst of the raging emotions warring within his soul.

At this point, the transcendent act of integration takes place in Luke. Placing himself—his ego-ideal—fully on the altar of sacrifice, Luke redeems his shadow. Here, the mythological hero enters the redemptive myth as Luke sacrifices his innocence, righteousness, and purity to save his soul from the one-sidedness that will damn his quest for wholeness. This act can be motivated only by love and compassion. Luke has embraced his shadow and is now drawing it into the light through love and sacrifice. Vader responds, but is unsure how to react.

In the meantime, the Emperor himself unleashes a brutal barrage of electrical torture calculated to destroy Luke. As Vader witnesses the suffering of his son, the goodness in him is brought to light—the light that shined all along in the darkness, but was not comprehended. In the very moment the Emperor is about to finish his murder of Luke, Vader embraces the light and the goodness within himself, and destroys the evil Emperor. The shadow, Vader, is now purified by Luke's love and acceptance, completely unmasked in the light and finally united with the ego,

Luke. Father and son, the unconscious and conscious aspects of the Self, are integrated. Luke assimilates the shadow and leaves a "jedi knight"—a whole, individuated person.

By not working with our shadow, we abandon ourselves. Self-abandonment includes punishing ourselves for our reactivity, as well as suppressing or denying whatever goes on inside of us that we, or others, don't like. Instead, we need to experience, embrace, and deal with our shadow compassionately and consciously, subjecting it to the values of our conscience as we strive to stay in relationship with ourself and others.

Not long ago, after an enjoyable week's vacation with my family, I paid the price for not acknowledging and working with my shadow. Unfortunately, so did my family. I had spent the week exercising all my pleasantness, trying to make sure we all had a good time. We spent the week with my brother and his family, who are very dear to me. There were times during the week when I experienced various "calls from the soul" to attend to my needs and feelings. I noticed how my brother's children seemed better behaved than ours, how he and his wife seemed more "on top of things" and more composed, and how his family seemed more organized and harmonious than mine. I knew logically that such comparisons were not valid or "healthy," and this, of course, made me feel worse. Somewhere in my unconscious I was making these observations. The shadow includes family dynamics, and my reactions had a lot to do with my family system and the roles my brother and I had played in it. The roots of my reactivity went way back.

As the week passed by, I had focused on being positive and had ignored the stirrings of the shadow. Feelings of inferiority, and then moral superiority, filled my breast. I felt waves of anger toward my brother, his wife, and their children, and also toward Annette and our children. I didn't take the time to work with the darkness. Instead, I willfully forced myself to be nice, affirming, pleasant, and loving. But the more I ignored my shadow, the harder it was to be positive.

Finally, the week was over. On the way back home, all hell broke loose. In the middle of a conversation with Annette, T. J. interrupted. I severely accused, chastised, and wounded him. Then Annette came to T. J.'s rescue and corrected me. Normally, I would acknowledge my reactivity and correct myself. But this time I didn't; the beast emerged. I verbally attacked Annette viciously. Then I attempted to apologize to T. J. and wound up attacking him again. The shadow was out—and it was ugly. I had not taken the time to listen to my soul's complaint and work with myself, and now I—and the rest of my family—was paying the price. Ironically, the topic of my conversation with Annette when all this happened was the importance of acknowledging the shadow.

So, how can we acknowledge the shadow and care for ourselves when negative shadow forces begin to stir? One of the most effective ways I have found in doing this is through internal dialogue. Whenever we become aware of feeling impelled (or compelled) to act or feel anxious, fearful, angry, threatened, defensive, offended, or overwhelmed by emotion, we can keep the shadow in check by asking our "reactive" self to answer the following questions:

- What are you feeling right now?
  Answer by labeling the feeling.
- How are you seeing this?
  Our feelings come from our judgments and assumptions. Tell your story.
- Why are you seeing it this way?
  Identify the memories this experience evokes to get back to the complex that is shaping your perception.
- What are some other ways to see it?
  Use your imagination to generate other options.
- What information are you missing to make a more accurate judgment?
- What are you inclined to do, and what might happen if you do it?
  Visualize reacting the way you normally do and picture the consequences vividly in your mind. Check your feelings, then ask:

- Is this what you want?
  What don't you want? What do you want?
- What's the right thing to do?
  —in expressing your feelings?
  —in resolving this issue?
  —in satisfying your needs?
  As you answer this question, visualize your feelings again
  and ask, "Is this the way I would want to be treated?"

With these questions, we hold the tension of competing values while succumbing to neither, and we ethically interact with our shadow by engaging the "feeling function" of the psyche. The feeling function is, according to Jungian analyst John Sanford: "Our inner means of ascertaining the value of something. [It] tells us what is desirable and not desirable, but it's not an ego judgment." He continues:

> The ego determines what's good and bad from the
> point of view of its own concerns: That which tends
> to support our egocentric defense system is what we
> deem to be good; that which is antithetical to it, we
> deem to be evil. When the Puritans infected the Native
> Americans with diseases that killed them, the Puritans
> saw it as a good thing and preached sermons about
> how God was paving the way for them to settle the
> land. Of course, the Indians who were dying of small-
> pox would have had a very different judgment of the
> good and evil in the situation.
>
> The feeling function is free of egocentric contam-
> ination. It is a pure feeling evaluation, but it's not
> always heard. The fact that the American public even-
> tually turned against the Vietnam War was due to the
> rise of the feeling function—an increasing number of
> people came to a *feeling* judgment that the war was
> wrong and terrible, even if it supposedly served our
> political aims. And of course they were right.
>
> The value judgment of the feeling function is a
> reliable determiner of the good and evil in a situa-
> tion—*provided that it has the right information.* If it

doesn't have all the information, or sees only a part of the whole situation, the feeling function is perfectly capable of arriving at an erroneous conclusion.[29]

This, of course, speaks to both the value and the limitation of conscience. Without exercising the "feeling function" *with the right information*, the conscience is limited and easily can be mistaken, even if accompanied by conviction.[30]

As we have learned, the strengths that make us successful make us most vulnerable to failure or difficulty in our relationships, unless we recognize the shadow qualities of our strengths and deal with them effectively. The following exercise will help you do so:

1. List the character and personality strengths that you feel have contributed to your success over the years. Next to each strength, identify the shadow qualities (i.e., the "flip side of the coin").
2. List the stressful situations at work or at home that tend to trigger a reactive response.
3. For each of the situations listed in number 2, identify the personal strengths you employ in such situations and the related, or corresponding, negative shadow qualities that emerge or become evident as you cope with the situation.
4. Finally, for each situation, determine how you might ethically deal with the situation in a way that would effectively use your strengths while avoiding shadow extremes.

This exercise can help bring the darkness to light. It also can help you exercise your imagination in visualizing new ways to respond *in strength* and stay conscious, thus avoiding dark extremes.

Finally, we can integrate the shadow and experience deep, spiritual healing through reexperiencing and grieving the past. Such grief work is about healing the wounds that caused the formation of our reactive complexes. It involves what Swiss psychotherapist J. Konrad Stettbacher refers to as a "healing confrontation" with our past, and defuses those complexes that put us out of relationship with ourselves and others. The subject of "grief work" is presented in more depth in Chapter Six.

The Problem of Conscience and Collision of Duty. In working with the hidden agenda, the problem of conscience shows itself at an even deeper level, sometimes creating a conflict between our conscience and the moral code. In all our relationships, at home and in the workplace, we are faced with "collisions of duty" as we struggle to decide between competing goods, or between doing what we are told and what we believe is right or feel we need to do. According to Aniela Jaffé:

> Because of this psychological complication, a man's ethical attitude is an indispensable precondition of any confrontation with the shadow. But even for the ethical personality, or perhaps for it in particular, there are difficult or tragic situations in life when, against all reason and will, and in defiance of consciousness, conscience sides with the shadow, the inferior personality, and questions the value of conforming to the moral code. In situations like this, the unity of the personality falls apart. Instead of a wholehearted affirmation of the generally accepted tradition, an individual conflict supervenes with all its suffering. We get, as Jung puts it, into a collision of duties. Obligation is pitted against obligation, will against will.[31]

For example, in the workplace a manager is given a directive by her boss to fire someone whom she feels should not be fired. She tries to persuade her boss to change his mind or find another alternative, but he is adamant. In another example, an employee has committed to his young daughter that he will be home on Saturday to attend her birthday party. In past years he has missed her parties because of last-minute work requirements. This year the coast is clear. But, on Friday afternoon, his boss informs him that he needs to work on Saturday. The employee explains his situation, but to no avail. He is told either to show up on Saturday or not bother showing up again. These are just two minor examples of collision of duty.

Sometimes we can experience the feeling value of such colli-sions of duty by placing ourselves in extreme, hypothetical situ-ations, referred to earlier as "ethical isometrics." Below are two such situations excerpted from Gregory Stock's *Book of Questions*. In answering these questions, engage your full imag-ination and deal with the word "would" instead of "should." Your answers can be very revealing, even if imagining is not the same as experiencing.

- A cave-in occurs while you and a stranger are in a concrete room, deep in a mine shaft. Before the phone goes dead, you learn the entire mine is sealed and the air hole being drilled will not reach you for another 30 hours. If you both take sleeping pills from the medicine chest, the oxygen will last for only 20 hours. Both of you can't survive; alone, one of you might. After you both realize this, the stranger takes several sleeping pills, says that it is in God's hands, and falls asleep. You have a pistol; what would you do?
- If you could prevent either an earthquake in Peru that would kill 40,000 people, a crash at your local airport that would kill 200 people, or an automobile accident that would kill a loved one of yours, which would you choose?[32]

In the motion picture "Fail Safe," the President of the United States is faced with a monumental decision. A computer error has resulted in an order to drop a nuclear bomb on Moscow. The command is irreversible. After numerous unsuccessful attempts to stop the pilot from completing his mission, the President is faced with the dilemma of preserving world peace in the face of such a disastrous accident. His obligation to the world is pitted against his obligation to his own people. From the dark and deep regions of the shadow, he makes the most dif-ficult ethical decision of his life. He orders that a nuclear bomb be dropped on New York City after the destruction of Moscow is confirmed. He knows that millions of Americans will be killed, including his own wife who is visiting the city on that fateful day.

Certainly, life has taught us that such "collisions of duty" do not necessarily lend themselves to established mores, pat formulas, "timeless principles," or traditional thinking. Even the "feelings" or convictions of moral conscience are not always reliable; we might, in times of great ethical demand, recoil from doing what we sense at a deeper level is right. Here, the shadow becomes a two-edged sword that must be wielded consciously, carefully, and with all the wisdom we can obtain. With respect to conscience, it becomes important under such circumstances to acknowledge the difference between its moral and ethical aspects. According to Jung:

> "Conscience," in ordinary usage, means the consciousness of a factor, which in the case of a "good conscience" affirms that a decision or an act accords with morality and, if it does not, condemns it as "immoral." This view, deriving as it does from the *mores*, from what is customary, can properly be called "moral."
>
> Distinct from this is the ethical form of conscience, which appears when two decisions or ways of acting, both affirmed to be moral and therefore regarded as "duties," collide with one another. In these cases, not foreseen by the moral code because they are mostly very individual, a judgment is required which cannot properly be called "moral," or in accord with custom. Here, the decision has no custom at its disposal on which it could rely. The deciding factor appears to be something else: It proceeds not from the traditional moral code, but from the unconscious foundation of the personality. The decision is drawn from dark and deep waters.
>
> It is true these conflicts of duty are solved very often and very conveniently by a decision in accordance with custom, that is, by suppressing one of the opposites. But this is not always so. If one is sufficiently conscientious, the conflict is endured to the end, and a creative solution emerges which . . . pos-

sesses that compelling authority not unjustly characterized as the voice of God.[33]

Hearkening to the ethical conscience in resolving collisions of
duty requires what Andrew Samuels refers to as "moral imagination." The moral imagination transcends original morality and, in
a sense, fulfills the law. It requires consciousness, wisdom, maturity, and a deep appreciation for the countervalues of the soul.[34]

Exercising the moral imagination wholeheartedly is, no
doubt, characteristic of individuals who are both psychologically
and spiritually mature, and thus empowered to meet the challenges and opportunities of these complex, demanding times.
Such individuals realize that in certain, very difficult situations—
or even in response to the call of their own soul—their primary
commitment to the truth within might require obedience to a
higher law, making imperative that which was once inconceivable,
or perhaps even forbidden, by the moral code. As with shadow
work, so it is with ethical decision making: In order to rise
above, we must be willing to descend below.

Attending to the Needs of the Soul

The final dimension of working beneath the surface
addressed in this chapter is attending to the needs of the soul.
Taking time to care for ourselves does much more than improve
productivity; it also enables us to listen to the voice of our soul.

The voice of the soul is the voice of need. Our need to be
fully alive—to love and be loved, to learn and grow, to create
and fulfill our destiny—is at the heart of our hidden agenda for
wholeness. Shadow work helps empower us to attend to our
needs and fulfill our hidden agenda. Soul work attends to our
needs. This level of inner work puts us in deeper relationship
with our Self and others, reconciling and unifying the opposing
masculine and feminine aspects of our personality toward ultimate wholeness, fulfillment, and joy.[35] If the voice of the soul is
the voice of need, it is also the voice of neglect.

Understanding this, we need to depart from our regimented obsession with curing the personality and being rescued, or "saved," from our "false self," and return to the art of caring for the soul. According to Thomas Moore:

> The great malady of the twentieth century, implicated in all of our troubles and affecting us individually and socially, is "loss of soul." When the soul is neglected, it doesn't just go away; it appears symptomatically in obsessions, addictions, violence, and loss of meaning. Our temptation is to isolate these symptoms or to try to eradicate them one by one; but the root problem is that we have lost our wisdom about the soul, even our interest in it. . . . The emotional complaints of our time . . . include:
>
>> Emptiness
>> Meaninglessness
>> Vague depression
>> Disillusionment about marriage, family, and relationships
>> A loss of values
>> Yearning for personal fulfillment
>> A hunger for spirituality
>
> All of these symptoms reflect a loss of soul and let us know what the soul craves. We yearn excessively for entertainment, power, intimacy, sexual fulfillment, and material things, and we think we can find these things if we discover the right relationship or job, the right church or therapy. But without soul, whatever we find will be unsatisfying, for what we truly long for is the soul in each of these areas. Lacking that soulfulness, we attempt to gather these alluring satisfactions to us in great masses, thinking apparently that quantity will make up for lack of quality.[36]

In *Care of the Soul,* Thomas Moore proposes "a therapeutic way of life that is not a self-improvement project." Such a way of life includes:

- Learning to listen deeply to and honor the soul's hidden agenda without fear, shame, or negative judgment. This requires self-awareness and imagination.
- Learning to appropriately and effectively nurture and care for ourselves by consciously and conscientiously attending to our needs.[37]

In living this "therapeutic way of life," I propose the ongoing consideration of three questions:

1. *What conditions (physical, emotional, or spiritual) am I experiencing right now that concern or distract me?*

These conditions might be symptoms of self-neglect, as well as the natural expression of the soul's needs and evolution. They are not necessarily negative; they are simply part of life. Instead of denying these symptoms or eradicating them, seek to honor the soul by patiently and compassionately observing how the soul expresses itself to you. Some examples of such expressions might be: lack of energy, laziness, moodiness, irritability, impatience, restlessness, desire, anxiety, frustration, worry, obsessiveness, hostility, anger, boastfulness, defensiveness, guilt, sorrow, sadness, suspicion, jealousy, fear of being alone, loneliness, emptiness, sickness, disillusionment, hunger for spirituality, crisis in faith, emotional sensitivity, numbness, and so forth.

While telling the story of my own soulful pursuit of vocation in one of my seminars, a man in the front row began to cry. When his crying progressed to sobbing and he could not contain himself, he left and returned to his hotel room, where he began to write out what was going on inside of him. Later, after he returned, he shared his experience. My own story had resonated with his soul's complaint of "playing it safe" and his yearning for fulfillment. He had neglected his calling and was now paying a dear price.

2. What is my soul trying to communicate through these symptoms or conditions?

Using the technique of active imagination, try to enter into a dialogue with the symptom you are experiencing. Don't be concerned with "shoulds," but rather listen to your unconscious mind, and then consider the various possibilities. Personify the symptom. Then ask it who it is and what it needs or wants. Seek to understand what your soul is trying to tell you and what you can learn about your needs from the conditions you're experiencing. Finally, be an advocate for the need. In support of this approach, Thomas Moore writes:

> One effective "trick" in caring for the soul is to look with special attention and openness at what the individual rejects, and then to speak favorably for the rejected element. . . . We all tend to divide experiences into two parts, usually the good and the bad. But there may be all kinds of suspicious things going on in this splitting. We may simply have never considered the value in certain things that we reject. Or, by branding certain experiences negative, we may be protecting ourselves from some unknown fears. We are all filled with biases and ideas that have snuck into us without our knowing it. Much soul can be lost in such splitting, so that care of the soul can go a long way simply by recovering some of this material that has been cut off.[38]

The powerful forces of the soul are made dark by our neglect and self-disdain. We make the darkness productive by infusing it with light, not by suppressing, denying, or shaming it through moralizing. Returning to the discussion about my family vacation, you will recall that my first inclination was to label my comparisons of my brother's family with mine as wrong, or "unhealthy." To be more "perfect," I attempted to rid myself of these thoughts and negative emotions. When I finally acknowledged my shadow and listened to my soul's complaint, I discovered the meaning of these symptoms and how I had been abandoning myself during the week. This opened the way to new insight and care in dealing with these hidden wounds.

3. How can I best respond to the call or complaint of my soul?

Again, consult the symptom and imagine better ways to nurture and care for yourself. Remember, caring is not merely *curing*, and the objective here is not to "fix it," but rather to explore ways you can appropriately meet your needs. Sometimes what we need is not obvious or desirable, and may even seem grievous. For example, guilt, sorrow, and anxiety might need to be fully experienced—without interference—to correct a course and establish greater integrity of soul. Or, in order to assist the soul in its quest for greater consciousness, we might need to go against our natural inclinations and hold patiently the tension between competing wants.

Finally, be prepared to conceive the inconceivable, for the heart has reasons the mind cannot always understand. This may require the courageous reexamination of your values with the intent to do what is right for you, while honoring the welfare and needs of others. Throughout my life and in the lives of many others, many promptings of the soul have resulted in significant life changes.

Nearly twenty years ago, while driving home from work, I passed a local bank branch and suddenly found myself sitting in the branch manager's office asking for a loan to start a consulting practice. I had a fine job at the time, working as director of strategic planning with a hotel chain. For years, I had dreamt of one day being a self-employed consultant. Now, without any deliberation, I was applying for a loan. I didn't even have an account with this bank.

The branch manager, who later became a dear friend, was a man named Richard Bentley. He asked what I wanted the loan for. I told him I wanted to quit my job and start my consulting practice. He then asked a series of questions: Did I have any clients, any other sources of income, any assets other than my home, a forecast or plan? I answered "No" to each question. He asked how I planned to repay the loan. I told him that I would earn enough from clients—the clients I didn't have—to repay the loan.

Richard finally looked at me and, with incredulousness in his voice, said, "Mr. Riskas, with all due respect, there is no way I can lend you any money if you quit your job and start a consulting practice." I told him I understood and assured him that I really believed I could repay the loan. He nodded, and I got up, shook his hand, and turned to leave.

As I was about to walk out of his office, he stopped me. As I looked at him, tears filled his eyes. His entire countenance had changed. He said, "I have no idea why, but I'm going to give you the loan." This was the story I told in the seminar that stirred another man to tears. I am constantly reminded of our need for aliveness and meaning in life, and such vitality can be found as we respond faithfully to the promptings and callings of the soul. Even if we fail, we can celebrate the experience.

In caring for ourselves we reach for greater wholeness and integrity and a more meaningful, enriching life. This is not a project, but a process that, in addition to responding to the call of the soul, honors the sacredness of everyday life. Somehow, we instinctively know what we need, if we are willing to listen with a sincere heart and real intent.

For example, we need to avoid toxic substances and excess. We need physical exercise, recreation, adequate rest, and good nutrition. We need to exercise our intellect and imagination. We need to be touched and enjoy the company of family and friends. We need to be spiritually nourished by nature, prayer, reflection, service, and worship. We need to respond to the call of fate. We need to be out in nature, work with our hands, create, attend to the "routine," hold babies, play with children, and care for pets. These are some of the things that nourish, strengthen, and enable us to live a full, rich life with meaning. We find such sacredness only when we descend from the lofty heights of worldly or spiritual ambition into the rich simplicity of daily life and true relatedness.

Aside from our personal lives, it isn't difficult to see how these three questions might be useful to the mature leader in caring for the soul of an organization. With only slight modification, these questions become the basis of conscious observation and inquiry that gradually shifts the emphasis from cure to care. Such a shift affects the very nature of human interaction, promotes increased community consciousness (and therefore responsibility), and results in the flourishing of imagination, creativity, and productivity.

This work is often stifled by excessive regimentation in our lives. Regimentation is the result of our tendency to organize complexity, chaos, and risk out of our lives and our organizations. This is the dark side of our need for order, safety, and structure, which robs the soul of vitality, spontaneity, creativity, and spiritual growth.

Recently I visited the prison of Alcatraz with my family. As I toured the prison grounds, studied the rules and regulations of inmates, and learned of the "life of a prisoner," a sad darkness came over me. I wondered how people could be rehabilitated when their souls suffocated under the inhuman regimentation of prison life. My mind then turned to organizational life as I considered the increasing regimentation of church, state, and enterprise. Excessive rules, regulations, policies, procedures, and laws of every kind lead not only to the "death of common sense," as Philip Howard suggests, but to the death of the soul as well.[39]

Polarized leaders, extolling the virtues of control, order, and safety, create one-sided concentration camps occupied by automatons who no longer exercise sound judgment or experience the richness of life. Our fears have crippled and deluded us into believing that, through regimentation, we can become invulnerable to suffering and that such invulnerability preserves life and is good. It is not. I echo the sentiments of Harry Williams, that "to be invulnerable [or safe] is not to be immortal. It is only to be dead."

The soul's answers to the haunting questions that reflect its malaise—which includes a lack of passion, commitment, and accountability—can be found in a paradox. The revelation we need is not more rules (or interpretations of rules), but the higher vision of eternal purpose, individual destiny, and the call of fate, along with a deep understanding of how opposites come together as one and, in their unity, reveal the higher truths that simultaneously release the spirit and ground the soul. This higher vision and understanding will lead to a *mindful obedience*, not the blind obedience that kills the soul.

As we mature, we ultimately shed the scales of "shoulds" and "thou shalts," and respond ethically to our own needs and the needs of others, moving to a wholeness and fulness of life and its potential. We faithfully respond to our callings in life as we consult the moral law that has been written on the tablets of the heart, and then apply this law consciously, creatively, and with wisdom. We then learn from our experience—and from the knowledge and wisdom of others—and thereby educate our conscience to a higher level. This is the way of "mindful" obedience.

For all of us engaged in the quest for wholeness, this means that chaos, diversity, uniqueness, dissent, risk, inaction, mistakes, and failure are valued as much as their counterparts. The ability to integrate such opposites into a "compound in one" is the essence of inspired, enlightened living and leadership. We need to trust in a higher order that embraces divergent, individual journeys as well as the "straight and narrow path," which provides ultimate safety through the mindful obedience that honors necessary risk taking, and which embraces ethical disobedience as a way to divine morality and constructive dissent as a way to greater commitment and unity. We must see things differently, more truthfully. And to do so, we need—as part of caring for the soul—to continually strive to clear the past and act responsibly, with integrity and wisdom. Such is the path of the true hero and the way to greater spiritual power.

Chapter Six

BEYOND HABITS . . .

Responding Honestly to Our Needs for Deep Spiritual Healing and Renewal

"There is an inextricable relationship between who we are inside, and how we behave with others around us. But unless we begin first with the tidying up inside each human being, we are deceiving ourselves. What is the good of drawing up rules of social behavior if we know in fact that our greed, cowardliness, ill temper, and self-conceit are going to prevent us from keeping them?"

—*C. S. Lewis*

"Do you so love the truth . . . that you welcome . . . the idea of an exposure of what in you is yet unknown to yourself?"

—*George MacDonald*

To be completely free from the lies we live and fully present in our relationships, we need to clear the past. Clearing the past is ultimately about death and renewal. It's about bringing resolution or closure to the unfinished business in our lives that alienates us from ourselves, God, and others. It requires a special kind of confidence and humanness characterized by humility, meekness, and submissiveness.

Far from negative, stereotyped notions, humility, meekness, and submissiveness speak to a spiritual strength that relatively few possess. *Humility* is simply a correct understanding of our strengths and limitations, requiring us to descend into the world and embrace our humanity. It is a realistic sense of our humanity and a healthy dependence on God. *Meekness* is that state of self-possession characterized by patience, long-suffering, and the mastery of desires, appetites, and passions. It also means being teachable and faithfully holding the tension of conflicting needs and values until a higher perspective or solution emerges. As one prominent religious leader, Howard W. Hunter, once said:

> In a world too preoccupied with winning through intimidation and seeking to be number one, no large crowd is standing in line to buy books that call for mere meekness. But the meek shall inherit the earth, a pretty impressive corporate takeover—and done *without* intimidation.[1]

Submissiveness is the willingness to consciously and ethically subordinate our will for a greater good or truth—as we know it, or as it might be revealed. It is also a willingness to let go of our need for control and to respond wholeheartedly to the callings of the soul.

Without humility, we fall prey to the hubris of success and the dark extremes of our strengths. Without meekness, we become impatient, rush natural processes, and close ourselves off to essential learning. Without submissiveness, we become willful and controlling and, ironically, slaves to our own appetites and limitations. These qualities call for further work beyond the integration of the shadow—work which moves beyond psychic empowerment to spiritual empowerment.[2]

As we have discussed, shadow work humbles us, empowers us, and facilitates greater consciousness. Still, in order to clear the pathways of spiritual communication and access the Voice of Wisdom, we must be right inside and reconciled to Truth. Our conscience must be free from offense toward self and others. The "forgotten wedges" need to be removed. Guilt, resentment, fear, and despair need to be washed away.

Hidden Wedges

Samuel T. Whitman tells the story of a young farm boy who placed an iron faller's wedge between the limbs of a young walnut tree his father had planted. The boy left it there because he was late for dinner, intending to take the wedge to the shed after dinner. He never did. The years passed, and the young boy became an old man. The tree grew over the iron wedge. Then, in a particularly severe ice storm one winter, one of the three major limbs of the tree "split away from the trunk and crashed to the ground. . . . When the storm was over, not a twig of the once-proud tree remained." The old farmer went out the next day "to mourn his loss." Then, his eyes caught sight of something in the splintered ruins. "The wedge," he muttered reproachfully. The man realized that the forgotten wedge, left between the limbs of the young walnut tree years ago, "had prevented the limb fibers from knitting together as they should."[3]

Are there forgotten, hidden wedges in your life? Such would be our unresolved mistakes, acts of self-betrayal, offenses, and wrongdoing, as well as the wounds we received in our family of origin and throughout our lives. We all have them, but not all of us desire to remove them, or even admit they are there. Such work, however, must be done if we are to end our patterns of self-defeating behavior and live with dignity and peace. Remember: To rise above, we must descend below. This is a call to honesty and sacrifice that faces us all.

Clearing the past is deeply private and personal. It involves psychological and spiritual healing and reconciliation. Such healing and reconciliation cannot be accomplished cheaply or easily. I agree with Colorado journalist Marc Barasch, who wrote: "Spirituality, as repackaged for the new age, is a confection of love and light, purified of pilgrimage and penance, of defeat and descent, of harrowing and humility."[4]

In the workshops I teach, participants reflect deeply on their lives. In one part of the course, the participants begin to clarify their values and figure out what they really stand for and what is

most important to them. During one session, one of the participants approached me privately after class had ended. He related
how, during the values exercise, he came to understand how
much his wife truly meant to him. He was a big man, and I could
tell he did not have much experience dealing with his emotions.
He was self-conscious, but needed to talk. He went on to tell me
that after he had completed the assignment, he had called home.

"What did you say?" I asked.

"I told my wife I had realized that, throughout our marriage,
she had done all the giving and I had done all the taking, that I
had taken her for granted, and that she was the most important
person in my life."

I could sense the sacredness of the moment. I was standing
on hallowed ground. "What did she say?" I asked.

"There was a long pause," he said. "And then she asked, 'Is
this my husband?'" This big man's lips began to quiver, and
tears filled his eyes. By now, tears were in my eyes as well.

"What happened next?" I asked.

Then, he bowed his head and said simply, "I asked for her
forgiveness." This man didn't know it, but he was involved in
the sacred, healing work of clearing the past. This work requires
suffering—sometimes great suffering and anguish of soul.

Healing the Spirit

> "No man is condemned for anything he has done: He
> is condemned for continuing to do wrong. He is con-
> demned for not coming out of the darkness, for not
> coming to the light."
>
> —*George MacDonald*

Healing the wounds in the spirit caused by wrongdoing
involves six essential steps:

1. Recognize our selfishness, the pride of our self-righteousness and one-sidedness, and our acts of wrongdoing.

This requires the humility to acknowledge our fears, laziness, insecurities, and pride, as well as the honesty to see them as triggering our selfish behaviors. Such behaviors include deliberately doing things that are wrong, not doing what we know is right, or not responding with integrity to the demands of the soul to love others. Other behaviors might include: shaming others, taking advantage of others, wrongfully judging others, accusing or gossiping about others, and not forgiving others. They also include more serious moral transgressions such as unethical or selfish acts that cause harm to ourselves and others.

We commit wrongdoings in countless ways. We know we have much clean-up work to do because of our feelings and self-protective behaviors, especially once we become familiar with the shadow. If we take an honest, moral inventory of ourselves and our relationships, we will find sensitive or painful memories that need to be attended to. Such sensitive memories include the many faces of pride, as well as wrongdoing, offenses, transgressions, and sins—terms that certainly are neither comfortable nor popular in today's "politically correct" society, but which are more relevant than ever before.

According to the late O. Hobart Mowrer, past president of the American Psychological Association, the connection between sin and mental and spiritual illness merits thoughtful consideration:

> In our time, two seemingly unrelated things have happened: On the one hand, mental illness has defied our best efforts to understand and control it; and, on the other hand, we have developed a widespread distrust of moral law and principle. Only recently, within the last few years, have we come to realize that there may be a very vital and important connection here. Some of us now suspect hidden guilt as being the central problem in all psychopathology. Integrity and integration, we

note, come from the same root, and it now appears that we cannot have one without the other. Cheating and chiseling erode character as they devitalize society. . . .

Traditionally, sin has been thought of as whatever causes one to go to Hell; and since Hell, as a place of otherworldly retribution and torment, has conveniently dropped out of most religious as well as secular thought, the concept of sin might indeed seem antiquated and absurd. But . . . Hell is still very much with us in those states of mind and being which we call neurosis and psychosis; and I have come increasingly, at least in my own mind, to identify anything that carries us toward these forms of perdition as sin. Irresponsibility, wrongdoing, immorality, sin: What do the terms matter if we can thus understand more accurately the nature of psychopathology and gain greater practical control over its ramified forms and manifestations? . . .

What is generally overlooked here, it seems, is that recovery (constructive change, redemption) is most assuredly attained, not by helping a person reject and rise above his sins, but by helping him accept them. This is the paradox which we have not at all understood and which is the very crux of the problem. Just so long as a person lives under the shadow of real, unacknowledged, and unexpiated guilt, he *cannot* (if he has any character at all) "accept himself"; and all our efforts to reassure and accept him will avail nothing. He will continue to hate himself and to suffer the inevitable consequences of self-hatred. But the moment he (with or without "assistance") begins to accept his guilt and his sinfulness, the possibility of radical reformation opens up; and with this, the individual may legitimately, though not without pain and effort, pass from deep, pervasive self-rejection and self-torture to a new freedom, of self-respect and peace.[5]

When we truly recognize our acts of wrongdoing, we will naturally feel remorse, sadness, and regret. These are signs that the cleansing and healing process has begun.

2. *Admit our acts of wrongdoing.*

Confession, in some form, is essential to the healing process. The notion of accountability justifies the need for us to admit our wrongdoings. We are naturally accountable to those we love and are truly committed to. Admission of wrongdoing is also an act of embracing truth, which frees us from the bondage of alienation and pride. It helps restore a healthy sense of shame, or humility, and brings the healing sorrow and contrition to the surface.

Whenever we hurt someone, whether we do it intentionally or inadvertently, admitting our wrongdoing to the person is an essential part of clearing the past. In addition, admitting our wrongdoings to God, if it is done sincerely and with a real desire to turn away from wrongdoing and change our errant course, is a humbling experience that promotes inner healing.

3. *Sincerely apologize for the wrongs we have done.*

Whenever our wrongdoings affect others, we can feel a great healing power by expressing a heartfelt apology to those we have wronged, and they, in turn, can also be healed from their wounds. Genuine apologies come from the heart and bear the imprint of true sorrow and contrition. There are no strings attached to genuine apologies—even if they are not accepted. They remain tokens of true reconciliation.

Sincere apologies free the soul and enable both parties to heal. Knowing this, why is it so hard to apologize? In a word, pride. Our fear of shame and appearing weak or vulnerable invariably gets in our way as we attempt to clear the past. This is particularly true whenever we have intended to do wrong or hurt others in the past. In actuality, sincere apologies are acts of honesty and signs of character strength and courage. The story of my father in Chapter Four is a perfect example of the power of a sincere apology.

4. Make direct amends, whenever possible, to those we have harmed.

Although sincere apologies can do much to repair the damage done to others' feelings, they still might not be enough. Additional work may be required to repair the breach and to restore trust and inner peace. Sometimes such reparations involve a literal restoration of what was stolen, lost, or destroyed. For example, a damaged car can be paid for and restored, as can a broken window. Damaging another person's character through gossip, accusation, or public embarrassment can be repaired, at least in part, by a public retraction. However, some damage can be difficult, if not impossible, to restore. For instance, how can we restore the loss of a child killed by reckless driving? In such cases, any attempt at restoration must be indirect: Dedicating our time and resources to prevent such losses to others would be an example. In any case, it is important to understand the real "message of our guilt," which is that "we must take steps to rectify the damage we have created, insofar as this is reasonably possible."[6]

5. Commit to a life of greater integrity.

If the recognition and admission of wrongdoing are sincere, and the subsequent apology and restitution are honest and complete, then such contrition will result in a change of heart that will involve forsaking hurtful, dishonest behaviors and making a deep commitment to greater integrity. Integrity is not merely acting according to our beliefs. Integrity means: (1) making good-faith efforts to consciously discern right from wrong, and then pursuing the right solutions or courses of action, (2) acting according to our convictions in good conscience, and (3) accepting full responsibility for all consequences that come as a result of such efforts and convictions.

To act with integrity on a consistent basis requires ongoing inner work and the suffering that comes with honest self-examination. It also requires that we exercise great faith, and that we apply our faculties of reason, reflection, and discernment. A commitment to integrity results in an attitude of obedience to the highest laws of our conscience. Such obedience is an honest, affirmative, conscious, and conscientious response made in relation to our core values and commitments.

When we are true to ourselves we are obedient, or submissive, to the truth that is in us. Such obedience—which I previously referred to as "mindful obedience"—is not merely following the rules or blindly doing what one is told, expected, or counseled to do. This highest form of integrity might entail the ethical disobedience or nonconformity to a lower law to obey a higher law or ethical imperative. To do so requires great moral courage. It involves collision of duty and is the stuff of which true commitment to integrity is made. In this regard, it is important to keep in mind that integrity has nothing to do with the correctness of decisions. One can act with integrity and still be mistaken.

As painful and difficult as it can be at times to achieve and maintain personal integrity, it is one of the greatest fruits that comes from truly clearing the past and undergoing a change of heart. One crucial aspect of integrity that is often overlooked involves following our destiny when we are called by the Voice of Fate. Not to do so is certainly a wrong committed against the Self. Regarding such callings, Jung writes:

> What is it, in the end, that induces a man to go his own way to rise out of unconscious identity with the mass as out of a swathing mist? . . . It is what is commonly called vocation: an irrational factor that destines a man to emancipate himself from the herd and from its well-worn paths. . . .Vocation acts like a law of God from which there is no escape. . . . Anyone with a vocation hears the voice of the inner man: He is called, . . . [and] unless one accepts one's fate . . . there is no individuation; one remains a mere accident, a mortal nothing.[7]

Admittedly, such "following," or responding to fate, has its risks. Integrity at this level, though essential to our wholeness, can be dangerous. Again from Jung:

> When one follows the path of individuation, when one lives one's own life, one must take mistakes into the bargain; life would not be complete without them. There is no guarantee—not for a single moment—that we will not fall into error or stumble into deadly peril. We may think there is a safe road. But that would be the road of death. Then nothing happens any longer— at any rate, not the right things. Anyone who takes the safe road is as good as dead.[8]

Finally, the commitment to a life of greater integrity will require the peaceable fruit of forgiveness, which necessarily brings with it the call to forgive. This requirement is the sixth and last step in this ongoing process.

6. Forgive ourselves and those who have offended us.

For many people, this is the most difficult step. Yet we need to understand that if we refuse to forgive others, we commit a grave offense, even worse than the one committed against us. Our blame and condemnation trigger their blame and condemnation, and distract them from looking inward and accepting personal responsibility. It blocks the healing process and can lead to increased resentment. To forgive does not mean to excuse from wrongdoing or to release from consequences. Nor does it necessarily require the restoration of trust. Forgiveness is the release of condemnation through compassion. When we forgive, we promote healing and reconciliation.

As with step five, this step requires a change of heart. While I believe there is much we can do to prepare ourselves to forgive others, ultimately we need help—divine help. To get such help we must humble ourselves and be willing to give up the "victim role." We cannot forgive ourselves or others as long as we see ourselves as victims or as shameful, degraded human beings. We are fallible and wounded, but not depraved. As long as we remain victims, we will continue to accuse ourselves and others. Accusation breeds resentment and blocks the power to forgive.

In one of my seminars, a participant shared with me in private a deep bitterness she felt toward her husband, who had abandoned her and her children for another woman. She said she had been praying for years, to no avail, for the ability to forgive him. As we talked, it became evident to both of us that she was still in the victim role, horribilizing her ex-husband and accusing him in her heart. She said she had "gotten over most of it," but the hidden wedge was still there. She was unable to forgive, in part, because she was not willing to let go of the victim role.

One excellent exercise to help facilitate forgiveness is "The Love Letter Technique" designed by John Gray. This exercise allows you to experience and express your feelings toward emotional healing and the resolution of emotional conflict, within yourself and in your relationships:

> To write a *Love Letter*, begin by expressing the first level of emotion, and then allow yourself to move through the other levels until you get down to the love. The lead-in phrases are intended to help get you started in one level and facilitate transition to the next.

1. Anger and Blame

I don't like it when . . .
I resent . . .
I hate it when . . .
I'm fed up with . . .
I want . . .

2. Hurt and Sadness

I feel sad when . . .
I feel hurt because . . .
I feel awful because . . .
I feel disappointed because . . .
I want . . .

3. Fear and Insecurity
I feel afraid . . .
I'm afraid that . . .
I feel scared because . . .
I want . . .

4. Guilt and Responsibility
I'm sorry that . . .
I'm sorry for . . .
Please forgive me for . . .
I didn't mean to . . .
I wish . . .

5. Love, Forgiveness, Understanding, and Desire
I love you because . . .
I love it when . . .
Thank you for . . .
I understand that . . .
I forgive you for . . .
I want . . .[9]

Clearly, some affronts are easier to forgive than others. We must be careful not to assume we have cleared the past simply because it doesn't bother us anymore. Time alone does not heal such wounds. Often, we confuse the absence of negative emotion and active "stewing," or resentment, as resolution. Even if we never see the offender again, unresolved resentment will likely transfer to someone else later, or transform itself into some other form of negative energy, such as cynicism and bitterness. Harboring resentment—even if it is inactive—will canker the soul.

The inability to forgive others goes beyond a failure to understand certain principles. For example, we can understand and agree with the principle that others cannot hurt us without our permission, and yet be unable to pull ourselves out of the victim role. The same holds true for our inability to forgive ourselves: We might understand and agree with the truth that we're only human, that "to err is human," yet be unable to stop punishing ourselves for our failings.

Our inability to forgive can be attributed in part to a faulty understanding of how to clear the past. Instead of faithfully applying ourselves to the first five steps, we attempt either to let "bygones be bygones" and "forget it," or to "cope with our guilt . . . by stoically enduring . . . self-blame and depression in the hope that a time will come when the weight of [our] suffering will finally cancel out the gravity of our misdeeds."[10] This, of course, speaks to the second cause of our inability to forgive, which is related to the wounded, unintegrated personality. Both the presence and persistence of the "victim" and "martyr" are indicators of a wounded personality.

The Wounded "Fisher King"

The legendary Fisher King, leader of the Grail castle, has been severely wounded, and his entire kingdom suffers with him. The myth tells us that the Fisher King is wounded in the thigh (just like, in the Bible, Jacob was wounded in the thigh while wrestling an angel). This wound impairs the King's capacities to create and relate, as well as his ability to feel love, appreciate beauty, or experience joy. Wounded people are driven with an insatiable appetite for external power, status, validation, acceptance, recognition, and control. These external "fixes" are often pursued to ease the suffering of wounds that most people are not even aware of.

The wound in the Fisher King's thigh is the existential wounding that every person suffers to some degree. Such are the wounds of our humanity—the psychic wounds that disempower us, making our faith and talents far less productive than they could be. (See the diagram of the five existential wounds of the soul and the corresponding discussion in Chapter Two.)

Our wounds give birth to our reactive complexes and fears. If we do not consciously seek to face, heal, and overcome our fears, our complexes will continue to get the best of us.

To be human is to be wounded. We are wounded so we can grow and live abundantly by being more serviceable to others and to God. Some people are more wounded than others. Many great individuals have been deeply and extensively wounded and then healed of their wounds. Their healed wounds give birth to greater compassion, consciousness, wisdom, maturity, and spirituality. Healing is painful. It requires the inner work of integration ("shadow work") and the cleansing work of reconciliation. It also requires some form of "grief work," or mourning our losses.

According to legend, "The court fool had prophesied long ago that the Fisher King would be healed when a wholly innocent fool arrived in the court and asked a specific question."[11] The "wholly innocent fool," on a psychological level, is the lost child of the soul who is to be seen and not heard. Likewise, according to biblical wisdom, "Whosoever therefore will humble himself as this little child, the same is greatest in the kingdom of heaven."[12] The "greatest" are those who are whole, complete, and healed.

We must return to the child within to be emotionally healed. And when we do, the healing question is asked: "How is it that I suffer so?" Beyond this, on a spiritual level, the "wholly innocent fool" is He who was willingly humiliated and mortally wounded for all mankind, that those who come to Him might be saved—spiritually healed and strengthened. From Him comes the question: "To what end do you live and suffer?", followed by the invitation, "Come unto me, all ye that labor and are heavy laden, and I will give you rest."[13] As with the first question, so it is with the second: "To ask well is virtually to answer."[14] We can never find the answer or healing solution without first asking the right question. In "asking well" we invoke the revelation of meaning that enables us to face the painful truth, grieve the past, and be emotionally healed.

Healing the Personality

Grief work, or "original pain work," is a form of therapy that enables us to heal the childhood wounds received in our family of origin and early life experiences. It is another way to clear the past. According to Alice Miller:

> The achievement of freedom . . . is hardly possible
> without the felt mourning. This ability to mourn, i.e.,
> to give up the illusion of a happy childhood, can
> restore vitality and creativity. . . . If a person is able to
> experience that he was never loved as a child for what
> he was, but for his achievements, success, and good
> qualities . . . and that he sacrificed his childhood for
> this love, this will shake him very deeply.[15]

The objective of grief work and its counterpart, legitimate
suffering, is to restore a healthy sense of shame, or humility, and
establish the basis for genuine self-acceptance toward self-
renewal. Although there are many ways to do this work and
many ways in which it happens, any approach or therapy that
limits the process to mere conceptual insights will be insufficient.
I agree with Alice Miller on this point, when she says:

> Only the mourning for what he has missed, *missed at
> the critical time*, can lead to real healing. . . . Problems
> cannot be solved with *words*, but only through *expe-
> rience*, [and] not merely corrective experience as an
> adult, but . . . through a reliving of early fear (sadness,
> anger). . . . Mere words, however skilled, . . . will
> leave the split from which he suffers unchanged or
> even deepened.[16]

To be effective, grief work must evoke the painful memories
of past events so that we can see the truth, experience the emotions, confront and challenge the actions of others, set up our
boundaries, and articulate our needs. This can be done alone or
with an enlightened friend, counselor, or therapist. One
approach you can use blends the Gestalt "empty chair" technique with an expansion of J. Konrad Stettbacher's four-step
approach.[17] You will need a private room with two chairs facing
each other. Then, allow yourself plenty of time—at least an hour
or two—to work through each issue. Also, you may want to
have a box of tissues on hand and make sure that you won't be
interrupted.

Step one involves identifying triggering events that "set you off" and make you enraged, angry, sad, or afraid. These triggers are symptomatic of wounds incurred through incidents of personal abuse. The following list of triggering events contains examples of wounds that are typical of someone who has been subjected to authoritarian abuse through the application of the rules of "corrupt patriarchy." These wounds often occur during childhood and are frequently and predominantly inflicted by controlling parents. I believe such abuse is common to all families, religious institutions, and organizations in society today. Although this list is long, it is not complete. Use your imagination to place yourself in each event listed below. Place a check mark in front of each event that causes an intense negative reaction in you, or that you know, when you demonstrate such behavior, causes an intense reaction in others.

Triggering Events Related to Authoritarian Abuse

I generally have intense negative reactions when:

- People intrude into my life or space without being invited, and without any consideration for my feelings or preferences.
- I'm told I can't do what I want to do because of some rule or policy that is irrelevant or capricious.
- People are inflexible in enforcing rules or policies without reason or explanation.
- People dismiss me or my ideas, feelings, beliefs, or needs, without any attempt to understand or work with me.
- People stubbornly hold to their opinions while refusing to consider my views.
- People "cut me down," make fun of me, or make me feel stupid and inferior, especially in front of others.
- People treat my serious concerns lightly by making "smart" remarks or by making light of my concerns.
- My thoughts or beliefs are attacked, discounted, or rejected "out-of-hand" without respectful consideration.

- My demands or requirements are ignored or disregarded.
- People treat me in a condescending or patronizing way and don't take me or my ideas, beliefs, feelings, or needs seriously.
- I'm pushed out of the way by those who interrupt me or cut in front of me in line.
- People insist that I do things their way.
- People are rude, discourteous, or demeaning.
- People tell me what I believe, what I'm feeling, what I'm thinking, or what I really mean.

Clearly any of these events could upset most people to some degree, even if they had not been abused as children. Therefore, it's important to distinguish between an intense reaction related to some wound and what would be common emotions toward such behavior. In my experience, our reactions toward abuse tend to overwhelm our consciousness and cloud our reason. We lose control, go into a trance, and react, after which we eventually return to ourselves. We find ourselves in the grip of a reactive complex—or "demon"—that takes control. We might "go ballistic" and lash out at others, go into a deep depression, feel conflicted and irritable, turn cold, or become paralyzed with fear, and we often feel powerless to stop these emotions. Incidently, we know the offended soon become the offenders. That is, those of us who were abused as children will likely abuse our own children and others in turn. How often do we catch ourselves doing to our children exactly what our parents did to us?

To help you identify triggering events that are unique to you, make a list. What sets you off? Keep an ongoing inventory of these triggers as they occur over time. They're like "reruns" of the unpleasant episodes in your life's drama. They continue to recur until you confront your wounds and heal them.

Step two involves selecting one of your triggering events that has powerful emotional energy behind it and allowing your memory to produce an actual situation. This might be a recent situation, a nagging problem that has been bothering you lately, or a reactive episode from the past. After selecting the situation, you can proceed with the healing confrontation. Bring an outline of the remaining steps with you to a private room with two chairs.

Step three begins the confrontation. Sit in one of the chairs and imagine that the other person is sitting in the other chair facing you. Then, imagine that you are looking at the other person in the eyes while you express your complaint. Tell the person what bothers you and what's on your mind as you reexperience the situation. Say what you are noticing, seeing, and hearing. For example: "I noticed you were smirking and rolling your eyes when I was sharing my thoughts in the meeting today. Other people saw your reaction and laughed at me."

After telling the person what you noticed, saw, heard, or perceived, share your feelings. Tell the person how his or her behavior has affected you. Stay with these thoughts until you can reconnect with your feelings as much as possible. You must reexperience your feelings. For example: "I was humiliated and totally pissed off. I felt like slapping the smirk off your face and walking out the door!"

In *step four,* substitute the person in the empty chair with one of your parents. Now imagine that your parent is in the chair. Deliver the exact same message to your parent, modifying only the situational context to conform to home life or some other experience. For example: "Sometimes you make fun of me in front of my friends. You make fun of things I say or do and make others laugh at me. It makes me want to run away and hide. I hate you when you make fun of me." Again, stay with these thoughts until you fully reexperience the anger, hurt, and hatred. Yell, scream, or cry if you feel like it. Let it out. Keep it going. What else is on your mind? What else are you feeling?

Step five involves demanding an explanation and justification from the parent by questioning his or her behavior. This step is a natural extension of step four. Ask: "Why are you doing this to me? What have I done? Tell me." After asking these questions, sit in the parent's chair and respond as the parent. Tell the child in the empty chair why you, the parent, did what you did. As you change chairs you will experience a transformation. In fact, you will find that you answer as though you actually were the parent. For example: "I'll tell you why I made fun of you—so you would stop acting so stupid and so you wouldn't embarrass yourself or me."

Now, move back to the child's chair and respond. "So, all you cared about was not being embarrassed? You didn't care about me, about how I felt? How dare you! How can you call yourself a mother (or father)? You're pitiful. I hate you! I'm so mad I could scream!" Let your feelings go. Get it all out. Then, when you're composed, proceed to step six.

In *step six,* make demands of your parent in the empty chair. Tell your parent what you want and don't want: "I need you to . . ." or "From now on, I don't ever want you to . . . again." For example: "I need you to protect and respect my feelings. From now on, you can coach me privately, but I don't *ever* want you to correct me or embarrass me in front of others again."

In *step seven,* take your parent out of the empty chair and imagine yourself in the chair as the parent. Now you, as the child, will talk to yourself as the internalized parent. Imagine looking at yourself in the empty chair as the parent and making a connection with the parent within you. Make the *exact same* demands of your internalized parent. Say it with conviction until you feel it in your heart. For example: "I want you to support me when I make a mistake or do something embarrassing. Don't ever be critical of me, make fun of me, call me stupid or any other name, ever again."

Finally, in *step eight,* sit in the chair of your internalized parent. Imagine looking at yourself in the other chair as the hurting child and making a connection with the wounded child within you. Commit to meeting your child's demands with all your heart. Feel after the child and sense the child's pain. Tell the child how much you love him or her. Reflect on what your child has been feeling. Apologize and ask for forgiveness.

I have experienced remarkable results with this process in my own life. It can be painful and exhausting, but it can be extremely effective in helping us heal the wounds of the past. Keep in mind there is no way to change what happened to us as children, nor is it necessary or advisable to confront your actual parents. As I have said before, this is where many people go wrong in this work. Grief work is not about blaming or confronting our parents. It's about healing our wounds and moving toward greater self-acceptance and wholeness. It's about breaking the cycle of self-abuse and the chains of corrupt patriarchy that bind us. It's about developing and strengthening our personal boundaries and internal authority. These are just a few of the benefits we can expect if we do this work at the right level—within our souls.

Healing the Loss of Loved Ones

Just as words alone are insufficient in healing the childhood wounds of the past, so too are words inadequate for mourning the loss of loved ones. Part of clearing the past includes the grieving of all personal losses. I experienced this indescribable grief with the loss of my father.

An individual who participated in one of my personal empowerment workshops shared an experience he had in clearing the past with his deceased brother:

> As I closed my eyes, I immediately thought of my brother, who was killed in an automobile accident nine years ago when he was only 18 years old. Since his death, I have been very angry at him. Angry for quitting, angry for deserting, and most of all, angry for hurting me. At the time of his death, we were best friends. This anger, I came to find, had more to do with me than it did with him. The weight of this . . . was overwhelming. As [I learned] the process of forgiveness, I felt the weight of all the anger disappear.

It struck me that the "weight" was "overwhelming." What else was in the "long bag"? He continued:

> For the past nine years, I have been wallowing in the
> role of the "victim." I deserted my faith, my religion,
> and my God. I realize now that I personally came very
> close to destroying my [self] by compromising my val-
> ues and beliefs.

How many people carry such burdens in their hearts and try
to cope and forget? Unless we are assisted, comforted, and
supported in our efforts to integrate such losses through the
necessary mourning and clearing the past, we cannot gain
strength from our experiences. Instead, we lose essential energy
and power that affect all parts of our life. For many, an active
faith in God, immortality, and the eternal continuation of family
relationships provides such needed perspective and comfort.

Much has been written on the various approaches to wholeness,
happiness, and psychological or spiritual well-being. This chapter,
along with the previous chapter, has presented some thoughts and
processes that are hardly original, yet very effective. I am convinced,
particularly, that clearing the past requires faith in God and divine
assistance, both of which are essential to the healing process.

Although some of the concepts and terminology I have
referred to have a religious connotation, it would be a grave error
to restrict their relevance to merely a "religious" domain.[18] To
quote Mowrer again: "Just so long as a person lives under the
shadow of real unacknowledged and unexpiated guilt he *cannot*
(if he has any character at all) 'accept himself'; and all our efforts
to reassure and accept him will avail nothing. He will continue to
hate himself and to suffer the inevitable consequences of self-
hatred."[19] This condition, which often affects us beneath the
surface of awareness, can undermine mental and physical health,
emotional stability, trust, commitment, and personal productivity.

The Mystery of Personal Renewal

In considering all of this, it's important not to lose sight of
the profound mystery that surrounds personal transformation.
Who can tell what may motivate a person to give up the past and

seek new life? In writing of Milton Erickson's imaginative approach to psychotherapy, John Bradshaw tells "The Story of Joe," which illustrates the mystery of personal change to which I refer. I was deeply impressed when I read this story. In providing some necessary background on "Joe," Bradshaw writes:

> There once was a boy named Joe, who at the age of 12 was expelled from school because of vandalism, incorrigible behavior, and brutality to other children. Joe had also tried to set his father's house and barn on fire and had stabbed all the animals on his father's farm with a pitchfork.
>
> His parents took Joe to court and had him committed to an industrial school for boys. At age 15, Joe was paroled, and on the way home, he committed some burglaries and was promptly returned to the industrial school, where he stayed until he was 21. The official records state that he was extremely violent and was kept in solitary confinement most of the time.
>
> At age 21, he was discharged with a suit and $10, and he headed for Milwaukee. He was soon arrested for burglary and was sent to the young men's reformatory in Green Bay. Again, the records show that he was aggressive and violent, and that he was kept in solitary confinement. The guards were so afraid of him that whenever he was allowed to go to the exercise yard, two guards accompanied him. When he was released, he went into the town of Green Bay and committed some more burglaries. The police picked him up, and he was sentenced to the state prison.
>
> The records at the state prison show that Joe beat up fellow convicts and spent most of his time in the dungeon. The dungeon was eight feet by eight feet, soundproof, and lightproof. The thick, heavy wooden door had a small slot at its base, through which, once a day, usually at 1:00 or 2:00 a.m., a tray of food was slipped. He completed every day of this sentence, was released, and went into the town and committed some more burglaries. He was arrested and sentenced to a second term in the state prison. He spent every day of

this sentence either in solitary confinement or in the darkness and silence of the dungeon.

Upon his release he returned to a village in Wisconsin. Milton Erickson lived nearby and was about ten years old at the time. Joe had been around for about four days. Milton was sent to town on an errand. He met some of his classmates, who told him "Joe is back!"[20]

Erickson picks up the story from here, stating, according to Bradshaw, "There was suspicion that Joe had already stolen some goods." Erickson continues:

> Now it happened that there was a farmer about three miles from the village, a farmer who had three hundred acres of company land. He was a very rich man, [and] had beautiful buildings. And to work three hundred acres it required a hired man. . . . His daughter, Susie, . . . was about five feet ten, and she could work alongside any man in the community. She could pitch hay, plow fields, help with the butchering, . . . any task she could handle.
>
> The entire community felt bad about Susie: She was a good-looking girl; she was famous for her housekeeping, her dressmaking, and her cooking; and she was an old maid at twenty-three years. And that should not be. Everybody thought Susie was too choosy.
>
> On that particular day, when I went to the village on an errand, Susie's father's hired hand quit because of a death in the family and said he would not be back. . . . Susie's father sent her into the village on an errand. Susie arrived, tied up the horse and buggy, and came walking down the street. . . . Joe stood up and blocked her pathway and . . . looked her up and down very thoroughly, quietly, . . . and Susie, with equal poise, looked him up and down very thoroughly. Finally, Joe said, "Can I take you to the dance next Friday?"
>
> Now the village always had a weekly dance on Friday nights for all the young people. . . . Susie was very much in demand at those dances, and she regu-

larly drove in and attended the dance. And when Joe said, "Can I take you to the dance next Friday?" Susie said coolly, "You can if you're a gentleman." Joe stepped out of her way. She performed her errand and went back. . . . The next morning the merchants were very glad to find boxes full of stolen goods at their front doors, . . . and Joe was seen walking down the highway toward Susie's father's farm.

Word soon got around that [Joe] had asked Susie's father for the job of hired hand, and he was hired and made a magnificent wage of $15 per month. He was allowed to have his meals in the kitchen with the family. . . . Susie's father said, "We'll fix a room for you in the barn." (In Wisconsin when the temperatures are down at 34 degrees below zero you really need a well-insulated room in the barn.)

Joe turned out to be the best hired hand that community had ever seen. Joe worked from sunup to long past sundown, seven days a week. Joe was six-foot-three, a very able-bodied man, . . .

Joe always walked to the village on Friday night to attend the dance. Susie drove in to attend the dance. And, much to the ire of the other young men, Susie usually danced with Joe every dance. Joe's size made them wary of pointing out to Joe the error of his way by appropriating Susie.

In just about a year the community was buzzing with gossip because Susie and Joe were seen going out Saturday evening for a drive, or "sparking," as the term was used. And there was even more gossip the next day—on Sunday—[when] Susie and Joe went to church together. And thereafter, [after] some months of this, Susie and Joe were married. . . . Joe moved from the barn into the house. He was still the best hired man imaginable, and Joe and his father-in-law, with some aid [from] Susie, ran the farm. . . . Joe was such a good worker that when a neighbor got sick, Joe was the first one to show up to help with the chores. And they soon forgot all about Joe's history of being an ex-convict. . . .

Eventually Susie's parents died, and Susie inherited the farm. Joe and Susie had no children, but Joe had no trouble getting hired men. He went to the state reformatory for young men and asked for any young, promising ex-convict from the reformatory. The reformatory was for first-time offenders. Some of those men lasted a day, a week, a month, and some for months. As long as they worked, Joe kept them around and treated them well, and he served to rehabilitate quite a number of ex-convicts. When I got my job as state psychologist for Wisconsin to examine all inmates in penal and correctional institutions, Joe was very happy for me.[21]

Bradshaw asks, "So what happened to change Joe?" What motivated this "incredible transformation" that had taken place in the life of this "seemingly incorrigible, chronic, and habitual criminal?" Erickson comments:

All the psychotherapy Joe received was "You can if you're a gentleman." He didn't need psychoanalysis for several years. He didn't need Carl Rogers' indirect psychotherapy. He didn't need five years of Gestalt therapy. All he needed was a simple statement: "You can if you're a gentleman." Psychotherapy has to occur within the patient; everything has to be done by the patient, and the patient has to have a motivation. And so when I became interested in psychiatry, Joe's history had a very strong influence on me.[22]

Finally, Bradshaw concludes:

The story of Joe speaks to my sense of the mystery of love. Our love for another can heal our broken lives. Joe's did. And no one knows exactly how or why. Pascal told us that "the heart has its reasons that reason cannot fathom." When we truly love, we are willing to change, and we do often change. We lose weight, start exercising, forgive our enemies, accept others, love ourselves, feel alive, believe that life is worthwhile. Eric Berne, the founder of a mode of therapy called

Transactional Analysis, termed love "nature's psychotherapy." I believe that love can dramatically heal our wounds and radically change our lives.[23]

Joe's change was, perhaps, initially sparked by an invitation that appealed to his needs for love, esteem, and acceptance. Susie spoke to his soul and called him to himself.

The mystery of transformation is reenacted in the lives of countless people in many different ways. Anwar Sadat experienced it in the isolation of prison. Saul of Tarsus experienced it on the road to Damascus. Many others experience it in different degrees, at unexpected times, and in unexpected ways. In the following story, we see how schoolteacher Jean Thompson and one of her young students were miraculously transformed by a small gift wrapped in brown paper:

On the first day of school, Jean Thompson told her students, "Boys and girls, I love you all the same." Teachers lie. Little Teddy Stollard was a boy Jean Thompson did not like. He slouched in his chair, didn't pay attention; his mouth hung open in a stupor; his eyes were always unfocused; his clothes were mussed; his hair unkempt, and he smelled. He was an unattractive boy, and Jean Thompson didn't like him.

Teachers have records, and Jean Thompson had Teddy's. First grade: "Teddy's a good boy. He shows promise in his work and attitude. But he has a poor home situation." Second grade: "Teddy is a good boy. He does what he is told. But he is too serious. His mother is terminally ill." Third grade: "Teddy is falling behind in his work. He needs help. His mother died this year; his father shows no interest." Fourth grade: "Teddy is in deep waters; he is in need of psychiatric help. He is totally withdrawn."

Christmas came, and the boys and girls brought their presents and piled them on her desk. They were all in brightly colored paper except for Teddy's. His was wrapped in brown paper and held together with scotch tape. And on it, scribbled in crayon, were the words, "For Miss Thompson, from Teddy." She tore open the brown paper, and out fell a rhinestone bracelet with most of the stones missing and a bottle of cheap perfume that was almost empty. When the other boys and girls began to giggle, she had enough sense to put some of the perfume on her wrist, put on the bracelet, hold her wrist up to the children, and say, "Doesn't it smell lovely? Isn't the bracelet pretty?" and, taking their cue from the teacher, they all agreed.

At the end of the day, when all the children had left, Teddy lingered, came over to her desk, and said, "Miss Thompson, all day long, you smelled just like my mother. And the bracelet—that's her bracelet. It looks real nice on you, too. I'm really glad you like my presents." And when he left, she got down on her knees, buried her head in her chair, and begged God to forgive her.

The next day when the children came, she was a different teacher. She was a teacher with a heart. And she cared for all the children, but especially those who needed help—especially Teddy. She tutored him and put herself out for him.

By the end of the year, Teddy had caught up with a lot of the children and was even ahead of some. Several years later, Jean Thompson got this note:

Dear Miss Thompson:
I'm graduating, and I'm second in my high school class. I wanted you to be the first to know.
Love, Teddy
Four years later, she got another note:

Dear Miss Thompson:
I wanted you to be the first to know. The university has not been easy, but I like it.
Love, Teddy Stollard
Four years later, there was another note:

Dear Miss Thompson:
As of today, I am Theodore J. Stollard, M.D. How about that? I wanted you to be the first to know.

> I'm going to be married in July. I want you to come
> and sit where my mother would have sat, because
> you're the only family I have. Dad died last year.
>
> And she went and she sat where his mother
> should have sat because she deserved to be there.[24]

Both Jean and Teddy were somehow healed by small acts of
giving and kindness. Selfless service also changes lives, especially
when, as Mother Teresa so beautifully put it, we "go on loving
and loving and giving and giving until it hurts."

Another simple yet profound way that lives are changed for the
better involves the power of self-revelation, as we wholeheartedly
articulate who and what we are in response to others and to the
demands of life and work. Here is yet another mystery: Giving the
soul expression through the voice has a powerful transforming effect.

As I teach the power of honest expression to others, I am
often confronted by the dark extreme of their realism, which is
cynicism. Being so honest and authentic, they say, would amount
to committing career suicide. But the fear goes much deeper: It is
a terrible thing to reveal oneself. "What if who I am isn't
enough?" we wonder.

For most of us, the fear of rejection is akin to the fear of
death. Yet the possibilities for a new life beckon from depths long
neglected. The idle words that we speak to "get along" in the
world will ultimately define and engulf us in the Thoreauvian
"desperation" of a life not fully lived, unless the truth of who we
are is finally given utterance. Perhaps such utterance is a simple,
yet honest "yes" or "no," "I know" or "I don't know," "I would
prefer" or "I would prefer not." Maybe it's an unpopular "I
agree" or "I don't agree." It might even be a courageous disclo-
sure of what's going on inside: "Right now I feel . . . about . . .
because . . ." Such expressions are what David Whyte so elo-
quently refers to as "Fire in the Voice":

> A man I know finds himself in a meeting room at the
> very edge of speech; he is approaching his moment of

reckoning, and he is looking for support from his fellow executives around the table. Strangely, at this moment, no one will look at him. The CEO is pacing up and down on the slate-gray carpet. He has asked, in no uncertain terms, for their opinion of the plan he wants put through: "I want to know what you all think about this," he demands, "on a scale of one to ten."

The CEO is testy; he makes it plain he wants everyone to say "ten," and damn whether they mean it or not. He is just plain tired, after all this time, of people resisting his ideas on the matter. He glares at them; he wants compliance. My friend thinks the plan is terrible and that there is too much riding on this solitary ego; everyone in the company will lose by it. He is sure, also, from talk he has heard, that half the other executives in the room think so, too.

As they go around the shamefaced table, the voices of those present sound alternatively overconfident, or brittle and on edge. Most say "ten," one courageous soul braves a "nine and a half," and my friend is the last to go. He reaches his hand toward the flame, opens his palm against the heat, and suddenly falters; against everything he believes, he hears a mouse-like, faraway voice, his own, saying "ten."

Courageous speech has always held us in awe—from the first time we spoke back to our parents as angry, stuttering teens, or had to stand tongue-tied before a roomful of people, feeling naked as the day we were born. There is, after all, something bare and revealing about speech. Perhaps because we intuit the physical intimacy behind the sound of words and the way they are spoken, and that much against our wishes our words tell the listener a good deal more than we would have them know about us.

The voice emerges literally from the body as a representation of our inner world. It carries our experience from the past, our hopes and fears for the future, and the emotional resonance of the moment. If it carries none of these, it must be a masked voice, and, having muted the voice, anyone listening knows intuitively we are not all there. Whether or not we try to tell the truth, the very act of speech is courageous because, no matter what we say, we are revealed. . . .

Imagine if my friend had said, to the fury of the CEO, "zero," on a scale of one to ten. There is a world of difference in the bodies of startled executives hearing zero pronounced in the room and those hearing a hesitant ten. The word zero would pass through the listeners like an emotional shock wave, galvanizing some to further acts of cowardice and others to the courage of their convictions. . . .

Saying the word zero, then, entails not just the pronunciation of a word, but a reentry into neglected portions of the body that can uphold the challenge and stand by it. . . .

The people who hear themselves say zero do not have the same lives ahead of them as those who gave the hesitant ten. Saying zero literally means they have guts, and their voice is resident in their guts. They have a vessel to hold their fire. They have a stomach for the consequences, a place to which their voice can belong no matter the outward change in circumstances. Ambition is not rejected, but replaced in the greater perspective of the soul, which again and again seems to choose a fuller experience of the here and now over a preordained trajectory through the corporate heavens. . . .

My friend had already figured out in his mind that the CEO's plan was not a good one. But the fire in our belly literally goes out until we find the courage or the circumstance to walk back into those parts of our bodies we have disowned and claim their earthly, grounded qualities for our own again.[25]

Not only are we reclaimed and transformed through such fire in the voice, but those who *hear* our truth are often transformed as well. A form of biogenesis takes place. As fire ignites fire, life begets life. The voice of one soul awakened awakens another. Somehow we, and those we touch, are never quite the same again.

When all else fails, the inner forces of the soul will move us, however unconsciously, to drastic measures in order to balance the account of an unbalanced life. For those who are too prideful or too deep in the sleep of their own fears and selfishness to stop, clear the past, and start over, the hidden agenda will provide the necessary wake-up calls. To the person who has neglected his or her body and health, illness might strike. To the individual who has neglected his or her marriage, infidelity or divorce might result. To parents who neglect or shame their children, tragedy might come in the form of delinquency or even suicide. The perpetrators of the "perfect" crime will somehow, at some time, unconsciously betray themselves and be brought to justice.

This, again, is the law of the hidden agenda: learn and grow, or suffer. Those who are too afraid or content to move on with their lives will be nudged—and even pushed—unmercifully forward through loss, trials, and heartache.

Spiritual Transformation and Beyond

The most essential aspect of individuation is spiritual in nature. The hidden agenda of wholeness involves not only numerous psychological "rebirth moments" that comprise the journey to psychic wholeness, but, at some point, a spiritual transformation which enables us to fill the full measure of our existence.[26] Such a transformation, or conversion, is a gift from God that comes through faith, sacrifice, reconciliation, and consecration, and results in a literal transformation of the spirit, along with an actual change in disposition, desire, direction, and purpose in life. Seeing this, and the realization of our limitless potential in this regard, it is clear that we must not only be in proper relationship with ourselves and others, but with God as well.

Although an in-depth treatment of this subject is beyond the scope of this book, many great people and leaders of every age throughout history and in every walk of life have acknowledged their relationship with God and have recognized a larger—or eternal—perspective. In my opinion, any work on the subject of human development that fails to include these aspects is, in my estimation, incomplete. Only with divine assistance can we be healed of our wounds, transgressions, infirmities, and weaknesses to a state of peace, spirituality, and true empowerment.

Even so, we need to keep our humanity in clear view. The work of wholeness does not end with spiritual conversion. As Carl Jung reminds us, "Even the Christian who feels himself delivered from evil will, when the first rapture is over, remember the thorn in the flesh, which even St. Paul could not pluck out."[27] The process of individuation includes spiritual conversion, but is much larger in scope. The "thorn in the flesh" indicates our capacity for evil, as well as the unconscious inner forces that necessarily compensate for our spirituality to bring it down to earth and make it soulful. This "thorn" remains, and even God will not remove it, "lest [we] be exalted above measure."[28]

Our work beneath the surface, then, involves not only the healing and integration of the mind (ego and shadow), the renewal of the spirit, or the unity of mind and spirit, but also the integration of mind, spirit, and body—including our capacity for evil and the desires, appetites, and passions of the flesh—to a state of wholeness.

As we faithfully embark on this journey to wholeness—psychically and spiritually—we will find ourselves "in relationship" with ourselves, others, and God. What emerges over time is a person and leader who is humble, meek, and submissive in the truest sense, and who is characterized by certain essential capacities that place him or her on higher ground, enabled to meet the accelerated demands, moral and ethical dilemmas, and opportunities of an increasingly challenging and troublesome future.

Chapter Seven

EMERGING FROM
THE DARKNESS:
Toward a Higher Vision of
Living and Leadership

"Our moment in history is indeed a pregnant one. As
a civilization and as a species we have come to a
moment of truth, with the future of the human spirit
and the future of the planet hanging in the balance. If
ever boldness, depth, and clarity of vision were called
for, from many, it is now."

—*Richard Tarnas*

The living soul emerges from the darkness. As it was with
physical birth, so it is with psychological and spiritual
rebirth. We come out of the darkness into the light. Such are the
true leaders of humanity—men and women who are striving for
individuation, or wholeness; wounded healers who have taken the
mythical journey of the hero to wholeness, and who, by their very
presence, help others transform to a higher level of consciousness.

As we move toward the twenty-first century, a new age of
wisdom, maturity, and higher consciousness will emerge, bringing forth those who have been resurrected—from the death of
traditionalism, fatalism, and mindless conformity—to a creative
life, free from the chains of past conditioning, and empowered
to meet the demands of the times. These people, though certainly
human and fallible, will nonetheless see and act in different,
unfamiliar ways—breaking the code of paradox, abolishing the
rules of corrupt patriarchy, changing what is deadening to society
into something life-giving, promoting unity instead of conformity

and commitment instead of compliance. They will "amaze and inspire us and help us reimagine the world we think we know so well, until we realize that something is so wrong with it that we have to create a new world."[1] They will promote the care and healing of the soul.

As we have learned, to be truly effective, productive, and ethical as human beings, and to be in relationship with ourselves and others, requires sufficient consciousness, wisdom, and maturity, with a genuine dedication to truth. Further, we now understand that these conditions of character are acquired and cultivated by working beneath the surface of ego and persona, and not merely by imitation, habit, or experience—although experience with understanding is certainly essential.

In this chapter I present several capacities of the individuating personality that naturally grow and develop as we work beneath the surface and respond to our hidden agenda for wholeness. They include the abilities to think in polarity, exercise 360-degree judgment, conceive the inconceivable, act with integrity, remain nonattached, "go straight around the circle," act in polarity, and be Self-directed.

Thinking in Polarity

The first capacity is the ability to *think in polarity*. Polarity is "opposites in unity"; it is the reality of opposition in all things. To think in polarity is to see both one side *and* its opposite as reality, and to hold such opposites in creative tension until a higher reality emerges. Reality is not either one side or its opposite. "Either/or" thinking is polarized, one-sided thinking, but polarity is balanced, whole, integrated thinking.[2]

When we see ourselves and others in polarity, we are better able to break the code of paradox. For example, how can the pursuit of trust diminish trust? How can the attempt to motivate demotivate? And how can efforts to empower disempower? These fundamental paradoxes are created by the dynamics of the social system and the polarity of the human psyche. An unwillingness to accept that, as human beings, we are part of larger systems and are at once trustworthy and untrustworthy sets us up for disillusionment, disappointment, and reactivity because of unrealistic expectations and one-sided extremism, which invites an unconscious takeover.

Polarized—either/or—thinking never deals with things or people as they really are. The polarized individual projects either the "ideal" image or the "degraded" image onto others because of a lack of self-knowledge. On the other hand, thinking in polarity, which comes with self-knowledge, enables us to reconcile apparent contradictions and bring opposing values and viewpoints into unity and harmony. Consider these questions:

- How can a person's weaknesses reveal the same person's strengths?
- How can obedience bring freedom?
- How can cruelty be an expression of care and concern?
- How can selfishness be an expression of generosity?
- How can dissent be an expression of support and commitment?
- How can criticism and chastisement be expressions of love and acceptance?
- How can inaction reflect commitment and a bias for action?
- How can indecision be a form of resolve?
- How can breaking the rules be an expression of obedience and, at the same time, a reflection of integrity or trustworthiness?
- How can an immoral act (i.e., an act that violates the moral code or rules of society) be right or ethical?
- How can two people with opposing viewpoints both be right with respect to the same issue?
- How can less be more or more be less?

Our capacity to answer such questions can help us hold the tension of opposites toward the accomplishment of the greatest good. This challenge faces all of us in the various roles we play in life. Consider the role of "leader." Whether at home, at work, in the community, at church, or in the management of our own private lives, we are leaders. How well we perform in this role depends in large measure upon how effectively we can hold and resolve the tension of certain opposing values toward the accomplishment of the greatest good. Some of these opposing values, which can make or break today's leaders, are listed in the following table.

Leadership Tensions

Order	Chaos
Control	Release
Conformity	Uniformity
Dissent	Individuality
Accept	Question
Safety	Risk
Performance	Growth
Logic	Creativity
Profit	Social responsibility
Follow orders and do what you're told	Follow your judgment and do what is right
Direct	Support
Mission	Margin
Action	Inaction
Unilateral decision making	Consensus or participative decision making
The good of the many	The good of the few, or the one
Position A	Position Z
Interests of A	Interests of B

To resolve these tensions, we first need to understand the difference between rationalization and reconciliation. Reconciling and transcending opposites to some higher truth does not involve rationalization or linear, logical thinking. It does, however, require thinking in polarity, which embraces a larger perspective for the highest good, and the maturity to balance assertiveness with consideration for others.

The unintegrated personality does not have the character strength to hold the tension, but tends to release one side of the tension in favor of the other side, which is favored due to safety, comfort, or familiarity. A more integrated person, conversely, sees the seed of each side in the other and values *both* opposites in proper context. Thus, for example, while from chaos comes order, yet from order also springs chaos, which ushers in a higher order. The issue is not either order *or* chaos, but rather, when chaos should be encouraged and allowed to bring about a new order, and how such chaos should be managed to optimize the effect.

Consider an example from the business sector involving competing stakeholder interests: Again, the answer is not found in either/or thinking. How many executives have crippled their organizations and needlessly harmed hundreds of people, directly and indirectly, by giving in to the tension between profits and social responsibility, resulting in unwise expense reductions and layoffs? This is one-sided thinking. Integrated leaders don't fall prey to such false dichotomies. New alternatives that unite these opposites will emerge for those who have the patience and moral courage to hold the tension and act with integrity. Only with such moral courage—and the ability and wisdom to think in polarity—can true synergy of thought be created to reconcile opposing values.

Although principles and processes are important in dealing with such dilemmas, they are insufficient. The capacity to think in polarity and hold the tension to resolve competing demands and conflicting duties is essential. With this capacity comes two others—the abilities to exercise *360-degree judgment* and *conceive the inconceivable*.

Exercising 360-Degree Judgment and Conceiving the Inconceivable

Inner work creates an attitude and aptitude for seeing things from all angles, helping us recognize that the truth has many faces, that blame begets blame, and that every action has far-reaching implications. In addition, four important facts are deeply internalized:

1. *Perception is projection.* The more repressed our shadow is, the more judgmental we are, and the more conviction we feel about our judgments of others.
2. *Things aren't always what they seem.* Appearances can be, and often are, deceiving.
3. *Our judgments are limited* by our experience, knowledge, wisdom, information, desires (how much we care), and human fallibility.
4. *We tend to look for and produce the necessary evidence* to justify our accusations and make us right.

In judging people and situations, we must be careful to look for differences as well as similarities. Categorizations, generalizations, outward appearances, patterns of behavior, circumstances, and even "red-handed" transgressions can be as deceptive as they are revealing. So, too, can feelings. Feelings are not facts, and, although they reveal the nature of the judgments that produced them, they do not prove the correctness of those judgments. Thus, even though we may feel a strong conviction or concern about someone, or about the "rightness" or "wrongness" of our own or other people's actions, it would be unwise to conclude that such judgments are absolutely correct.

Judging character based on precedents or patterns, especially in comparison with other people or situations, can be dangerous and damaging—particularly when such judgments take the form of criticism or accusation. We need to forget about judging people in this way—such judgments are usually, if not always, corrupted by our own ignorance. Instead, we can exercise better judgment in the following ways:

- Assessing ourselves through honest self-examination.
- Discovering how we might be part of the problems, concerns, and troublesome attitudes we experience with others.
- Determining how we might best help others, while respecting their dignity and uniqueness and honoring their moral agency.

- Resolving how best to act with integrity in furthering or protecting our own self-interests *and* the interests of others.
- Seeing the strengths in the apparent weaknesses of others.
- Serving as a resource to help others clear the past, stay in relationship, and think in polarity.

Exercising our capacity for judgment in these ways brings us full circle, as we return all of our projections to ourselves and stop criticizing, finding fault, labeling, blaming, accusing, and condemning others. In other words, we judge others the way we would want to be judged, for as we judge others so shall we be judged.

Clearly, there are times when, in doing our duty to protect the innocent and to uphold law and order, we must sit in judgment on others—as parents, teachers, managers, and concerned citizens. To do so under proper circumstances could rightly be seen as an ethical responsibility. In discharging such responsibilities, however, we must exercise great care, particularly before condemning others or meting out egregious consequences.

The responsibility to judge ethically places upon all of us, I believe, a burden of due diligence and self-knowledge far beyond present norms and standards. In my own life, I have felt the dark extremes of my desire for justice and mercy. The dark side of the desire for justice can be cruelty, vindictiveness, vengeance, close-mindedness, and a rush to judgment. On the other hand, the dark side of mercy can be leniency, permissiveness, and tolerance of wrongdoing. We must be aware and cautious of both extremes working within us as we sit in judgment on others.

Often, we find ourselves condemning others because of their attitudes. We feel that the accused should be cooperative, conciliatory, and contrite, but instead they are steadfast in their convictions, uncooperative, defensive, rebellious, unyielding, unrepentant. Because of these attitudes, we easily infer guilt. We react with a conviction of their wrongness and increase our resolve to see justice served. But how many of these attitudes are caused by the accusers and judges themselves? If the accused and their accusers are reacting to each other, then both sides will produce the evidence to validate their judgments. In response, then, to the negative attitudes of the accused, those who have a more integrated personality will carefully examine their own feelings, judgments, and attitudes toward the accused as part of the problem either *before* they make a judgment or in response to a judgment already made. Remember, our judging and accusing feelings will come across, even if we try to hide them.

Additionally, the capacity to exercise 360-degree judgment is helpful when we are faced with the dilemma of respecting another person's lifestyle or life choices on the one hand, and discharging our moral and ethical responsibility to exercise leadership when that person appears to be in need of perspective, direction, or correction on the other hand. According to M. Scott Peck:

> The dilemma can be resolved only by painstaking self-scrutiny, in which one examines stringently the worth of his or her "wisdom" and the motives behind this need to assume leadership. "Do I really see things clearly, or am I operating on murky assumptions? Do I really understand [the other person]? Could it not be that the path [this person] is taking is wise, and that my perception of it as unwise is the result of limited vision on my part? Am I being self-serving in believing that [the person] needs redirection?" These are questions that those who truly love [and lead] must continually ask themselves. This self-scrutiny, as objective as possible, is the essence of humility or meekness . . .
>
> There are, then, two ways to confront or criticize another human being: with instinctive and spontaneous certainty that one is right, or with a belief that one is probably right arrived at through scrupulous self-doubting and self-examination. The first is the way of arrogance; it is the most common way of parents, spouses, teachers, [managers,] and people generally in their day-to-day affairs; it is usually unsuccessful, producing more resentment than growth and other effects that were not intended. The second

is the way of humility; it is not common, requiring as it does a genuine extension of oneself; it is more likely to be successful, and it is never, in my experience, destructive.[3]

Finally, as discussed in Chapter Five, we are most serviceable and effective when we are able to conceive the inconceivable. This also requires the capacity to exercise 360-degree judgment, as well as to think in polarity. To ethically conceive the inconceivable requires an imagination for the illogical, irrational, and even evil.

The motion picture "Ransom" provides an excellent example of this capacity. After a wealthy man's son is kidnapped and it is determined that ransom, alone, won't return the boy to his parents, the boy's father, from deep within the shadow regions of his soul, conceives the inconceivable: He comes up with a plan to turn the tables on the kidnappers. Instead of paying the ransom, he offers the public a sizeable reward to anyone who provides information that leads to the capture of the kidnappers. Most people see the act as irresponsible, and even immoral, given that the boy could be killed if the ransom isn't paid. Such ideas are conceived in the irrational or unconscious regions of the mind and have the appearance of evil. After all, "How could a father risk the life of his child like that?" This is the outcry of the masses, but the plan is inspired by a higher source and calls everyone involved, including the boy's father, to the truth about themselves. (I'll let you discover the ending of this movie on your own.)

Such is the nature and purpose of this transcendent function of the psyche—to call us to the truth about ourselves and to greater wholeness. As we continue to mature, this capacity develops as a natural outgrowth of the individuating personality. In many instances it is a necessary condition for *acting with integrity*.

Acting with Integrity to Resolve Collisions of Duty

In Chapter Five, I introduced the subject of countervalues and "collision of duty," along with a brief treatment of the moral and ethical aspects of conscience.[4] I also alluded to such dilemmas in my discussion, earlier in this chapter, of the capacity to think in polarity and hold the tension of competing demands.

The ethical aspect of conscience—that aspect which enables us to resolve our collisions of duty—pertains essentially to the capacity to conceive the inconceivable and correctly discern right from wrong. To rise above the conflict between the moral and the ethical requires great insight, wisdom, maturity, and moral development. It involves a conscious, reflective descent into the very depths of our being. Part of us dies in such a descent, only to be resurrected to a higher state of consciousness and morality.

Ethically resolving collisions of duty is a rite of initiation into the highest realms of leadership and personhood, and an ongoing ritual in the lives of those who seek to fill the full measure of their existence. Such efforts stretch us upon the cross of conflict—not only between right and wrong, but between right and right—between the competing or conflicting truths of legitimate perspectives, and between the "general" rule and the soul's call for an exception to accomplish a needed outcome, fulfill its truth, or obey the laws of its progression and completion. In such situations, the "right" of conventional morality can come in conflict with the "right" of the situation, which asserts itself by another voice of conscience, commanding the individual to obey, even at the risk of "going astray" or suffering other grave consequences. This "other voice," which is also the voice of conscience, might be "right" or "false." According to Jung:

> In practice it is very difficult to indicate the exact point
> at which the "right" conscience stops and the "false"
> one begins, and what the criterion is that divides one
> from the other. But if [this other] voice of conscience is
> the voice of God, this voice must possess an incompa-
> rably higher authority than traditional morality.[5]

We all find ourselves grappling with ethical dilemmas more frequently than we suppose—or care to. We do not look for such opportunities; they find us, usually when we least expect them. "Do I tell the whole truth and risk irreparable and unnecessary harm to another, or should I tell a lie or withhold information to save a relationship or a human life?" To quote Jung again:

> In such dilemmas, we are certainly not obeying our conscience if we stick obstinately, and in all circumstances, to the commandment: Thou shalt not lie. We have merely observed the moral code. But if we obey the judgment of conscience, we stand alone and have hearkened to a subjective voice, not knowing what the motives are on which it rests. No one can guarantee that he has only noble motives. We know—some of us—far too much about ourselves to pretend that we are one hundred percent good and not egotists to the marrow. Always behind what we imagine are our best deeds stands the devil, patting us paternally on the shoulder and whispering, "Well done!"[6]

Other examples might include dissenting at the risk of severe reprisal, breaking the confidence of one person to benefit others, breaking one promise to keep another, entrapping or deceiving a friend or family member in order to help him or her, sacrificing a significant relationship by exposing the other person, stealing in order to survive, betraying a sacred trust in order to be true to oneself, sacrificing or taking a life to save many, and so on. The list is endless.

One woman faced such a collision of duty when, after a difficult divorce, her soul "called" her to relocate and pursue another life at the risk of losing full custody of her children to her ex-spouse. Her moral conscience, coupled with her own insecurities, resisted the call to follow her heart and the way that had opened to her. After all, what kind of a mother would move away from her children? Only a selfish one, of course. Then there was the insecurity of losing her children's love and loyalty. Yet, through her "ethical" conscience, she knew that if she did not follow the new path, she would somehow be making a huge mistake.

In business, such conflicts might include firing a friend or family member, breaking a personal promise to an employee to honor a fiduciary promise to the organization, laying off people who were just hired, closing a plant or division, not paying payroll taxes in order to make payroll, deciding not to disclose required information or conflicts of interest, or breaking certain laws to save jobs or stay in business. It's too easy to judge quickly situations like these or minimize their significance: hence, the need for 360-degree judgment and the feeling function of conscience.

To qualify as a true ethical dilemma or collision of duty, the person faced with the decision must stand alone in moral conflict, holding the tension of competing values and attempting to reconcile opposing internal forces in search of "higher ground." Such higher ground usually takes the form of a larger perspective that reconciles the two opposing aspects of conscience and brings calm, decisive resolution.

Carl Jung asks the great questions that face us all in considering such decisions: "Where does the true and authentic conscience, which rises above the moral code and refuses to submit to its dictates, get its justification from? What gives it the courage to assume that it is not a false conscience, a self-deception?"[7] These questions bring us to the heart of the matter, which is the subject of right and wrong and the process of discerning which is which, and which is the higher "right" in a true collision of duty. The relevance of this subject, along with our ability to make such determinations, is significant to us all, and particularly to those in leadership roles, who represent and serve multiple stakeholders with divergent and, at times, conflicting interests.

In striving to resolve ethical dilemmas, it is important first to place the situation in proper context and then see it in proper perspective. Truly, that which is wrong in one situation might be right in another, and vice versa. But beware: Taken at face value, such an assertion can, in many cases, amount to nothing more than "situational ethics," whereby we change the rules in a given situation to get what we want, and justify ourselves on the basis that the situation warrants such a change. Such a philosophy opens the door to delusion and self-deception through rationalization.

Even when we are sincere, subjectivity complicates the situation, leaving us standing on uncertain ground. Thus, *only by embracing the moral code can we make truly ethical decisions.* A justifiable exception to the rule requires first that we whole-heartedly accept the rule and maintain a mind-set or attitude of obedience, distinguishing between the letter of the law and the spirit, or intent, of the law.

Beyond this, our soul's need for integrity requires the mature, reflective exercise of good faith and good conscience in the decision-making process. When we do so, we act with integrity. To act in good faith means more than merely acting with good motives, because much of what truly motivates us works below the surface of awareness. One of my colleagues shared a story of a small business owner who withdrew $50,000 in cash at a great peril to his company. His conscious motive was to help his family through a difficult time by taking them on a much-needed vacation. Despite the fact that some of his key employees had to go without paychecks and his company had to violate some of its vendor payment agreements, he saw no indication that he had done anything wrong or even questionable. In his mind he had acted in "good faith," or with noble motives. Perhaps he did, yet he also allegedly refused to consider the possibility that he had acted selfishly or inconsiderately.

Because of hidden or unconscious motives and the likelihood of self-deception through rationalization, it is often not enough to be merely convinced of the "rightness" of a particular course of action, or even converted to the principles that support it. In cases in which much is at stake and the risks of error or loss are high, we must feel *compelled* to act—called or moved upon, as it were—by a higher law or power from within. Additionally, to be completely justified, we must exercise due diligence in the process of making decisions with integrity. These are defining moments, requiring not only great faith, but great humility and meekness.

"Good faith," then, requires that we *make and take* the time to do the following to the best of our ability:

- Study the situation as carefully and objectively as possible.
- Engage in internal debate against any options that would require a deviation from established standards and norms.
- Consider empathically how different options and deviations impact ourselves and others.
- Think deeply about what is really wanted in light of the possible consequences.
- Examine any considered deviations in light of established principles.
- Where possible and appropriate, seek counsel from others and listen carefully to them, particularly when they have opposing viewpoints.
- Finally—and initially as well—do what many great leaders do in such situations: Seek for divine confirmation, wisdom, and guidance.
- Be willing to "check back" again and again for mitigating circumstances, a change of heart, or a redefinition of duty. The willingness to reconsider, stop, and reverse one's course is a sign of honest duty to the Truth, and the essence of good faith in action.

When we respond reflectively, and in good faith, to a given situation, our response is right, or ethical, if our heart assents to it in "good conscience." Such assent is manifested in a whole-hearted response without internal rationalization, restraint, or hesitancy. When this happens, our response will result in a life experience that is good for all involved, regardless of how difficult or trying it might be.

Understanding the "feeling value" of internal assent is extremely important in the development of ethical character. What does "wholeheartedness" feel like? What about "rationalization," "restraint," and "hesitancy" of conscience? How do they *feel*? These things cannot be articulated sufficiently to be of any real value. They must be experienced to be known. This requires the exercise of self-awareness in the pursuit of greater insight or self-knowledge. All this is complicated when our "moral" conscience and "ethical" conscience collide.

As we are seemingly impelled to move forward by the psychic forces within, the moral conscience asks, "Is *this* right?" or warns, "*This* isn't right"—"this" referring to the act itself *in relation* to the content of the moral code or to established standards. Such internal voices or impressions are usually accompanied by fear or uneasiness. As these voices and feelings emerge, we often feel yet another force within that seems to call upon us to move forward with the assurance that to do so is needful and also right.

So now there are two competing forces within us—one tells us to stop, and the other to move forward. Which one is really the "right" response for us in such a situation? We can only know if we are quiet, calm, and passive. We must be humble enough to acknowledge that our ways are not necessarily Wisdom's ways, and be willing to conceive, and then consider, the inconceivable, and accept whichever course the soul might demand. Thus, if we exercise good faith, with the real intent to do what is right, we will be able to safely plumb the creative depths of our soul, see the situation in proper context, and thus find a higher ground.

From this higher ground—or, more accurately, "middle" place—the clear path will become evident, and with it, a new alternative that is not contrary in spirit to either truth, but which embraces them both. And although necessarily we may face conflict, such a new course will produce the greatest good—to which the Voice of Wisdom will speak and the voice of internal authority will assent. There will be peace at the center, a peace that enables us to stand alone if necessary and endure the terrible isolation that often accompanies a purely ethical decision.

Remaining Nonattached and "Getting in the Middle"

Another essential capacity that we can develop by working beneath the surface is the ability to *be nonattached and get in the middle of unconscious extremes*. The capacity for nonattachment is fundamental to all core capacities of the individuating personality. As we work beneath the surface to cultivate whole-ness and the integration of our personality, we mature to such a state of nonattachment, and we gradually let go of:

- Our incomplete or incorrect perceptions and perspectives.
- Our need for approval from others and the related fear of rejection.
- Preconceived notions of how things "ought" to be or work out.
- Inhuman ideals and expectations.
- The tyranny of the "should," including moral rigidity.
- Our need to be right.
- Our ego-ideal, or one-sided self-image.
- Obsession over results.
- One-sided extremism.

These limitations cloud our judgment and contaminate the decision-making process. Our thinking becomes polarized, our judgment linear, and our actions controlling. We miss the mark. Striving with the anxiety of achieving a particular outcome can alienate us from the outcome we are striving for and make it unattainable. This is the paradox of "hyper intentionality."[8] Chuang Tzu refers to this paradox in "The Need to Win":

> When an archer is shooting for nothing,
> He has all his skill.
> If he shoots for a brass buckle,
> He is already nervous.
> If he shoots for a prize of gold,
> He goes blind;
> Or sees two targets—
> He is out of his mind!
>
> His skill has not changed. But the prize
> Divides him. He cares.
> He thinks more of winning
> Than of shooting—
> And the need to win
> Drains him of power.[9]

The problem is not desiring the outcome or striving to obtain it, but striving *with the anxiety of achieving it*. One source of such anxiety might be the nature or timing of the desired outcome. If the pursuit of an outcome is inappropriate or the outcome itself is inappropriate, we generally will experience a natural anxiety or uneasiness of bad conscience.

Another source of performance anxiety might be a personal insecurity or sense of inadequacy that results in an identification with the outcome. In this case, our sense of identity or self-esteem depends in part—or entirely, in some cases—on how well we perform and how well others feel about our performance. If we do well, we are okay. If we do not, we are "less than" okay. This kind of "twisted thinking" produces anxiety and results in either self-shaming or the shaming of others.[10] (See this endnote for ten common thinking distortions.)

A third source of anxiety might be, and often is, an incorrect or limited perspective, resulting in inflating the importance of the outcome or our role in determining the outcome. Or, how we perceive the context and implications of an outcome in relation to our needs, values, and beliefs may also produce performance anxiety.

As anxiety increases, consciousness decreases. Without sufficient consciousness, we cannot respond to any given situation as it really is. Instead, we react, narrow our focus (go into a trance), tighten up, or attempt to achieve the desired outcome by controlling the situation and those involved in it. This, of course, begets blame and results in resistance and a breakdown of personal accountability.

Our anxiety also blinds us from seeing the clear path. And, even if we do see it—or someone shows it to us—our fears block us from doing the right thing. As my colleague and friend, Dan Caspersen, believes, until we are willing to lose our job, we can't do our job—a simple yet profound statement on the importance of nonattachment in the workplace. In a state of nonattachment, we are totally dedicated to truth and right action, whatever that might be. We are free from performance anxiety and the demands of external expectations and associations. The last resort is the voice of internal authority and wisdom where the will of God resides or is confirmed.[11]

Our ability to ethically let go and get in the middle of unconscious extremes (to find the higher ground of consciousness and right action) depends on our degree of wholeness or individuation. Nonattachment is one of the highest expressions of personal maturity, integrity, and true humility. It enables us to respond consciously, conscientiously, and effectively to difficult or challenging situations with faith that right actions will always produce the right outcomes, whatever those might be. We know from experience that sometimes integrity demands one course while wisdom demands another. In such cases, to favor the demand of wisdom entails the compromise of integrity at one level and the exercise of integrity at a higher level. There are many levels of integrity, and the highest level is obedience to the Voice of Wisdom, which obedience is the fruit of a nonattached state of being and a mature faith that is void of willfulness in the presence of Truth.

There is great wisdom in knowing when to act and when not to act, what to do and what not to do, how to act and how not to act. To access the wisdom of "right," or appropriate action, we must hold the tension of opposing values and views and be present, quiet, calm, passive, and indifferent to the form of the outcome. These are characteristics of a nonattached state of mind. When we attain this state, we then ask our questions in good faith and watch and listen for the answers.

Answers might come as sudden insights or ideas, impressions, promptings, or simply casual comments or suggestions. They might come through strange coincidences, dreams, or even through inadvertent slips of the tongue. Because answers can come in a variety of ways, we must be watchful, alert, and attentive. When the right answer comes, we will know it in our minds and in our hearts. If no answer comes, or if we are uncertain or confused, we then keep the question in mind, go about our business, and do nothing. Sometimes we impatiently seek for a way *out* when perhaps what is needed is a way *through*. We struggle with what to do when perhaps it is best to "not do." However, if we feel, through some prompting of conscience, that we must do something, then we must do only what we feel "good" about doing and then do it to the best of our ability.

Going "Straight Around the Circle" and Acting in Polarity

Other corollary decision-making capacities associated with nonattachment include the abilities to go "straight around the circle" and to ethically balance polar energies in right action.

To go "straight around the circle" means to flow *with* resistance, not oppose it. In this way, restraining forces are transformed into pulling forces of commitment. The Western mind exhausts itself in the exercise of sheer willpower to force a desired outcome. The driving, controlling mind-set often creates an illusion of progress as it pushes against the restraining forces of alternate or opposing viewpoints. This creates a paradox wherein the more we drive and push, the more powerful the resistance becomes.

In contrast, the nonattached mind-set has the flexibility either to be direct or to "go around the circle." The ego is not invested. We seek first to understand the resistance, and then act in context of it. If direction is needed, direction is given. If involvement is needed, involvement is solicited. If force is needed, force will be used. If silence is required, there will be silence. The wise person learns to read the social forces, and then goes with the flow, ethically balancing polar energies to do what is right. So it is that one who is nonattached can consciously and conscientiously act in polarity according to the demands of the situation. This means that the ethical yet nonattached person can be appropriately creative and destructive, active or passive, loving and hateful, healing and wounding, cruel and kind, tolerant and unyielding, compassionate and ruthless, innocent and shrewd, peaceful and wrathful, calm and violent, honest and deceptive, flexible and demanding, agreeable and disagreeable, compliant and rebellious, and so on.

The dark side of each virtue can be either denied and suppressed—wherein it becomes dangerous—or acknowledged, embraced, and integrated, thereby rounding out the personality and making the person whole in power and virtue. Although others might judge such polarity in action as being morally wrong, inconsistent, or untrustworthy, the person who acts appropriately in polarity—in love, wisdom, good faith, and good conscience—does so consciously, responsibly, and ethically, and therefore with integrity to the highest duties of the soul, which are sometimes above even natural feelings and affections. Such action is fraught with great risk, and is never justified without considerable due diligence, nor executed without some degree of natural concern, or even anguish and suffering.[12]

Being Self-Directed

The last capacity of the individuating personality that I want to address involves Self-direction. The term "Self," which I have interpreted to mean the divine center, or spirit within us, is capitalized to distinguish it from the notion of "self" that pertains to the ego. The Self (capital "S") is the *I am*, while the self (small "s") is who *I think I am*, or the small part of myself I am aware of.

Our unique work, calling, or vocation in life is, I believe, imprinted in the Self, or spirit, and comes with us, as the poet William Wordsworth so beautifully wrote, "from afar: Not in entire forgetfulness, . . . but trailing clouds of glory . . . from God, who is our home." To be Self-directed, then, means to be directed by the revelations or laws imprinted in our soul, which define and direct our work and calling in life, rather than by external laws or principles as many popular approaches would suggest. Being directed in this way involves being prompted, moved, called upon by the voice of God, to respond to events, opportunities, or coincidences that seem strangely pregnant with meaning or significance in our life. Sometimes such calls bring us face to face with genuine conflicts of duty that might separate us from the community in which we belong and painfully isolate us from all connections and privileges associated with them. In all cases, it would seem, such calls require sacrifice—a losing of our life to find our life.

The capacity for Self-direction involves our ability to consistently access, correctly interpret, and accurately confirm the voice of God as it directs us and calls us to action. It requires the ability to consciously rise to the highest heaven and descend to the lowest depths in the abyss of our own soul. This ability is the greatest of all heightened capacities that result from the process of individuation, and yet is wholly dependent on each of the others: To be Self-directed requires all the other abilities presented in this chapter. It also requires great faith, courage, humility, meekness, and submissiveness to the truth within us. It is the greatest of all capacities and is by far the most frightening, requiring our utmost respect and an attitude of "fear and trembling."

Our refusal to faithfully respond to our callings in life is certainly understandable. Nevertheless, such refusals are breaches of integrity that bring with them serious consequences. Of these consequences, Jolande Jacobi writes:

> For as soon as a man tries to escape every risk and prefers to experience life only in his head, in the form of ideas and fantasies, as soon as he surrenders to opinions of "how it ought to be" and, in order not to make a false step, imitates others whenever possible, he forfeits the chance of his own independent development. Only if he treads the path bravely and flings himself into life, fearing no struggle and no exertion and fighting shy of no experience, will he mature his personality more fully than the man who is ever trying to keep to the safe side of the road. . . .
>
> Not following one's destiny, or trying to avoid one's fate, is a frequent cause of numerous psychic difficulties. It may even be that the steady increase in the number of neurotics today is due to the fact that more

and more individuals are called upon by fate to work
for their psychic wholeness, but that fewer and fewer
of them are ready to do so. Any obstruction of the
natural process of development, any avoidance of the
law of life, or getting stuck on a level unsuited to one's
age, takes its revenge, if not immediately, then later at
the onset of the second half of life.[13]

Truly, after all we can do on our own, the need to follow
one's destiny requires an act of grace. It also requires, I believe,
an act of grace to enable us to *do* all that we can do. It is precisely
because such acts of integrity on our part are so difficult and so
gut-wrenching that they are crucial to our quest for wholeness,
including the further development of our ability to be Self-directed.
By working beneath the surface, all the essential capacities of
productive living and effective leadership can be gradually
reclaimed, healed, and developed in their wholeness. Although
all our capacities and qualities require development, the capacities
presented in this chapter are, to me, of singular importance with
respect to the challenges facing us today.

As social, cultural, political, and economic forces continue to
shift, change will become even more unpredictable, and our ability
to respond ethically and effectively in the moment will be taxed
to the limit. In fact, I believe it already is. In my experience the
capacities to think in polarity, exercise 360-degree judgment,
conceive the inconceivable, act with integrity, remain nonattached, "go straight around the circle," act in polarity, and be
truly Self-directed are all significantly unrealized in our Western
society. Are such capacities then really needed? I believe they are.

"Bias for action," which characterizes the popular notion of
success in our time, is often redundant and one-sided as we seek
to do what works within confined and inbred paradigms or
notions of effectiveness, appropriateness, or success. Meanwhile,
in our spiritually wounded and disempowered society, increased
demands upon us result in decreased commitment and accountability, and in increased cynicism, frustration, and insecurity.

Programs, laws, policies, and strategies for order and improvement are often undermined by unconscious restraining forces that are more powerful than we can possibly imagine. These restraining forces include people's instincts for survival and resistance, which are activated by prevailing assumptions and beliefs—many of which are incomplete, incorrect, and accusatory, as well as derogatory and distrusting in nature.

The Great Challenge

Effective living and leadership call for right action through wise and ethical decisions and conscious, meaningful interactions. This is the great challenge of our day. Every interaction with another human being is a moment of truth. And every decision that involves people is a moral and ethical decision that leaves a legacy. We need to understand that *right action is only what it must be in any given situation*, even if such action is to admit mistakes, ignorance, and powerlessness and to seek help and greater understanding.

Certainly, expanding competencies through knowledge, skills, and continuous improvement will always be necessary. Perhaps of even greater importance, however, will be our commitment to work beneath the surface. This, we now know, is the way to personal empowerment, sustained effectiveness, and wholeness, which in turn are prerequisites for love, commitment, abiding trust, and accountability in our relationships with one another and for fulfillment in our life's work.

The biblical caution against putting new wine in old containers is appropriate in considering our need for development. The *new wine* of advanced skills and capabilities such as Self-direction, thinking in polarity, 360-degree judgment, solving collisions of duty, remaining nonattached, and "going straight around the circle" cannot be contained in the old container. The *old container*, or unintegrated personality of the individual, cannot contain the new wine and will either release or corrupt it. In order to contain and pre-serve the new wine, the container must be renewed or transformed.

Those who diligently and consistently work their own hidden agenda of wholeness are the true leaders in our world today. These loving men and women of great vision, faith, and hope are highly conscious, humble, meek, and above all, dedicated to truth and submissive to the Voice of Truth. They are *in* the world but not *of* the world. They are nonattached, yet involved; powerful, yet unassuming and unpretentious; committed and passionate, yet self-possessed. They represent a new breed—more whole and human—whose sense of worth is not identified with nor determined by performance or results. They have great capacity to deal with their own imperfections and the imperfections of others, and to face challenges, by integrating them into a larger, even eternal perspective. Such capacity requires a true sense of one's humanity, as well as wisdom and a deep, well-grounded spirituality forged in the fires of legitimate suffering and refined over the years by reflection, experience, and diligently striving for greater integrity.

In all of this there is a profound dependence—a healthy dependence that transcends all earthly associations—a dependence fundamental to all the glorious capacities of one's being: a dependence on God. "I am the vine; ye are the branches: He that abideth in me, and I in him, the same bringeth forth much fruit, for without me ye can do nothing."[14] Truer words were never spoken.

Epilogue

THE HOPE FOR TOMORROW

"Things fall apart; the center cannot hold; mere anarchy is loosed upon the world. . . . Surely some revelation is at hand."

—*William Butler Yeats*

We can no longer avoid the inevitable.

I believe we are in a time when the paradoxical nature of the challenges we have encountered in the past will face us in full force and with greater complexity, compression, and magnitude than ever before. Further, such challenges will be resistant to present-day thinking and to many of the solutions and formulas that seemed to work in the past. We will be dealing with, in effect, a new strain of virus against which our current remedies are powerless. This virus is psychic and spiritual in nature, manifesting itself in a variety of symptoms such as feelings of powerlessness, inadequacy, and victimization. Other symptoms include increased violence, immorality, cynicism, criticism, resentment, contention, rebellion, need for control, blame assigning, obsession, compulsion, and so on.

These are all symptoms of soul sickness and psychic infection. The cure, as we have seen, is inspired care of the soul, spiritual regeneration, and wholeness. Those who work beneath the surface to honor the hidden agenda of the soul will not only integrate their own personalities, but will also withdraw their projections, repent of their lies and wrongdoings, and reduce the potency of collective evil in the process. By striving to become whole they will promote healing and wholeness in the world.

We all have work to do. It is a great work, a healing, transforming, and empowering work. In doing this work, our greatest hope—indeed our only hope, in my estimation—is to surrender our willfulness to the Truth and then work beneath the surface to find the truth, face the truth, and, to the best of our ability, live the truth. This cannot be accomplished by merely returning to traditional values or even to the dogmas of religion. Nor can it be attained by striving for greater accomplishment.

Moving from our current level of consciousness to a higher level of consciousness, the level required for humanity to deal effectively with the perilous times ahead, requires a journey into the darkness wherein one's *center* can shift from the ego to God, and from God to the Self. To those of us who embark on this journey and continue it faithfully, the Truth will be made known—the Truth that shall free us from the bondage of fear, ignorance, and wrongdoing. The questions: "What is truth? What is *my* truth? and What is *the* Truth?" must to be asked wholeheartedly—by our strivings, reflections, and soulful petitions—with the assurance that, as we sincerely ask and seek, so shall we find.[1]

To be sure, the hope for tomorrow can be found through personal wholeness in relation to the Truth—not in containment, regimentation, blind obedience, moralism, or one-sided idealism, and not in the benevolent authoritarianism that seeks its own by simply being nice or treating people right. Such wholeness is the basis of real character, and "Real character is formed in the midst of the battles for the soul."[2] These words of Hugh B. Brown are amplified by David O. McKay, who asked, "What progress [or hope] can there be for a man unconscious of his faults?" Then, in answer to his own question, he states, "Such a man has lost the fundamental element of growth, which is the realization that there is something bigger, better, and more desirable than the condition in which he now finds himself. In the soil of self-satisfaction, true growth has poor nourishment. Its roots find greater succor in discontent."[3] In such discontent and legitimate suffering we shall all find the peace, joy, and fulfillment we yearn for, and the hope of a glorious future together.

Notes

Preface

1. *The 7 Habits of Highly Effective People*® is a registered trademark of Franklin Covey Co.

2. Christian religion asserts that through His atoning sacrifice, Jesus Christ saves mankind *from* their sins on the condition of repentance, but such redemption from sin does not make us whole or remove from us our weaknesses and imperfections. These remain, as the apostle Paul described, as "thorns in the flesh" to provide the opposition we need to become whole and fully conscious. Only through the tension of opposing forces—spirit and body—and the reconciliation of both in a state of unity, can the soul be made whole, or "perfect," in the true sense of the term.

   Carl Jung made Christians painfully and uncomfortably aware of the cross they must take up and hang upon in order to be whole: He taught us that the way to wholeness, as prescribed and exemplified by Christ, requires reconciliation and unification of opposites, connection with God through consciousness of Self, and the imitation of Christ—not through modeling His behavior or duplicating His works, but by living our lives as truly as He lived His.

3. Friedrich Nietzsche, in *Thus Spake Zarathustra*, presents three transformations of the spirit. Manuel Komroff, ed., Thomas Common, trans. (New York: Tudor, 1934).

   Joseph Campbell summarizes these three transformations in his book, *The Power of Myth*, as follows:

   > In a kind of parable, Nietzsche describes what he calls the three transformations of the spirit. The first is that of the camel, of childhood and youth. The camel gets down on his knees and says, "Put a load on me." This is the season for obedience, receiving instruction and the information your society requires of you in order to live a responsible life.
   >
   > But when the camel is well-loaded, it struggles to its

feet and runs out into the desert, where it is transformed into a lion—the heavier the load that had been carried, the stronger the lion will be.

Now, the task of the lion is to kill a dragon, and the name of the dragon is "Thou Shalt." On every scale of this scaly beast, a "thou shalt" is imprinted: some from four thousand years ago; others from the morning's headlines. Whereas the camel, the child, had to submit to the "thou shalts," the lion, the youth, is to throw them off and come to his own realization.

And so, when the dragon is thoroughly dead, with all its "thou shalts" overcome, the lion is transformed into a child moving out of its own nature, like a wheel impelled from its own hub. No more rules to obey. No more rules derived from the historical needs and tasks of the local society, but the pure impulse to living of a life in flower. Joseph Campbell with Bill Moyers (New York: Anchor Doubleday, 1988): 191. Cited hereafter as Campbell, *The Power of Myth*.

As we mature spiritually we shift our center from ego to God and then from God to Self. We mature from being self—(or ego-) centered to being God-centered, and finally to being Self-centered and Self-directed. With these transformations the voice of authority changes from the external source to the internal truth. We ultimately mature to the level of holding our own authority according to the light and truth, or *Vox Dei*, that is in us. We as "lions" kill our dependency on external authority (the "dragon") to free the god within, a god I might add, that is very much like both a little child *and* a serpent.

4. Robert A. Johnson, *We: Understanding the Psychology of Romantic Love* (San Francisco, CA: Harper & Row, 1983): 28. Cited hereafter as Johnson, *We*.

5. Ibid, 33.

6. Thomas Moore, *Care of the Soul: A Guide for Cultivating Depth and Sacredness in Everyday Life* (New York: Harper Collins, 1992): 34. Cited hereafter as Moore, *Care of the Soul*.

Introduction

1. Carl G. Jung, *The Undiscovered Self with Symbols and the Interpretation of Dreams*, R. F. C. Hull, trans. (Princeton, NJ: Princeton University Press, 1990): 61. Cited hereafter as Jung, *The Undiscovered Self*.

Chapter One

1. James Hillman, *The Soul's Code: In Search of Character and Calling* (New York: Random House, 1996): 45-46.

2. The true greatness of leaders, as we shall see in Chapter Seven, is not in their track records, numbers of followers, or positive human qualities, but rather in their ability to think in polarity, exercise judgment based on a macro perspective, ethically resolve collisions of duty, and "go straight around the circle and get in the middle" of unconscious extremes. These capacities are developed through the crucible of inner work I refer to as "working beneath the surface."

3. St. Paul, "The Epistle of Paul the Apostle to the Romans," *The Jerusalem Bible*, Alexander Jones, ed. (Garden City, NY: Doubleday, 1966), 7:23.

4. Carl G. Jung, *C. G. Jung: Psychological Reflections: A New Anthology of His Writings, 1905-1961*, Jolande Jacobi and R. F. C. Hull, eds. 2nd ed. (Princeton, NJ: Princeton University Press, 1970): 27. Cited hereafter as Jung, *Psychological Reflections*.

5. Ibid, 211.

6. Ibid, 224.

7. Ibid, 218-19.

8. Jesus, cited in St. Matthew, "The Gospel According to St. Matthew," *The Holy Bible: King James Version*, 13:3-9.

9. Howard W. Hunter, in his book *That We Might Have Joy*, makes the following observations about the "Parable of the Sower":

> Sowing of seed is important; otherwise, there would be no harvest, and, as stated in the parable, there must be good ground to bring forth a good harvest. Plowing must have been done before the sowing, or there would have been no seedbed.
>
> Of all the work of the field, plow-work is the heaviest labor. It is primary and fundamental. A seed may be dropped anywhere, and there is no resistance; but put the blade of the plow into the ground, and a thousand forces join to oppose the change. To disturb the conventional, to overturn the traditional, or to attempt to make changes in the deep-rooted way of doing things in the lives of individuals requires toil and sweat. What a great change comes

over land that has been cleared and plowed—row after row of evenly spaced furrows, the subsurface loosened and exposed to the sun and air and the rains from heaven, ready to be broken up and planted to seed. The wilderness is conquered and subdued. . . .

Is it hard work? Of course, but that which is worthwhile is seldom easy. As individuals, we have a responsibility to plow. Some accept the opportunity, but some shrink from the responsibility. Some of those who commence cut only a short furrow and then leave the field for what appears to be escape from the toil. Their plowshares are left to rust in the furrow. (Salt Lake City, UT: Deseret Book, 1994): 166-67. Cited hereafter as Hunter, *That We Might Have Joy.*

10. Carl G. Jung, "A Psychological View of Conscience," in *The Collected Works of C. G. Jung*, Herbert Read, Michael Fordham, and Gerhard Adler, eds. 2nd ed. 20 vols. (New York: Pantheon; and Princeton, NJ: Princeton University Press, 1953-83), 10:447. Cited hereafter as Jung, *Collected Works.*

One more passage from Carl Jung will hopefully drive this point home:

Unfortunately there can be no doubt that man is, on the whole, less good than he imagines himself or wants to be. Everyone carries a shadow, and the less it is embodied in the individual's conscious life, the blacker and denser it is. If an inferiority is conscious, one always has a chance to correct it. Furthermore, it is constantly in contact with other interests, so that it is continually subjected to modification. But, if it is repressed and isolated from consciousness, it never gets corrected. . . .

It is a frightening thought that man also has a shadow side to him, consisting not just of little weaknesses and foibles, but of a positively demonic dynamism. The individual seldom knows anything of this; to him, as an individual, it is incredible that he should ever in any circumstances go beyond himself. But let these harmless creatures form a mass, and there emerges a raging monster; and each individual is only one tiny cell in the monster's body, so that for better or worse he must accompany it on its bloody rampages and even assist it to the utmost. Having a dark suspicion of these grim possibilities, man turns a blind eye to the shadow-side of human nature. Yes, he even hesitates to admit the conflict of which he is so painfully aware. Jung, *Psychological Reflections*, 240.

11. Eugene Pascal, *Jung to Live By: A Guide to the Practical Application of Jungian Principles for Everyday Life.* (New York: Warner Books, 1992): 169.

Chapter Two

1. Robert Bly, *A Little Book on the Human Shadow*, William Booth, ed. (San Francisco, CA: Harper San Francisco, 1988): 17-24. Cited hereafter as Bly, *A Little Book on the Human Shadow*. This is an excellent book, and a must-read.

2. I am told that recent evidence suggests such rejection—which may also come through the projection of the parents' shadow (inferior personality) to the child—can occur and be experienced by children while in the womb. Certainly it occurs as these children go through life trying to "measure up," or otherwise win and retain their parents' love and respect.

3. Bly, *A Little Book on the Human Shadow*, 24-25.

4. David Whyte, *The Heart Aroused: Poetry and the Preservation of the Soul in Corporate America* (New York: Currency Doubleday, 1994): 53. Cited hereafter as Whyte, *The Heart Aroused*.

5. Bly, *A Little Book on the Human Shadow*, 30-31.

Chapter Three

1. For more information on "self-fulfilling prophecy," see Robert K. Merton, *Social Theory and Social Structure*, enl. ed. (New York: The Free Press, 1968): 475-90. For more information on "deviation amplifying processes," see Magorah Maruyama, "The Second Cybernetics: Deviation-Amplifying Mutual Causative Processes," *American Scientist* 51 (1963): 164-79.

   My work in this field began years ago with my exposure to the unpublished work of C. Terry Warner, *Bonds of Anguish, Bonds of Love* (privately distributed by Arbinger Group of Salt Lake City, Utah). However, I have enlarged my understanding of what he calls "collusion" by relating reactive cycles to the creative instinct of individuation—what I call the soul's "hidden agenda"—which is played out destructively as an unconscious "death wish" through four levels of untruth. I have drawn extensively from the disciplines of social and depth psychology, as well as from cognitive and trans-actional psychotherapy.

2. Paul H. Wender, "Vicious and Virtuous Circles: The Role of Deviation Feedback in the Origin and Perpetuation of Behavior," *Psychiatry* 31 (1968): 315. Cited hereafter as Wender, "Vicious and Virtuous Cycles."

3. The concept of "advocacy loops" is inspired by the work of Chris Argyris and is represented in Peter M. Senge, *The Fifth Discipline: The Art and Practice of the Learning Organization* (New York: Currency Doubleday, 1990): 198-99. See also pages 81 and 384-85 for Senge's own concepts of "reinforcing processes" and "escala-tion." Eric Berne describes deviation amplifying processes as inter-personal "games." Regarding Berne's work, Paul Wender writes:

> Eric Berne has described stereotyped sequences of interper-sonal transactions which he has called "games." What is important, he states, is not only that an individual plays a role in such a game, but that he [or she] has a "script"—that is, he [or she] is capable of behaving, and does behave, in such a manner that he [or she] is able unconsciously to dic-tate the parts of the other actors in his little drama. Such compelling behavior acts in a manner similar to that by which expectations operate in a self-fulfilling prophecy. "Vicious and Virtuous Circles," 320-21.

See also Eric Berne, *Transactional Analysis in Psychotherapy: Systematic Individual and Social Psychiatry* (New York: Grove Press, 1961) and Eric Berne, *Games People Play: The Psychology of Human Relationships* (New York: Grove Press, 1964).

4. Karl E. Weick, *The Social Psychology of Organizing* (Reading, MA: Addison-Wesley, 1979): 86.

Chapter Four

1. James Redfield and Carol Adrienne, *The Celestine Prophecy: An Experiential Guide* (New York: Warner Books, 1995): 90. Cited hereafter as Redfield and Adrienne, *The Celestine Prophecy: An Experiential Guide*.

2. Chris Argyris, *Overcoming Organizational Defenses* (Needham, MA: Allyn and Bacon, 1990): 88-89.

3. See John Bradshaw, *Creating Love: The Next Great Stage of Growth* (New York: Bantam, 1994): 327-32. Cited hereafter as Bradshaw, *Creating Love.*

4. Ibid, 6-17.

5. Redfield and Adrienne, *The Celestine Prophecy: An Experiential Guide*, 155-56.

6. Aaron Lazare, "Go Ahead, Say You're Sorry," *Psychology Today* (January–February 1995): 40.

7. Daniel Goleman summarizes this difficulty very well in his book *Vital Lies, Simple Truths: The Psychology of Self-Deception*:

> Information that threatens the self—that does not support the story one tells oneself about oneself—threatens self-esteem. Such threats are a major source of anxiety. For animals, stress is most often in the form of a threat to life or limb. For humans, though, a challenge to self-esteem is enough to brew anxiety. . . .
>
> When a threat to the self-concept looms, anxiety can be warded off by . . . an artful maneuver or two. Events can be selectively remembered, reinterpreted, slanted. When the objective facts don't support the self-system, a more subjective recounting can: If I see myself as honest and good, and events don't support that view, then I can preserve self-esteem by skewing my rendering of them.
>
> As we have seen, the wherewithal to do this is entirely outside awareness. The self-system can sanitize its portrayal of events through the filtering that goes on prior to awareness. I need confront only a finished, polished view of myself; the dirty work goes on behind the scenes. . . . Such self-serving reinterpretations of reality go on for most of us some of the time, but we are rarely found out. After all, the dissembling goes on discreetly, behind the screen of the unconscious; we are only its recipients, innocent self-deceivers. A convenient arrangement.

Goleman then proceeds to catalogue some of the most common defense mechanisms, including denial and reversal, projection, rationalization, and selective inattention, and then concludes:

> The defenses—our bastions against painful information—operate in a shadow world of consciousness, beyond the fringes of awareness. Most often we are oblivious to their operation and remain the unknowing recipients of the ver-

sion of reality they admit into our ken. The craft of teasing
out and capturing defenses in vivo is a tricky endeavor.
While people can, perhaps, realize they have at one time or
another relied on a defense, without special conditions our
self-deceptions are largely impenetrable and unnoticed.
(New York: Simon & Schuster, 1985): 100-1, 123. Cited
hereafter as Goleman, *Vital Lies, Simple Truths*.

Chapter Five

1. This concept has reference to the myth of the "hero's quest" wherein
   each of us must descend below our ignorance and ego-ideal in order
   to become fully human and actualize our potential. To "rise above" is
   to transcend the darkness through that self-knowledge which brings
   us face to face with the *Imago Dei*, a self-knowledge that integrates
   the whole Self and can only be obtained—paradoxically—by descend-
   ing below the ego and into the darkness of the unconscious.

2. Aniela Jaffé, *The Myth of Meaning in the Work of C. G. Jung*, R. F.
   C. Hull, trans. (Zurich, Switzerland: Daimon, 1984): 85. Cited hereafter as Jaffé, *The Myth of Meaning*.

3. Jung, *The Undiscovered Self*, 5.

4. Langdon Gilkey, *Shangtung Compound: The Story of Men and
   Women Under Pressure* (New York: Harper & Row, 1966): 112.

5. Goleman, *Vital Lies, Simple Truths*, 184-85, paraphrasing Irving
   Janis.

6. Ibid, 188.

7. Jaffé, *The Myth of Meaning*, 81, 95-96.

8. According to Carl Jung:

   > Since it is universally believed that man is merely what his
   > consciousness knows of itself, he regards himself as harm-
   > less, and so adds stupidity to iniquity. He does not deny that
   > terrible things have happened and still go on happening, but
   > it is always "the others" who do them. And, when such
   > deeds belong to the recent or remote past, they quickly and
   > conveniently sink into the sea of forgetfulness, and that state
   > of chronic woolly-mindedness returns which we describe as
   > "normality.". . . None of us stands outside humanity's black
   > collective shadow, . . . and one would therefore do well to
   > possess some "imagination for evil," for only the fool can

permanently disregard the conditions of his own nature. In fact, this negligence is the best means of making him an instrument of evil. . . .

Recognition of the shadow, on the other hand, leads to the modesty we need in order to acknowledge imperfection. . . . The perfect have no need of others, but weakness has, for it seeks support and does not confront its partner with anything that might force him into an inferior position and even humiliate him. This humiliation may happen only too easily when high idealism plays too prominent a role.

What our age thinks of as the "shadow" and inferior part of the psyche contains more than something merely negative. . . . Through self-knowledge, that is, by exploring our own souls, we come upon the instincts and their world of imagery. [This] should throw some light on the powers slumbering in the psyche, of which we are seldom aware so long as all goes well. They are potentialities of the greatest dynamism, and it depends entirely on the preparedness and attitude of the conscious mind whether the irruption of these forces, and the images and ideas associated with them, will tend towards construction or catastrophe. *The Undiscovered Self*, 52-53, 55-58.

9. The impact of false Christian tradition on psychological and spiritual wholeness is profoundly examined by Carl Jung in his *Collected Works*. Jungian analyst Murray Stein summarizes Jung's analysis of Christianity in the following statements:

The central argument is as follows: The Christ symbol, which lies at the center of Christianity, came into being because an archetype of the collective unconscious was constellated in the times of Jesus of Nazareth. The stories and images that gathered around the historical Jesus eventually created a symbol that compensated the collective consciousness of the times. This Christ symbol represented the self, but only partially, because the self was split into good and evil components. The resulting religion and its doctrine created a tradition, and ultimately a culture, in which the splits and unreconciled oppositions of the originating images were lived out by multitudes of men and women. . . .

In the course of Christian theology's development, beginning with Origen, the "dark side of things" was deprived of substance and came to be regarded as mere absence of good. This was the product of denial, which caused an aspect of human psychology reality to be repressed and lose its relationship to consciousness, to disappear from the world of substance into the realm of shades and shadows, into the unconscious. . . .

To say that anyone or anything is absolutely good or absolutely evil is a distortion by conscious judgment, which will inevitably be accompanied by the opposite judgment being placed on someone or something else (equally a distortion). This is the essential dynamics of psychological splitting. Theological doctrines that divide good and evil so sharply, as some of Christianity's doctrines have done, encourage believers similarly to make black/white discriminations about aspects of themselves (instinct versus Spirit, for example) and about others ("us" versus "them" in politics and society). This describes a psychologically unhealthy condition. *Jung's Treatment of Christianity: The Psychology of a Religious Tradition* (Wilmette, IL: Chiron Publications, 1985): 148, 150, 152. Cited hereafter as Stein, *Jung's Treatment of Christianity.*

10. Connie Zweig and Jeremiah Abrams, eds. *Meeting the Shadow: The Hidden Power of the Dark Side of Human Nature* (Los Angeles, CA: Jeremy Tarcher, 1991): xxiv-xxv. Cited hereafter as Zweig and Abrams, *Meeting the Shadow.*

11. The following is an excerpt of a conversation between Bill Moyers and Joseph Campbell concerning the nature and deeds of the hero:

Moyers: Why are there so many stories of the hero in mythology?

Campbell: Because that's what's worth writing about. Even in popular novels, the main character is a hero or heroine who has found or done something beyond the normal range of achievement and experience. A hero is someone who has given his or her life to something bigger than oneself.

Moyers: So, in all of these cultures, whatever the local costume the hero might be wearing, what is the deed?

Campbell: Well, there are two types of deeds. One is the physical deed, in which the hero performs a courageous act in battle or saves a life. The other kind is the spiritual deed, in which the hero learns to experience the supernormal range of human spiritual life and then comes back with a message.

The usual hero adventure begins with someone from whom something has been taken, or who feels there's something lacking in the normal experiences available or permitted to the members of his society. This person then takes off on a series of adventures beyond the ordinary, either to recover what has been lost or to discover some life-giving elixir. It's usually a cycle, a going and a returning.

But the structure and something of the spiritual sense of this adventure can be seen already anticipated in the puberty or initiation rituals of early tribal societies, through which a child is compelled to give up his or her childhood and become an adult—to die, you might say, to his or her infantile personality and psyche, and come back as a responsible adult. This is a fundamental psychological transformation that everyone has to undergo. We are in childhood in a condition of dependency under someone's protection and supervision for some fourteen to twenty-one years—and, if you're going on for your Ph.D., this may continue to perhaps thirty-five. You are in no way a self-responsible, free agent, but an obedient dependent, expecting and receiving punishment and rewards. To evolve out of this position of psychological immaturity to the courage of self-responsibility and assurance requires a death and a resurrection. That's the basic motif of the universal hero's journey—leaving one condition and finding the source of life to bring you forth into a richer or more mature condition.

Moyers: So, even if we happen not to be heroes in the grand sense of redeeming society, we still have to take the journey inside ourselves, spiritually and psychologically.

Campbell: That's right. Otto Rank, in his important little book, *The Myth of the Birth of the Hero*, declares that everyone is a hero in birth, where he undergoes a tremendous psychological as well as physical transformation, from the condition of a little water creature living in a realm of amniotic fluid into an air-breathing mammal which ultimately will be standing. That's an enormous transformation, and had it been consciously undertaken, it would have been, indeed, a heroic act. And there was a heroic act on the mother's part, as well, who had brought this all about.

Moyers: Then heroes are not all men?

Campbell: Oh, no. The male usually has the more conspicuous role, just because of the conditions of life. He is out there in the world, and the woman is in the home. But, among the Aztecs, for example, who had a number of heavens to which people's souls would be assigned according to the conditions of their death, the heaven for warriors killed in battle was the same for mothers who died in childbirth. Giving birth is definitely a heroic deed, in that it is the giving over of oneself to the life of another.

Moyers: Don't you think we've lost that truth in this society of ours, where it's deemed more heroic to go out into the world and make a lot of money than it is to raise children?

Campbell: Making money gets more advertisement. You know the old saying: If a dog bites a man, that's not a story, but if a man bites a dog, you've got a story there. So the thing that happens and happens and happens, no matter how heroic it may be, is not news. Motherhood has lost its novelty, you might say.

Moyers: That's a wonderful image, though—the mother as hero.

Campbell: It has always seemed so to me. That's something I learned from reading these myths.

Moyers: It's a journey—you have to move out of the known, conventional safety of your life to undertake this.

Campbell: You have to be transformed from maiden to a mother. That's a big change, involving many dangers.

Moyers: And when you come back from your journey, with the child, you've brought something for the world.

Campbell: Not only that, you've got a life job ahead of you. Otto Rank makes the point that there is a world of people who think that their heroic act in being born qualifies them for the respect and support of their whole community.

Moyers: But there's still a journey to be taken after that.

Campbell: There's a large journey to be taken, of many trials.

Moyers: What's the significance of the trials, tests, and ordeals of the hero?

Campbell: If you want to put it in terms of intentions, the trials are designed to see to it that the intending hero should really be a hero. Is he really a match for this task? Can he overcome the dangers? Does he have the courage, the knowledge, the capacity, to enable him to serve?

Moyers: In this culture of easy religion, cheaply achieved, it seems to me we've forgotten that all three of the great religions teach that the trials of the heroic journey are a significant part of life, that there's no reward without renunciation, without paying the price. The Koran says, "Do you think that you shall enter the Garden of Bliss without such trials as came to those who passed before you?" And Jesus said in the Gospel of Matthew, "Great [strait or restricted] is the gate and narrow is the way which leadeth to life, and few there be who find it" [Matthew 7:13]. And the heroes of the Jewish tradition undergo great tests before they arrive at their redemption.

> *Campbell:* If you realize what the real problem is—losing yourself, giving yourself to some higher end or another— you realize that this, itself, is the ultimate trial. When we quit thinking primarily about ourselves and our own self-preservation, we undergo a truly heroic transformation of consciousness.
>
> And what all the myths have to deal with is transformations of consciousness of one kind or another. You have been thinking one way; you now have to think a different way.
>
> *Moyers:* How is consciousness transformed?
>
> *Campbell:* Either by the trials themselves or by illuminating revelations. Trials and revelations are what it's all about.
> In Campbell, *The Power of Myth*, 151-55.

12. The "Self," as used in analytical psychology, is analogous to the theological concept of spirit, or the divine in man. It is the *Imago Dei*. Edward F. Edinger explains the concept of Self and relates it to the ego:

> Jung's most basic and far-reaching discovery is the collective unconscious, or archetypal psyche. Through his researches, we now know that the individual psyche is not just a product of personal experience. It also has a pre-personal or transpersonal dimension which is manifested in universal patterns and images such as are found in all the world's religions and mythologies. It was Jung's further discovery that the archetypal psyche has a structuring or ordering principle which unifies the various archetypal contents. This is the central archetype of wholeness which Jung has termed "the Self."
>
> The Self is the ordering and unifying center of the total psyche (conscious and unconscious), just as the ego is the center of the conscious personality. Or, put in other words, the ego is the seat of *subjective* identity while the Self is the seat of *objective* identity. The Self is thus the supreme psychic authority and subordinates the ego to it. The Self is most simply described as the inner empirical deity and is identical with the *Imago Dei*. Jung has demonstrated that the Self has a characteristic phenomenology. It is expressed by certain typical symbolic images called mandalas. All images that emphasize a circle with a center, and usually with the additional feature of a square, a cross, or some other representation of quaternity, fall into this category.
>
> There are also a number of other associated themes and images that refer to the Self. Such themes as wholeness, totality, the union of opposites, the central generative point, the world navel, the axis of the universe, the creative point where God and man meet, the point where transpersonal

energies flow into personal life, eternity as opposed to the temporal flux, incorruptibility, the inorganic united paradoxically with the organic, protective structures capable of bringing order out of chaos, the transformation of energy, the elixir of life—all refer to the Self, the central source of life energy, the fountain of our being, which is most simply described as God. Indeed, the richest sources for the phenomenological study of the Self are in the innumerable representations that man has made of the deity. . . .

Jung originally described the phenomenology of the Self as it occurs in the individuation process during the second half of life. More recently, we have begun to consider the role of the Self in the early years of life. Neumann, on the basis of mythological and ethnographical material, has depicted symbolically the original psychic state prior to the birth of ego consciousness as the *uroborus*, using the circular image of the tail-eater to represent the primordial Self, the original mandala-state of totality out of which the individual ego is born. Fordham, on the basis of clinical observation of infants and children, has also postulated the Self as the original totality prior to the ego.

It is generally accepted among analytical psychologists that the task of the first half of life involves ego development with progressive separation between ego and Self; whereas the second half of life requires a surrender or at least a revitalization of the ego as it experiences and relates to the Self. The current working formula, therefore, is, first half of life: ego-Self separation; second half of life: ego-Self reunion. This formula, although perhaps true as a broad generality, neglects many empirical observations made in child psychology and in the psychotherapy of adults. According to these observations, a more nearly correct formula would be a circular one, which could be diagramed thus (see Figure 3):

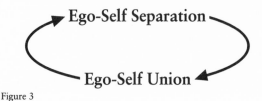

Ego-Self Separation

Ego-Self Union

Figure 3

The process of alternation between ego-Self union and ego-Self separation seems to occur repeatedly throughout the life of the individual both in childhood and in maturity. Indeed, this cyclic (or better, spiral) formula seems to express the basic process of psychological development from birth to death. *Ego and Archetype: Individuation and the Religious Function of the Psyche* (Boston, MA: Shambhala, 1992): 3-5.

13. "Toxic shame" is a term used by John Bradshaw to distinguish the healthy shame of humility, which comes from human fallibility, from the demeaning and degrading shame that attacks and deteriorates one's self-worth as a human being, resulting in personality dysfunction.

14. Bly, *A Little Book on the Human Shadow*, 42.

15. John R. O'Neil, *The Paradox of Success: When Winning at Work Means Losing at Life: A Book of Renewal for Leaders* (New York: Tarcher-Putnam, 1993): 66-67. "Flip Side of the Coin" is O'Neil's term.

16. R. D. Laing, cited in Zweig and Abrams, *Meeting the Shadow*, xix.

17. Ibid (Laing).

18. William Miller, "Finding the Shadow in Daily Life," cited in Ibid, 43-44.

19. Anthony Stevens, *On Jung: A New and Authoritative Introduction to Jung's Life and Thought* (New York: Penguin Books, 1990): 39, citing Carl Jung.

20. To provide you with a brief overview of Jungian dream interpretation, I have prepared a summary quote of Robert A. Johnson's four-step process, along with his four principles for validating interpretations, which are included in his excellent book entitled *Inner Work*. For a necessary, more detailed understanding of how to apply his process to your dreams, I urge you to read his whole book.

> 1. *Go through the dream and write out every association that you have for each dream image.*
>
> 2. *Connect each dream image to a specific dynamic in your inner life.*
>
> 3. *Interpret the dream.* Ask: What is the central, most important message that this dream is trying to communicate to me? What is it advising me to do? What is the overall meaning of the dream for my life?
>
> 4. *Do something physical to honor your dream.* Don't just keep it in your head. Perform some ritual. But use common sense and don't act irresponsibly.

Four Principles for Validating Interpretations

> 1. *Choose an interpretation that shows you something you didn't know.* Opt for the interpretation that teaches you something new, rather than one that seems to confirm your ingrained opinions and prejudices.
>
> 2. *Avoid the interpretation that inflates your ego or is self-congratulatory.* . . . If you find yourself writing an interpretation of your dream that has you preening your feathers and congratulating yourself on how wonderful you are, how high above other mortals, then your interpretation is not accurate. Dreams don't give us those kinds of signals, and they don't invite us into ego inflations.
>
> 3. *Avoid interpretations that shift responsibility away from yourself.* . . . Our dreams are not concerned with pointing out the faults of other people, or where other people need to change. . . .
>
>   If your dream comments on an external situation, it will focus on the contributions of *your* attitudes and unconscious behavior patterns.
>
> 4. *Learn to live with your dreams over time—fit them into the long-term flow of your life.* . . . If, after all your work, you can't honestly choose one definitive interpretation of your dream, then consent to live with it for a while. Be willing to live with the ambiguity of your dream just as we sometimes have to live with the ambiguity of life. You can legitimately say: "It may mean this, or it may mean that. It may go this way, or it might go another way. Only time will tell." *Inner Work: Using Dreams and Active Imagination for Personal Growth* (San Francisco, CA: Harper San Francisco, 1986): 94-96 (51-134).

21. Ibid, 24-26.

22. Ibid, 160.

23. See Anne S. Harris, *Living with Paradox: An Introduction to Jungian Psychology* (Pacific Grove, CA: Brooks/Cole, 1996): 115-124.

    The indispensable role of transference and countertransference in healing and transforming the personality is well-established in the fields of psychoanalysis and analytical psychology. Although these healing phenomena are traditionally framed within the context of "patient" and "therapist," it has been my experience that some degree of transformation can, through transference and countertransference, take place through non-traditional channels, such as with a friend, leader, or even a complete stranger. Jungian analyst Murray Stein writes:

> The term *transference*, softened now by usage into psycho-logical jargon, refers to a type of emotional reaction on the part of patients to their therapists. The pioneers of psycho-analysis found this reaction to occur fairly regularly during therapeutic treatment. [Sigmund] Freud, the first to name this reaction, interpreted it as a "carryover" (the literal translation of his *Übertragung*) from childhood. In Freud's original understanding, transference referred to a relation-ship in the present (typically in adulthood) with a stranger (a professional therapist, in this case), which reflected the emotional climate of childhood, and particularly the patient's relationships to parents. Transference creates a sort of illusory relationship between two people, generating assumptions and expectations that are based on the projec-tion of parental figures.
>
> Typically, transference is characterized by feelings of dependency, awe, anger or hostility, sexual attraction or repulsion, veneration, and ambivalence. To a person experi-encing this type of emotional reaction, there is a close resemblance to the childhood relationship to parents. In this emotional nexus a patient repeats the experiences of child-hood in the present. . . . The object of working through the transference, Jung felt, is to free the patient's ego from the domination of the inner parental figures and from infantile wishes and fears related to them. . . .
>
> Jung was, from the beginning of his association with Freud and psychoanalysis, keenly aware of the cultural task that psychoanalysis was performing in freeing modern men and women from a traditional (and, to analysts, an infantile) rela-tion to authority. . . . Jung speculated that transference in ther-apy is useful not only because it eventually may lead to greater moral autonomy, but also because it creates a psychological milieu in which the patient's conscious attitudes can be restruc-tured. . . . Transference, therefore, creates an opportunity for the patient to repeat earlier phases of development. . . .
>
> Like transference, countertransference has entered the lexicon of technical jargon through years of usage. If there is transference, there is bound to be countertransference, as the analyst is forced to react emotionally to the impact of transference. This reaction may be defensive and aimed at fending off disturbing effects, or it may pave the way for a dialectical process of mutual influence between analyst and patient. Of these two possible directions, Jung recommend-

ed the latter, on the grounds that the analyst's influence "can only take place if the patient has a reciprocal influence on the doctor. You can exert no influence if you are not susceptible to influence. . . ."

As Jung saw it, then, it was within the transference-countertransference process between patient and analyst that transformation takes place. Transformation in the patient depends critically on the analyst's openness to influence and to the patient's demon of sickness, then on the analyst's ability to undergo an inner transformational process and to return the result of this to the patient via the inductive effect ("influence") of his or her personality on the patient.

(It should be noted that the patient is open to the analyst's influence at this level because of the initial bridge thrown between them by the transference.) This transference-countertransference loop may remain largely unconscious, or unspoken, but it is often vividly observed in the dreams of patients and analysts. *Jung's Treatment of Christianity*, 52-63.

24. "Ecclesiastes, or The Preacher" *The Holy Bible: King James Version*, 3:1(1-8).

25. Jolande Jacobi, *The Way of Individuation*, R. F. C. Hull, trans. (New York: Harcourt, Brace & World, 1967): 40, citing Carl Jung. Cited hereafter as Jacobi, *The Way of Individuation*.

26. The question of defining and succumbing to good or evil and the need to acquire an "imagination for evil" to protect ourselves from it is treated with great clarity and insight by Carl Jung:

> Touching evil brings with it the grave peril of succumbing to it. We must, therefore, no longer succumb to anything at all, not even to good. A so-called good to which we succumb loses its ethical character—not that there is anything bad in it on that score, but to have succumbed to it may breed trouble. Every form of addiction is bad, no matter whether the narcotic be alcohol or morphine or idealism. We must beware of thinking of good and evil as absolute opposites. The criterion of ethical action can no longer consist in the simple view that good has the force of a categorical imperative, while so-called evil can resolutely be shunned. Recognition of the reality of evil necessarily relativizes the good, and the evil likewise, converting both into halves of a paradoxical whole.
>
> In practical terms, this means that good and evil are no longer so self-evident. We have to realize that each represents

a *judgment*. In view of the fallibility of all human judgment, we cannot believe that we will always judge rightly. We might so easily be the victims of misjudgment. The ethical problem is affected by this principle only to the extent that we become somewhat uncertain about moral evaluations. Nevertheless, we have to make ethical decisions. The relativity of "good" and "evil" by no means signifies that these categories are invalid, or do not exist. Moral judgment is always present and carries with it characteristic psychological consequences.

I have pointed out many times that as in the past, so in the future, the wrong we have done, thought, or intended will wreak its vengeance on our souls. Only the contents of judgment are subject to the differing conditions of time and place and, therefore, take correspondingly different forms. For moral evaluation is always founded upon the apparent certitudes of a moral code which pretends to know precisely what is good and what is evil. But once we know how uncertain the foundation is, ethical decision becomes a subjective, creative act. We can convince ourselves of its validity only *Deo concedente*—that is, there must be a spontaneous and decisive impulse on the part of the unconscious. Ethics itself, the decision between good and evil, is not affected by this impulse, only made more difficult for us. Nothing can spare us the torment of ethical decision. Nevertheless, harsh as it may sound, we must have the freedom in some circumstances to avoid the known moral good and do what is considered to be evil, if our ethical decision so requires. In other words, again: We must not succumb to either of the opposites.

A useful pattern is provided by the *netineti* of Indian philosophy. In given cases, the moral code is undeniably abrogated, and ethical choice is left to the individual. In itself there is nothing new about this idea; in pre-psychology days, such difficult choices were also known and came under the heading of "conflict of duties."

As a rule, however, the individual is so unconscious that he altogether fails to see his own potentialities for decision. Instead, he is constantly and anxiously looking around for external rules and regulations which can guide him in his perplexity. Aside from general human inadequacy, a good deal of the blame for this rests with education, which promulgates the old generalizations and says nothing about the secrets of private experience. Thus, every effort is made to teach idealistic beliefs or conduct which people know in their hearts they can never live up to, and such ideals are preached by officials who know that they themselves have never lived up to these high standards and never will. What is more, nobody ever questions the value of this kind of teaching.

Therefore, the individual who wishes to have an answer to the problem of evil, as it is posed today, has need, first and foremost, of *self-knowledge*, that is, the utmost possible knowledge of his own wholeness. He must know relentlessly how much good he can do, and what crimes he is capable of, and must beware of regarding the one as real and the other as illusion. Both are elements within his nature, and both are bound to come to light in him, should he wish—as he ought—to live without self-deception or self-delusion.

In general, however, most people are hopelessly ill-equipped for living on this level, although there are also many persons today who have the capacity for profounder insight into themselves. Such self-knowledge is of prime importance, because through it we approach that fundamental stratum or core of human nature where the instincts dwell. Here are those pre-existent dynamic factors which ultimately govern the ethical decisions of our consciousness. This core is the unconscious and its contents, concerning which we cannot pass any final judgment. Our ideas about it are bound to be inadequate, for we are unable to comprehend its essence cognitively and set rational limits to it. We achieve knowledge of nature only through science, which enlarges consciousness; hence, deepened self-knowledge also requires science, that is, psychology. No one builds a telescope or microscope with one turn of the wrist, out of goodwill alone, without a knowledge of optics.

Today we need psychology for reasons that involve our very existence. We stand perplexed and stupefied before the phenomena of Nazism and Bolshevism because we know nothing about man, or at any rate have only a lopsided and distorted picture of him. If we had self-knowledge, that would not be the case. We stand face to face with the terrible question of evil and do not even know what is before us, let alone what to pit against it. And even if we did know, we still could not understand "how it could happen here." With glorious naivete a statesman comes out with the proud declaration that he has no "imagination for evil." Quite right: *We* have no imagination for evil, but *evil has us in its grip*. Some do not want to know this, and others are identified with evil. That is the psychological situation in the world today; some call themselves Christian and imagine that they can trample so-called evil underfoot by merely willing to; others have succumbed to it and no longer see the good. Evil today has become a visible Great Power . . .

Our myth has become mute, and gives no answers. The fault lies not in it as it is set down in the Scriptures, but solely in us, who have not developed it further, who rather have suppressed any such attempts. The original version of the myth offers ample points of departure and possibilities of development. For example, the words are put into Christ's mouth: "Be ye therefore wise as serpents, and harmless as doves." For what purpose do men need the cunning of serpents? And what is the link between this cunning and the innocence of the dove? "Except ye . . . become as little children . . ." Who gives thought to what children are like in reality? By what morality did the Lord justify the taking of the ass which he needed in order to ride in triumph into Jerusalem? How was it that, shortly afterward, he put on a display of childish bad temper and cursed the fig tree? What kind of morality emerges from the parable of the unjust steward, and what profound insight, of such far-reaching significance for our own predicament, from the apocryphal logion: "Man, if thou knowest what thou dost, thou art blessed; but if thou knowest not, thou art accursed and a transgressor of the law"? What, finally, does it mean when St. Paul confesses: "The evil which I would not, that I do"? *Memories, Dreams, Reflections*, Aniela Jaffé, ed., Richard and Clara Winston, trans., rev. ed. (New York: Vintage, 1989): 329-33, citing Jesus in St. Matthew, "The Gospel According to St. Matthew," 10:16 and 18:3, *The Holy Bible: King James Version*, and referring to incidents recorded in 21:1-7 and 18-22, and St. Luke, "The Gospel According to St. Luke," 16:1-13; also citing *Codex Bezae ad Lucam*, 6:4, and St. Paul, "The Epistle of Paul the Apostle to the Romans," 7:19.

27. Jung, *Psychological Reflections*, 239-40.

28. John Bradshaw, *Healing the Shame That Binds You* (Deerfield Beach, FL: Health Communications, 1988): 148-49.

29. John A. Sanford, as cited in D. Patrick Miller, "What the Shadow Knows: An Interview with John A. Sanford," in Zweig and Abrams, *Meeting the Shadow*, 23.

30. John A. Sanford insightfully expands on the need for adequate information in making value judgments by sharing the following story from the Koran:

> Helpful though it is in freeing our sense of right and wrong from the tyranny of the ego, the feeling function is not always a reliable guide, because it must operate on the information it has at its disposal. If we could always see situations completely in all their meaning, we might always arrive at valid value judgments through the feeling function.

But what if our information of our conscious perspective is incomplete, or even incorrect? Then our feeling function, healthy enough in itself, might still err, simply because it was misinformed about the facts.

The Koran tells the story of Moses and the angel Khidr. They are traveling together when they come upon a fishing village. Khidr, seemingly out of pure malice, sinks all the villagers' boats, and Moses is horrified and complains about it. Khidr explains that, unknown to Moses, robbers were on their way to the village to steal their boats. If Khidr had not sunk them, the robbers would have taken them; as it is, all the villagers have to do now is raise them up again and repair them. In another incident Khidr falls upon a young man and brutally kills him. Again, Moses is horrified and objects, but Khidr tells him that this young man was going to murder his father and mother that evening and, if he had done so, his soul would have been condemned to hell forever. By killing the youth, Khidr saved the parents from death and the young man from everlasting damnation. In these tales, Moses' feeling function filled him with a sense of horror and moral repulsion at the acts of Khidr, but when he understood why the angel acted as he did his value judgment changed.

One of the results of the process of becoming whole, that Jung called individuation, is that we come to see the overall pattern of our lives. This leads to a certain kind of wisdom and a conscious perspective that helps us see many things in a different light. As a result, our value judgments change. *Jung and the Problem of Evil: The Strange Trial of Mr. Hyde* (Boston, MA: Sigo Press, 1993): 85-86.

31. Jaffé, *The Myth of Meaning*, 96.

32. Gregory Stock, *Book of Questions* (New York: Workman, 1987): 153, 170

33. Jung, *Psychological Reflections*, 247.

34. Andrew Samuels' treatment of the moral imagination is summarized well by John Beebe:

Samuels explains the conscience as an interplay between two psychological faculties: one that he calls original morality and another which he terms the moral imagination. Havel's "quiet restlessness" impressed Heinrich Boll; the original morality is the "quiet," and the moral imagination the "restlessness." In *Paradise Lost*, this pair is God and Satan. Original morality is "some kind of innate moral sense," but, as Samuels points out: "Insufficient for the leading of a moral life; it can be experienced as harsh, vengeful, primitive, and cold. In an adult, original morality can take the form of a profound suspiciousness of others, a tendency to jump to the worst possible conclusions, to rejoice in the other's misery when it seems deserved, and, ultimately, to retreat into the wilderness to feed on locusts and honey."

This is surely a good description of Puritanism at its worst: belief in God as an endless occasion for guilt. Moral imagination, by contrast, is the "means by which we consider complex social and political issues." [John] Milton's unforgettable image of Satan summoning all the gods of antiquity like so many fallen angels to decide how to interfere in God's newest creation, man, emphasized how central a role the shadow plays in such deliberations. Samuel's own example of the nihilism implicit in the moral imagination is the prayer read at the start of the Jewish Day of Atonement service:

All vows, bonds, devotions, promises, obligations, penalties, and oaths; wherewith we have vowed, sworn, devoted, and bound ourselves; from this Day of Atonement unto the next Day of Atonement; lo, all these, we repent us to them. They shall be absolved, released, annulled, made void and of none effect: They shall not be binding, nor shall they have any power. Our vows shall not be vows; our bonds shall not be bonds, and our oaths shall not be oaths.

The Yom Kippur prayer, as Samuels points out, cancels resolutions "at the very moment of making them: indicating that "a recognition of the unlivable nature of original morality on its own lies at the heart even of Judaism," the religion which is "so often unfairly castigated . . . as the source of repressive and legalistic moralism." This paradoxical prayer epitomizes moral imagination because it "contains an intuitive and psychological understanding of what a moral principle really is," for example, that it is sometimes "morally permissible to tell lies," "to break promises," and to refuse to give help. Moral imagination is characterized by "forgiveness, and not blame." And moral imagination "typically requires a weighing of conflicting claims."

It is the capacity to articulate the relation between original morality and moral imagination that concerns us, a capacity that rare figures like Havel and Milton model for us. As Samuels puts it, "Moral imagination enables us effectively to use original morality; original morality guarantees the depth and authenticity of moral imagination." Both "are equally archetypal; both have to become personal and express themselves in human relationships at all stages of life. . . . Neither is divine; if it lies anywhere, divinity lies in their conclave." Their conclave is what a developed Puritan sensibility would have meant by integrity, and we recover the archetype of purity when we engage in an authentic moral process. *Integrity in Depth* (New York: Fromn International, 1995): 56-57.

35. Robert A. Johnson provides an excellent overview of the Jungian concept to the androgynous psyche in his book, *We: Understanding the Psychology of Romantic Love*:

> Jung found that the psyche is *androgynous:* It is made up of both masculine and feminine components. Thus, every man and every woman comes equipped with a psychological structure that in its wholeness includes the richness of both sides, both natures, both sets of capacities and strengths. The psyche spontaneously divides itself into complementary opposites and represents them as a masculine-feminine constellation. It characterizes some qualities as being "masculine" and certain others as being "feminine." Like *yin* and *yan* in ancient Chinese psychology, these complementary opposites balance and complete each other. No human value or trait is complete in itself: It must be joined with its masculine or feminine "mate" in a conscious synthesis if we are to have balance and wholeness.
>
> The psyche sees our capacity for relatedness and love as a "feminine" quality, emanating from the feminine side of the psyche. By contrast, it views the ability to wield power, control situations, and defend territory as strengths that we find in the "masculine" department of the psyche. To become a complete man or woman, each of us must develop both sides of the psyche. We must be able both to handle power and to love, both to exert control and to flow spontaneously with fate—each value in its season.
>
> When we speak of "feminine" in this sense, we obviously do not mean "pertaining to woman." We are speaking of inner, psychological qualities that are common to both men and women. When a man develops the strengths of his inner feminine, it actually completes his maleness. He becomes more fully male as he becomes more fully human. The strongest man is the one who can genuinely show love to his children, as well as fight his battles in the business world during the work day. His masculine strength is augmented and balanced by his feminine capacity to be related, to express his affection and his feelings.
>
> In each of us there is a potential for wholeness, for bringing the conflicting parts of ourselves together in a syn-

thesis. We have a simple name for this totality of the individual: Jung called it the "self."

The self is the sum of all the divergent forces, energies,
and qualities that live within you and make you who you
are—a unique individual. The self is the balanced, harmonious, symmetrical unity at the very center of one's being,
which each of us senses within. But we rarely experience the
self with our conscious mind; we rarely have that sense of
unity and wholeness. We feel ourselves usually as a chaotic
mass of conflicting desires, values, ideals, and possibilities,
some conscious and some unconscious, pulling us in many
directions at once.

The work of "enlightenment" is to make conscious
these divided and conflicting parts of ourselves, to wake up
to the primordial unity that joins them. To awaken to the
unity of the self is the great goal of our psychological evolution, the Pearl Without Price, the object of our deepest
longings. It is this possibility that is manifested by the dual
masculine-feminine nature of the psyche. pp. 17-19.

36. Moore, *Care of the Soul*, xi, xv, and xvii.

37. What does caring for the soul have to do with "shadow work,"
morality, conscience, and ethical decision making? Everything. I
return to Thomas Moore again for valuable insight:

What I am talking about here is a version of Jung's theory
of shadow. For Jung, there are two kinds of shadow: One
consists of the possibilities in life that we reject because of
certain choices we have made. The person we choose to be,
for example, automatically creates a dark double—the person we choose not to be. This compensatory shadow varies
from one person to the next.

For some people sex and money are looming shadows,
while for others they are simply part of life. Moral purity
and responsible living can be shadow aspects to some. Jung
also believed there is an absolute shadow, not relative to our
life choices and habits. In other words, there is evil in the
world and in the human heart. If we don't recognize this, we
have a naive attitude that can get us into trouble. Jung
thought the soul could benefit by coming to terms with both
kinds of shadow, losing some of its naive innocence in the
process. It appears to me that as we open ourselves to see
what our soul is made of and who we really are, we always
find some material that is a profound challenge. . . .

To some extent, care of the soul asks us to open our
hearts wider than they have ever been before, softening the
judging and moralism that may have characterized our atti-

tudes and behavior for years. Moralism is one of the most effective shields against the soul, protecting us from its intricacy. There is nothing more revealing, and maybe nothing more healing, than to reconsider our moralistic attitudes and find how much soul has been hidden behind their doors. People seem to be afraid that if they reflect on their moral principles they might lose their ethical sensitivity altogether. But that is a defensive approach to morality. As we deal with the soul's complexity, morality can deepen and drop its simplicity, becoming at the same time both more demanding and more flexible. Ibid, xvii-xviii, 16-17.

38. Ibid, 16.

39. See Philip K. Howard, *The Death of Common Sense: How Law Is Suffocating America* (New York: Random House, 1994).

Chapter Six

1. Hunter, *That We Might Have Joy*, 9.

2. Spiritual empowerment implies the need for divine assistance through an active faith in God and by allowing God to work in our life. On this point, Jung acknowledged:

> The individual who is not anchored in God can offer no resistance on his own resources to the physical and moral blandishment of the world. For this he needs the evidence of an inner, transcendent experience which alone can protect him from the otherwise inevitable submersion in the mass. Cited in Jaffé, *The Myth of Meaning*, 134.

3. Spencer W. Kimball, *Hidden Wedges* (Salt Lake City, UT: Deseret Book, 1969): 5.

4. Marc Barasch, cited in Zweig and Abrams, *Meeting the Shadow*, 130.

5. O. Hobart Mowrer, *The Crisis in Psychiatry and Religion* (Princeton, NJ: Van Nostrand, 1961): 146, 148, 154.

6. Lewis Andrews, *To Thine Own Self Be True: The Relationship Between Spiritual Values and Emotional Health* (New York: Doubleday, 1989): 41. Cited hereafter as Andrews, *To Thine Own Self Be True*.

7. Carl Jung, cited in Jacobi, *The Way of Individuation*, 115.

8. Ibid (Jung), 119.

9. John Gray seminar handout.

10. Focusing on this form of "therapy," Lewis Andrews continues:

> And, if this "common sense" trade-off therapy ignores the real correctional imperative of our guilt, it also ignores the secret pleasure we occasionally derive from substituting self-blame for rectification. For all the depression we inevitably suffer, our guilt does have a strangely addicting quality, an appeal based on the degree to which it flatters our ego's manipulative powers.
>
> How can we feel guilty, after all, unless we have done "something big" to feel guilty about? The woman who feels so terribly upset about breaking up some poor man's marriage is also saying to herself, "It's *because* of me. I did that!" However guilty a child may feel about behaving so badly at school that his [or her] parents have to spend hours with school counselors—no matter how much a husband regrets that his "willful stupidity" has caused everything to go wrong at home—both secretly revel in their abilities to bring about such major family catastrophes.
>
> Tennessee psychologist Richard Driscoll has even seen cases where egotistic self-criticism evolves into a kind of arrogant morality. Deploring one's sins, Driscoll finds, is really a way of insisting that we are beyond reproach, that our standards are never relaxed, that we in fact are *morally superior*. . . . Today we see the powerful grip of egotistically "trading-off" in the familiar stories of wives who quietly endure abusive marriages, of men who seem to enjoy humiliating intimidation, and in all people who repeatedly play the role of patsy without apparent complaint. *To Thine Own Self Be True*, 41.

11. Robert A. Johnson, *He: Understanding Masculine Psychology*, rev. ed. (New York: Harper & Row, 1989): 11. Cited hereafter as Johnson, *He*.

12. St. Matthew, "The Gospel According to St. Matthew," *The Holy Bible: King James Version*, 18:4.

13. Ibid, 11:28.

14. See Johnson, *He*, 80.

15. Alice Miller, cited in John Bradshaw, *Bradshaw on: The Family: A Revolutionary Way of Self-Discovery* (Deerfield Beach, FL: Health Communications, 1988): 212.

16. Ibid (Miller), 213.

17. J. Konrad Stettbacher, *Making Sense of Suffering: The Healing Confrontation with Your Own Past.* Simon Worrall, trans. (New York: Dutton, 1991).

18. An interesting twist on the meaning of religion is provided by Robert A. Johnson, in *Owning Your Own Shadow: Understanding the Dark Side of the Shadow:*

> Our error (thank God there is an error or life would be unendurable!) is that we use the world "religious" in a wrong way. The word "religion" stems from the Latin roots *re*, meaning "again," and *ligare* meaning "to bind, bond, or bridge." Our common word *ligature*, comes from the same root. Religion means, then, "to bind together again." It can never be affixed to one of a pair of opposites. . . . [Much of the problem has to do with] the secular versus the religious attitude. This is a flaming, flagrant error and is the seat of most of the neurotic suffering in humankind. To think that one way of action is profane and another sacred is to make terrible misuse of the language. There is no such thing as a religious act or list of characteristics. There can only be a religious insight that bridges or heals. This is what restores and reconciles the opposites that have been torturing each of us. The religious faculty is the art of taking the opposites and binding them back together again, surmounting the split that has been causing so much suffering. It helps us move from contradiction—that painful condition where things oppose each other—to the realm of paradox, where we are to entertain simultaneously two contradictory notions and give them equal dignity. Then, and only then, is there the possibility of grace, the spiritual experience of contradictions brought into a coherent whole—giving us a unity greater than either one of them.
>
> To say that it is better to give than to receive is to indulge in the same kind of error that proves that 2 equals 3. To focus on one of a pair of opposites as "religious" is truly a mistake. It is only the realm of synthesis that is worthy of the adjective.
>
> We must restore the word *religious* to its true meaning; then it will regain its healing power. To heal, to bond, to join, to bridge, to put back together again—these are our sacred faculties. (San Francisco, CA: Harper San Francisco, 1991): 83-85:

19. O. Hobart Mowrer, cited in Andrews, *To Thine Own Self Be True*, 40.

20. Bradshaw, *Creating Love*, 178-79.

21. Milton Erickson, cited in ibid, 179-81.

22. Ibid (Erickson), 181.

23. Ibid (Bradshaw).

24. Deval L. Patric, "Struggling for Civil Rights Now: Let Us Recapture Our Perspective," *Vital Speeches of the Day* (November 15, 1994): 93.

25. Whyte, *The Heart Aroused*, 119-20.

26. A psychological "rebirth moment" is a new realization of truth with respect to one's personality. It involves the death of some ego-ideal. See Jacobi, *The Way of Individuation*, 61.

27. Jung, *Collected Works*, 14: 169.

28. See St. Paul, "Second Epistle of Paul the Apostle to the Corinthians," *The Holy Bible: King James Version*, 12:7.

Chapter Seven

1. Edward Tivnan, *The Moral Imagination: Confronting the Ethical Issues of Our Day* (New York: Simon & Schuster, 1995): 254.

2. The concept of polarity versus polarized thinking is articulated well by Sydney Harris in his book, *The Authentic Person: Dealing with Dilemma*:

> On a gray, bleak day, I walk down a crowded downtown street and look at the faces passing me, and I feel that the public is truly a rabble—ignorant, prejudiced, incompetent, unattractive, stupid, slothful, inconsiderate, incapable of governing themselves with the kind of excellence that Jefferson envisioned for a democratic society.
>
> Then, on another day, a lovely summer afternoon, the very same faces seem vital and warm, repositories of goodwill, sharing with me a common hope and dream, endowed with a native shrewdness and sense of values, and filled with the potentialities for realizing the hope of Jefferson and his colleagues.
>
> *Now it seems to me that both views are right and both are wrong, at the same time and in the same way.* And this is the paradox at the heart of the commonwealth. The false aristocrat sees the people only in the shadow of the gray day; the false liberal sees them bathed only in the sentimental radiance of the sunny day.

> What neither of them is capable of doing—and what is so really hard to do—is to hold both these concepts in tension at once, to recognize that both are right and both are wrong, depending upon what one is asking of people, on what one is trying to do *with* them, or *for* them, or *against* them.
>
> People are stupid; they are also shrewd. As the number of people in any group increases, the average intelligence quotient goes down; but at the same time, the average level of judgment goes up. People are kind, cruel, generous, and selfish. What we call human nature is like a vast organ, capable of the deepest or highest tones, of magnificent harmonies or ear-splitting cacophonies. (Niles, IL: Argus, 1972): 39-45.

3. M. Scott Peck, *The Road Less Traveled: A New Psychology of Love, Traditional Values, and Spiritual Growth* (New York: Simon & Schuster, 1978): 151-52. Cited hereafter as Peck, *The Road Less Traveled.*

4. To summarize this subject, I rely once again on the insight of Carl Jung:

> Conscience is a psychic reaction which one can call *moral* because it always appears when the conscious mind leaves the path of custom, of the *mores*, or suddenly recollects it. Hence, in the great majority of cases, conscience signifies primarily the reaction to a real or supposed deviation from the moral code, and is, for the most part, identical with the primitive fear of anything unusual, not customary, and hence "immoral." As this behavior is instinctive and, at best, only partly the result of reflection, it may be "moral," but can raise no claim to being *ethical*. It deserves this qualification only when it is reflective, when it is subjected to conscious scrutiny. And this happens only when a fundamental doubt arises as between two possible modes of moral behaviors, that is to say, in a conflict of duty. A situation like this can be "solved" only by suppressing one moral reaction, upon which one has not reflected till now, in favor of another. In this case the moral code will be invoked in vain, and the judging intellect finds itself in the position of Buridan's ass between two bundles of hay. Only the creative power of the ethos that expresses the whole man can pronounce the final judgment. . . .
>
> The concept and phenomenon of conscience thus contains, when seen in a psychological light, two different factors: on the one hand a recollection of, and admonition by, the *mores*; on the other, a conflict of duty and its solution through the creation of a third standpoint. The first is the moral, and the second the ethical, aspect of conscience. "A Psychological View of Conscience," in *Collected Works*, 10: 453-55.

5. Ibid, 445.

6. Ibid, 444.

7. Ibid.

8. See Victor E. Frankl, *Man's Search for Meaning: An Introduction to Logotherapy,* 3rd ed. (New York: Simon & Schuster, 1984): 125.

9. Chuang Tzu, cited in Thomas Merton, *The Way of Chuang Tzu* (New York: New Directions, 1965): 107.

10. Here, according to David Burns, are "The Ten Forms of Twisted Thinking":

> *1. All-or-nothing thinking.*
> You see things in black-or-white categories. If a situation falls short of perfect, you see it as a total failure. When a young woman on a diet ate a spoonful of ice cream, she told herself, "I've blown my diet completely." This thought upset her so much that she gobbled down an entire quart of ice cream!
>
> *2. Over-generalization.*
> You see a single negative event, such as a romantic rejection or a career reversal, as a never-ending pattern of defeat by using words such as "always" or "never" when you think about it. A depressed salesman became terribly upset when he noticed bird dung on the windshield of his car. He told himself, "Just my luck! Birds are *always* crapping on my car!"
>
> *3. Mental filter.*
> You pick out a single negative detail and dwell on it exclusively, so that your vision of all of reality becomes darkened, like the drop of ink that discolors a beaker of water. Example: You receive many positive comments about your presentation to a group of associates at work, but one of them says something mildly critical. You obsess about his reaction for days and ignore all the positive feedback.
>
> *4. Discounting the positive.*
> You reject positive experiences by insisting they "don't count." If you do a good job, you may tell yourself that it wasn't good enough or that anyone could have done as well. Discounting the positive takes the joy out of life and makes you feel inadequate and unrewarded.
>
> *5. Jumping to conclusions.*
> You interpret things negatively when there are no facts to support your conclusion.

Mind-reading: Without checking it out, you arbitrarily conclude that someone is reacting negatively to you.

Fortune-telling: You predict that things will turn out badly. Before a test you may tell yourself, "I'm really going to blow it. What if I flunk?" If you're depressed you may tell yourself, "I'll never get better."

6. Magnification.

You exaggerate the importance of your problems and shortcomings, or you minimize the importance of your desirable qualities. This is also called the "binocular trick."

7. Emotional reasoning.

You assume that your negative emotions necessarily reflect the way things really are: "I feel terrified about going on airplanes; it must be very dangerous to fly," "I feel guilty; I must be a rotten person," "I feel angry; this proves I'm being treated unfairly," "I feel so inferior; this means I'm a second-rate person," or "I feel hopeless; I must really be hopeless."

8. "Should" statements.

You tell yourself that things *should* be the way you hoped or expected them to be. After playing a difficult piece on the piano, a gifted pianist told herself, "I shouldn't have made so many mistakes." This made her feel so disgusted that she quit practicing for several days. "Musts," "oughts" and "have to's" are similar offenders.

"Should" statements that are directed against yourself lead to guilt and frustration. Should statements that are directed against other people or the world in general lead to anger and frustration: "He shouldn't be so stubborn and argumentative."

Many people try to motivate themselves with shoulds and shouldn'ts, as if they were delinquents who had to be punished before they could be expected to do anything. For example, a woman might tell herself, "I shouldn't eat that doughnut." This usually doesn't work because all these shoulds and musts make people feel rebellious, and they get the urge to do just the opposite. Albert Ellis has called this "musterbation"; I call it the "shouldy" approach to life.

9. Labeling.

Labeling is an extreme form of all-or-nothing thinking. Instead of saying, "I made a mistake," you attach a negative label to yourself: "I'm a loser." You might also label yourself "a fool" or "a failure" or "a jerk." Labeling is quite irrational because you are not the same as what you do. Human beings exist, but "fools," "losers," and "jerks" do not. These labels are just useless abstractions that lead to anger, anxiety, frustration, and low self-esteem.

You may also label others. When someone does something that rubs you the wrong way, you may tell yourself: "He's an S.O.B." Then you feel that the problem is with that person's "character" or "essence" instead of with the person's thinking or behavior. You see the person as totally bad. This makes you feel hostile and hopeless about improving things and leaves little room for constructive communication.

10. Personalization and blame.

Personalization occurs when you hold yourself personally responsible for an event that isn't entirely under your control. When a woman received a note that her child was having difficulties at school, she told herself, "This shows what a bad mother I am," instead of trying to pinpoint the cause of the problem so that she could be helpful to her child. When another woman's husband beat her, she told herself, "If only I were better in bed, he wouldn't beat me." Personalization leads to guilt, shame, and feelings of inadequacy.

Some people do the opposite. They blame other people or their circumstances for their problems, and they overlook ways that they might be contributing to the problem: "The reason my marriage is so lousy is because my spouse is totally unreasonable." Blame usually doesn't work very well because other people will resent being scapegoated, and they will just toss the blame right back in your lap. It's like the game of hot potato—no one wants to get stuck with it. *The Feeling Good Handbook* (New York: Plume, 1989): 8-11.

11. In her book, *Thick Face Black Heart: The Path to Thriving, Winning, and Succeeding.* Chin-Ning Chu refers to nonattachment as the capacity for "detachment." She presents an evolutionary process for detachment as "The Seven Stages of Unfolding":

1. The desire to do right.

You feel the intense desire to do good, to do the right thing.

2. Confusion and negativity.

Eventually you begin to gain insight. Up to this point you think you have been making a noble sacrifice, when in fact you have not been sacrificing at all. Rather, you have been denying and depriving yourself, afraid to acknowledge your needs.

Before you are a son, daughter, husband, wife, employee, executive, politician, entrepreneur, lawyer, or policeman, you are a human who possesses natural and basic human needs. By ignoring your individual needs and totally catering to the needs of others in accordance to the role you are playing, you have betrayed your inner nature and sacrificed your well-being. In fact, you have victimized yourself through self-denial. This was done under the noble pretense of self-sacrifice.

You begin to feel anger and resentment, and at the same time you feel guilty about these despicable emotions, which are unfit for people of your character.

3. The battle for surrender.

You finally reach the conclusion that it is too painful to live your life without the liberty of self-expression and self-nurturing. You cannot contribute to anyone if you cannot contribute to yourself. The pain of living under others' standards has become intolerable.

By now you are persuading yourself to accept your "despicable" emotions. Anger and guilt fill you, and are part of you for the time being. You have reached the conclusion that life is just as painful whether you practice self-denial by living up to others' expectations or practice self-expression and feel guilty about it. At least, you feel, the latter option creates the opportunity for movement within you.

4. Acceptance of your imperfect perfection.

You are evolving to the point where you are less judgmental about your anger and resentment. You start to see yourself as imperfectly perfect. You experience love for your perfection and your imperfections. You begin to be aware that a great courage exists within you, the power of courage that enables you to acknowledge your own existence and your own needs.

You are in ecstasy over the possible new realms that await you, but also in agony over the abandonment of the old. Just like the moment before parachuting from an airplane, you are full of fear and excited anticipation. Yet during this transition period, it will be painful at times.

5. The new possibilities.

At this stage, you have begun to develop the natural power that gives you the strength to stand up against your automatic, habitual actions and thoughts and venture into the new frontier. As each event crosses your path, you will take a moment to reach within yourself for guidance and discover the best course of action.

At first, this is a slow process, and often your habitual response gets ahead of your conscious effort.

6. The inner harmony.

By breaking through your notion of others' standards and expectations, you find a new surge of inner harmony; the unfamiliar emotion of peace and tranquility.

You begin to experience genuine compassion for others not because you are supposed to, or because you feel guilty if you don't, but rather through your own love for yourself. You recognize that the flame of love burning within you is equally present in others, even though they may not perceive it themselves.

At this stage, when others slap you in the face, you no longer feel like a victim of your sense of morality. You have a choice: to slap back twice, or turn the other cheek. The decision of how to react will be in accord with the result that you are looking for.

7. Detachment: The power source of magnetism.

The highest code of living is detachment. There is no power higher than the power of detachment. When one masters the state of detachment, he becomes the embodiment of dispassion and fearlessness. At this stage, nothing he possesses will possess him. He becomes the master of his possessions, rather than being possessed by them. (Mill Valley, CA: AMC Publishing, 1992): 304-9.

12. According to M. Scott Peck:

Spiritually evolved people, by virtue of their discipline, mastery, and love, are people of extraordinary competence, and in their competence they are called on to serve the world, and in their love they answer the call. They are inevitably, therefore, people of great power, although the world may generally behold them as quite ordinary people, since more often than not they will exercise their power in quiet or even hidden ways. Nonetheless, exercise power they do, and in this exercise they suffer greatly, even dreadfully. For to exercise power is to make decisions, and the process of making decisions with total awareness is often infinitely more painful than making decisions with limited or blunted awareness (which is the way most decisions are made and why they are ultimately proved wrong).

Imagine two generals, each having to decide whether or not to commit a division of ten thousand men to battle. To one the division is but a thing, a unit of personnel, an instrument of strategy, and nothing more. To the other it is these things, but he is also aware of each and every one of the ten thousand. For whom is the decision easier? It is easier for the general who has blunted his awareness precisely because he cannot tolerate the pain of a more nearly complete awareness. It may be tempting to say, "Ah, but a spiritually evolved man would never become a general in the first place." But the same issue is involved in being a corporation president, a physician, a teacher, a parent. Decisions affect-

ing the lives of others must always be made. The best decision makers are those who are willing to suffer the most
over their decisions but still retain their ability to be decisive.
One measure—and perhaps the best measure—of a person's
greatness is the capacity for suffering. Yet the great are also
joyful. This, then, is the paradox. . . .

The problem is that the more loving one is, the more
humble one is; yet the more humble one is, the more one is
awed by the potential for arrogance in exercising power.
Who am I to influence the course of human events? By what
authority am I entitled to decide what is best for my child,
my spouse, my country, or the human race? Who am I to
play God? *That* is the risk. For whenever we exercise power
we are attempting to influence the course of the world, of
humanity, and we are thereby playing God. Most parents,
teachers, leaders—most of us who exercise power—have no
cognizance of this. In the arrogance of exercising power without
the total self-awareness demanded by love, we are blissfully
but destructively ignorant of the fact that we are playing God.
But those who truly love, and therefore work for the wisdom
that love requires, know that to act is to play God. Yet they
also know that there is no alternative except inaction and
impotence. Love compels us to play God with full consciousness
of the enormity of the fact that that is just what we are doing.
With this consciousness the loving person assumes the
responsibility of attempting to be God and not to carelessly
play God, to fulfill God's will without mistake. We arrive,
then, at yet another paradox: Only out of the humility of love
can humans dare to be God. *The Road Less Traveled*, 75-76.

13. Jacobi, *The Way of Individuation*, 115.

14. Jesus, cited in St. John, "The Gospel According to St. John," *The
Holy Bible: King James Version*, 15:5. (See also all of Chapter 15 of
St. John, and St. Luke 5:36-39 for other allusions referred to here.)

Epilogue

1. The "Truth" referred to here refers to St. John, "The Gospel
According to St. John," *The Holy Bible: King James Version*, 14:6,
wherein Jesus refers to Himself as "the Way, the Truth, and the Life."

2. Hugh B. Brown, *Conference Report of The Church of Jesus Christ
of Latter-day Saints* (April 1964): 55.

3. David O. McKay, *Gospel Ideals: Selections from the Discourses of
David O. McKay* (Salt Lake City, UT: Bookcraft, 1953): 12.

About the Author

Over the past twenty years, Tom Riskas has enjoyed a rich professional life teaching, coaching, and counseling in the field of human and organizational development both nationally and internationally. For five years he served as a Vice President and Senior Consultant of the renowned Covey Leadership Center, where he contributed significantly as an executive and senior presenter, speaker, and facilitator to *Fortune* 1000 clients worldwide.

Some of the organizations Tom has worked with include: Merck & Co., Marion Merrell Dow, TAP Pharmaceuticals, Andersen Consulting, NutraSweet, Frito Lay, AT&T, U.S. West Communications, Conoco, Dayton Hudson Corporation, American College of Cardiology, Synergon Health Care Systems, Franciscan Sisters Health Care Systems, Cincinnati Milacron, and many others.

Riskas completed his undergraduate degree at the University of San Francisco and his graduate degree at Golden Gate University. For two and a half years he served as an adjunct professor of management at Arizona State University.

Thomas resides in Provo, Utah, with his wife, Annette, and their four children: Nicole, T. J., Tyson, and Tessa.

About Thomas Riskas & Associates

Thomas Riskas is founder and president of Thomas Riskas & Associates, Inc., a consulting firm dedicated to the healing and empowerment of individuals, families, and organizations and to the development of leadership capability throughout the world. This work is carried out through public seminars and workshops, as well as through a variety of other services including:

- Working Beneath the Surface Personal Empowerment Course (1–3 day)
- The Relationship Course (2 days)
- Overcoming Barriers to Sustained Effectiveness (1 day)
- Personal Visioning and Life Balance (1 day)
- High-Performance Team-Building sessions (including outdoor leadership exercises)
- Conflict Resolution sessions for teams and individuals
- Relationship-Building sessions for greater trust, interdependence, and synergy
- Customized leadership development workshops and seminars
- Organizational and management consulting
- Executive coaching and counseling
- Keynote speeches and other presentations

For more information, please contact:

Thomas Riskas & Associates, Inc.

3917 North Quail Run Drive
Provo, UT 84604
phone: (801) 379-3300
fax: (801) 229-2320